Ethiopian Yearbook of International Law 2016

Editor-in-Chief

Dr. Zeray Yihdego

Editors

Prof. Dr. Melaku Geboye Desta
Dr. Fikremarkos Merso

Assistant Editors

Jülide Bredee
Jasmin Hansohm
Emily Hirst

Editorial Advisory Boards

Prof. Dr. Daniel Abebe, University of Chicago Law School, Chicago, CA, USA
Dr. Musa Abseno, Independent Consultancy and Law Practice, Addis Ababa, Ethiopia
Prof. Dr. Jean Allain, Monash University, Clayton, VIC, Australia
Prof. Dapo Akande, University of Oxford Faculty of Law, Oxford, UK
Dr. Yacob Arsano, Addis Ababa University, Addis Ababa, Ethiopia
Dr. Mulugeta Mengist Ayalew, Prime Minister's Office, Addis Ababa, Ethiopia
Dr. Mohamed Abdelsalam Babiker, University of Khartoum Faculty of Law, Khartoum, Sudan
Dr. Assefa Fiseha, Addis Ababa University, Addis Ababa, Ethiopia
Prof. Dr. James Thuo Gathii, Loyola School of Law, Chicago, IL, USA
Ambassador Minelik Alemu Getahun, World Intellectual Property Organisation (WIPO), Geneva, Switzerland
Prof. Dr. L. van den Herik, Leiden University, Leiden, The Netherlands
Ambassador Ibrahim Idris, Addis Ababa University, Addis Ababa, Ethiopia and Ethiopian Ministry of Foreign Affairs, Addis Ababa, Ethiopia
Prof. Dr. Jeremy Levitt, Florida A & M University College of Law, Orlando, FL, USA
Prof. Dr. Makane Moïse Mbengue, University of Geneva, Geneva, Switzerland
Dr. Benyam Dawit Mezmur, Dullah Omar Institute of the University of the Western Cape, Western Cape, South Africa and UN Committee on the Rights of the Child, Geneva, Switzerland
Prof. Sean Murphy, George Washington School of Law, Washington, DC, USA and International Law Commission (ILC), Washington, DC, USA
Prof. Dr. Makau Mutua, The State University of New York (SUNY) Buffalo Law School, Buffalo, NY, USA
Prof. Dr. John Paterson, University of Aberdeen Law School, Aberdeen, UK
Prof. Chris Maina Peter, International Law Commission (ILC), Washington, DC, USA and University of Dar es Salaam, Dar es Salaam, Tanzania
Dr. Salman Salman, International Water Resources Association (IWRA), Khartoum, Sudan
Prof. Dr. Wenhua Shan, Xi'an Jiaotong University, Shaanxi Sheng, China
Judge Abdulqawi A. Yusuf, International Court of Justice, The Hague, Netherlands and Institut de Droit International, Geneva, Switzerland

The Ethiopian Yearbook of International Law (EtYIL) is a peer-reviewed academic journal that publishes scholarly works of the highest standard in the field of international law broadly defined, but with a focus on Ethiopia and the Horn of Africa region. International law presents both opportunities and challenges to developing countries; however, their role in the making of the law and the scholarly analysis and debate that informs and underpins its evolution remains marginal. By choosing Ethiopia as its geographical focus, this Yearbook aims to contribute towards filling this gap and the long-term goal of rebalancing the narrative of international law in a manner that better reflects the diversity of its actors and subjects. With this in mind, EtYIL welcomes contributions in all areas of international law and relations. Particular issues of interest to the Yearbook include sustainable development law, the law of international trade and investment, the peaceful settlement of disputes, the sharing and preservation of transboundary resources, regional integration, peace and security, humanitarian law and human rights, and regional and international institutions.

More information about this series at http://www.springer.com/series/15093

Zeray Yihdego • Melaku Geboye Desta •
Fikremarkos Merso
Editors

Ethiopian Yearbook of International Law 2016

Editors
Zeray Yihdego
School of Law
University of Aberdeen
Aberdeen, United Kingdom

Melaku Geboye Desta
Faculty of Business
De Montfort University
Leicester, United Kingdom

Fikremarkos Merso
College of Law and Governance Studies
Addis Ababa University
Addis Ababa, Ethiopia

Ethiopian Yearbook of International Law
ISBN 978-3-319-55897-4   ISBN 978-3-319-55898-1   (eBook)
DOI 10.1007/978-3-319-55898-1

Library of Congress Control Number: 2017908136

© Springer International Publishing AG 2017
This work is subject to copyright. All rights are reserved by the Publisher, whether the whole or part of the material is concerned, specifically the rights of translation, reprinting, reuse of illustrations, recitation, broadcasting, reproduction on microfilms or in any other physical way, and transmission or information storage and retrieval, electronic adaptation, computer software, or by similar or dissimilar methodology now known or hereafter developed.
The use of general descriptive names, registered names, trademarks, service marks, etc. in this publication does not imply, even in the absence of a specific statement, that such names are exempt from the relevant protective laws and regulations and therefore free for general use.
The publisher, the authors and the editors are safe to assume that the advice and information in this book are believed to be true and accurate at the date of publication. Neither the publisher nor the authors or the editors give a warranty, express or implied, with respect to the material contained herein or for any errors or omissions that may have been made. The publisher remains neutral with regard to jurisdictional claims in published maps and institutional affiliations.

Printed on acid-free paper

This Springer imprint is published by Springer Nature
The registered company is Springer International Publishing AG
The registered company address is: Gewerbestrasse 11, 6330 Cham, Switzerland

Contents

Part I Introduction

Towards Rebalancing the Narrative of International Law 3
Zeray Yihdego, Melaku Geboye Desta, and Fikremarkos Merso

Part II Articles

The South West Africa Cases: 50 Years Later 11
Makane Moïse Mbengue and Najib Messihi

**Decolonisation as the Source of the Concepts of *Jus Cogens*
and Obligations *Erga Omnes*** 35
Jean Allain

The Place of International Law in the Ethiopian Legal System 61
Getachew A. Woldemariam

Ethiopia's WTO Accession at the Crossroads 95
Derk Bienen

**Competition for Natural Resources and International
Investment Law: Analysis from the Perspective of Africa** 117
Melaku Geboye Desta

**The Global Goals: Formalism Foregone, Contested Legality
and "Re-imaginings" of International Law** 151
Duncan French

**Developing Countries Under the International Climate
Change Regime: How Does the Paris Agreement Change
Their Position?** 179
Olivia Woolley

Part III Current Development

The Declaration of Principles on the Grand Ethiopian Renaissance Dam: An Analytical Overview..................................... 203
Salman M.A. Salman

The South Sudan Crisis: Legal Implications and Responses of the International Community..................................... 223
Jasmin Hansohm and Zeray Yihdego

Part I
Introduction

Towards Rebalancing the Narrative of International Law

Zeray Yihdego, Melaku Geboye Desta, and Fikremarkos Merso

The Ethiopian Yearbook of International Law (EtYIL), like many others in the field, is a peer-reviewed academic journal that publishes scholarly works of the highest standard in the field of international law broadly defined. However, unlike most journals, EtYIL is dedicated to those issues of international law that are of particular interest to the African continent in general and Ethiopia and the Horn in particular. EtYIL's point of departure is the fact that these countries do not just lack adequate representation at the table where international law is made and interpreted; their ability to contribute to the evolution of international law is also severely constrained owing, in part, to their absence from the scholarly debate in the field. A key mission of EtYIL is therefore to provide a platform for purpose-oriented scholarly analysis and debate on issues of particular significance for these countries so as to enhance their capacity to contribute to this evolution. More generally, the Yearbook aims to contribute towards the long-term goal of rebalancing the narrative of international law in a manner that better reflects the diversity of its actors and subjects.

At this juncture, one may ask: Why Ethiopia? A student of the modern history of international law is likely to encounter Ethiopia in the context of, first, its joining the League of Nations in 1923 as the second African country to do so (Liberia was a founding member) and, second, its invasion by Italy in 1935 in violation of the then established law of international relations in the form of Articles X to XII of the

---

Z. Yihdego (✉)
School of Law, University of Aberdeen, Aberdeen, UK
e-mail: zeray.yihdego@abdn.ac.uk

M.G. Desta
Faculty of Business, De Montfort University, Leicester, UK
e-mail: melaku.desta@dmu.ac.uk

F. Merso
College of Law and Governance Studies, Addis Ababa University, Addis Ababa, Ethiopia
e-mail: fikremarkosm@yahoo.co.uk

Covenant of the League of Nations of which both the aggressor and the aggressed were members. Ethiopia's feeling of betrayal by the League can be gleaned from its early faith in international law, which it articulated in the 1923 request to join the League:

> We know that the League of Nations guarantees the independence and territorial integrity of all the nations in the world, and maintains peace and agreement among them; that all its efforts are directed towards the strengthening of friendship among the races of mankind; that it is anxious to remove all the obstacles to that friendship which give rise to wars when one country is offended; that it causes truth and loyalty to be respected.[1]

However, and despite that experience, Ethiopia became one of the signatories of the 1942 Declaration of the United Nations and later a founding member of the United Nations in 1945, and a host of other multilateral institutions that were established in the aftermath of World War II, including the World Bank and the International Monetary Fund. The Post-War period in many ways promised renewed hope for parts of the world still under colonial rule. The same international law that had been used to justify colonialism by denying the attribute of sovereignty to non-European parts of the world accepted *inter alia* the principle of self-determination so as to accommodate what Anthony Anghie called "the disconcerting prospect of Africans and Asians acquiring sovereignty in the 1950s and 1960s".[2] And Ethiopia played a leading role in the struggle for the self-determination of the African people and their liberation from colonial rule, which made the country a model of resistance by leaders of the independence movement, many of whom later adopted variants of its tri-coloured flag (green, yellow and red) for their respective national flags following independence. Ethiopia also used different political and legal forums to pursue this goal, one of the most notable being the case it brought, together with Liberia, against Apartheid South Africa before the International Court of Justice in the famous West Africa cases. That Ethiopia is the seat of the African Union (AU)—and its predecessor the Organisation of African Unity (OAU)—is also a further testament to the role it played—and continues to play—on the Continent. Finally, as its active participation in global peacekeeping and peace enforcement operations dating back to the Korean war in the early 1950s and the Congo and Rwandan conflicts in the early 1960s and 1990s, respectively, to its current involvement in peacekeeping operations in Sudan, South Sudan and others testifies, Ethiopia has been in the vanguard of the effort to maintain international peace and security in Africa and beyond.

Yet, long-term engagement with foreign states based on international law does not necessarily signify active participation in the making and development of international law. Arguably, Ethiopia has been a taker and, on many occasions, a victim of international law norms rather than a maker or beneficiary thereof. In this sense Ethiopia's experience is hardly distinguishable from those faced by any of its fellow developing countries in general and African countries more particularly. Its

---

[1]Quoted in Stern (1936), pp. 199–200.
[2]Anghie (1999), p. 4.

borders were defined by colonial forces that encircled it and left it landlocked; its major wars—from the Battle of Adwa in 1896 all the way to the latest war with Eritrea over a hundred years later—arose out of conflicts relating to those borders and colonisation, amongst other major factors; its economic fortunes suffered arguably as a direct result of the asymmetric system of economic governance implemented through the instrumentality of international law, although the embryonic endeavour made by Ethiopia to grow its economy in the last decade or so uses the very same international law frameworks in the fields of trade, investment and finance, etc. In trying to advance its social and economic interests, today's Ethiopia, like its fellow African states, finds itself hobbled by the challenges that international law brings to developing countries.

However, with all its constraints and problems, international law remains an indispensable tool for peaceful co-existence and cooperation among sovereign nations, large and small. With its unequivocal stance on the sanctity of human rights and human dignity,[3] coupled with the principles of rule of law and the peaceful settlement of disputes, today's international law represents a significant achievement in human history. At the same time, to exploit the enormous potential and promise of international law to the full and rectify its shortcomings, Ethiopia and its fellow African states cannot afford to continue to stay on the periphery of the scholarly debate that shapes existing international law and its future. EtYIL aims to contribute to this goal by working closely with scholars from all over the world who share our vision of international law that is inclusive, protects the interests of the weaker party, and continues to work for the establishment of a fairer and more just international political and economic order. With this in view, and already in this maiden issue, we offer scholarly views and analyses on some of the critical issues facing Ethiopia and the Continent authored by leading scholars and practitioners in their respective fields of research.

We start this volume by looking half a century back to when Ethiopia, together with Liberia, attempted—unsuccessfully—to use international law to advance the causes of freedom and justice for the people of South West Africa and indeed Africa more generally. As Makane Mbengue and Najib Messihi argue in *The South West Africa Cases: 50 Years Later*, the 1966 decision of the International Court of Justice on the South West Africa Cases has been considered as the most controversial judgment in the Court's history that led to a long period of mistrust by African States towards the ICJ. This historical investigation then goes broader and deeper into some of the recent adaptations of international law with Jean Allain's *Decolonisation as the Source of the Concepts of Jus Cogens and Obligations Erga Omnes*, where he traces the development of *jus cogens* and obligations *erga omnes*[4] as part of the effort to accommodate Newly Independent States.

---

[3]See e.g. UN High-level Panel on Threats, Challenges and Change Report: "A More Secure World, Our Shared Responsibility", December 2, 2004 http://www.un.org/en/peacebuilding/pdf/historical/hlp_more_secure_world.pdf. Trindade (2013).
[4]Barcelona Traction case, ICJ Repts 1970.

Once we have a flavour of some of the historical and theoretical issues, we turn specifically to Ethiopia with Getachew A. Woldemariam's contribution on *The Place of International Law in the Ethiopian Legal System*, which describes the process of reception of international law into the Ethiopian legal system and analyses its status and relationship with domestic law once it has been so received. For a country such as Ethiopia that has been relatively active on the international plane, its absence from the General Agreement on Tariffs and Trade (GATT) in the past and from the World Trade Organisation (WTO) today has been a matter of interest for a while. This issue is tackled head on with Derk Bienen's contribution on *Ethiopia's WTO Accession at the Crossroads*, which provides an update on Ethiopia's ongoing WTO accession negotiations.

The series of Ethiopia-specific articles is then followed up with contributions of a more regional significance, starting with Melaku Geboye Desta's piece on *Competition for Natural Resources and International Investment Law*, which discusses the history and development of modern international investment law as an innovative antidote designed to circumscribe the reach of the principle of permanent sovereignty over natural resources in the hands of newly-independent states. Two further contributions then address two of the most pressing issues of development and climate change. In his contribution on *The Global Goals: Formalism Foregone, Contested Legality and "Re-imaginings" of International Law*, Duncan French examines the legal status of Sustainable Development Goals (SDGs) and concludes by challenging the wisdom of the use of the political, as opposed to the legal, avenue to express these Goals and why international law has not been viewed as an acceptable conduit for the advancement of global development. Olivia Woolley's contribution on *Developing Countries under the International Climate Change Regime* explains the change and continuity that the Paris Agreement represents for developing countries.[5]

Finally, we conclude the maiden issue with two current development pieces—the first by Salman Salman on *The Declaration of Principles on the Grand Ethiopian Renaissance Dam (GERD)* and the second one by Jasmin Hansohm and Zeray Yihdego on *The South Sudan Crisis: Some Legal Developments and Responses of the International Community*. As editors, we are, of course, cognizant of the recent declaration of a state of emergency in Ethiopia, which will have international law dimensions and implications; however, because of tight publishing schedule for this maiden issue, we have decided to defer our current developments piece on this subject to the next issue of the Yearbook.

To conclude, without denying the universal value and benefits of, and opportunities from, international law for developing countries and their citizens, the challenges facing Ethiopia and other countries in the region relating to international law are serious and need to be matched with equally serious commitment from all of us. To that end, we would like to seize this opportunity to invite international law scholars and practitioners in all fields to consider the EtYIL for publishing their

---

[5]See also AfDB (2012).

research work of general or specific relevance to the aims and scope of the Yearbook.

The completion of this issue within schedule was possible only because of the unreserved support, guidance and encouragement we received from members of the EtYIL Advisory Board. We also extend our appreciation to the external reviewers who did an excellent job and yet have to remain anonymous for obvious reasons. Our assistant editors—Jasmin Hansohm, Emily Hirst and Jülide Bredee—have been tireless and meticulous; we are grateful.

References

AfDB (2012) Solutions for a Changing Climate The African Development Bank's Response to Impacts in Africa. http://www.afdb.org/fileadmin/uploads/afdb/Documents/Generic-Documents/The%20Solutions%20for%20a%20Changing%20Climate%20The%20African%20Development%20Bank's%20Response%20to%20Impacts%20in%20Africa.pdf. Accessed 13 Dec 2016

Anghie A (1999) Finding the peripheries: sovereignty and colonialism in nineteenth-century international law. Harv Int Law J 40(1):1–71

Barcelona Traction case, ICJ Repts 1970

Stern WB (1936) The treaty background of the Italo-Ethiopian dispute. Am J Int Law 30:189–203

Trindade AAC (2013) The Hague Academy of International Law Monographs: international law for humankind: towards a new jus gentium. Martinus Nijhoff, Leiden

UN High-level Panel on Threats, Challenges and Change Report: "A More Secure World, Our Shared Responsibility", December 2, 2004. http://www.un.org/en/peacebuilding/pdf/historical/hlp_more_secure_world.pdf

Part II
Articles

The South West Africa Cases: 50 Years Later

Makane Moïse Mbengue and Najib Messihi

Abstract The following article is designed as an anniversary retrospective on the South West Africa cases, the first dispute brought by African States before the International Court of Justice (ICJ). By summarising the content of the judgments of 1962 and 1966, exposing the background against which they were adopted and envisaging the various critical reactions they generated among governments and international law experts, it aims at explaining why the decision of 1966 has been considered as the most controversial judgment in the history of the ICJ and was followed by a relatively long period of mistrust of African States towards the Court. Moreover, it purports to show how the controversy surrounding the South West Africa cases had a significant impact on the ICJ itself, notably by compelling it to review its rules of procedure and its position regarding the question of *ius standi*.

1 Introduction

The 1966 judgment of the International Court of Justice (ICJ) in the South West Africa cases, the first dispute brought before it by African States, has been considered as the most controversial decision in the history of the Court.[1] The 50th anniversary of this 'disaster,' to borrow the terms of Georges Abi-Saab, as well as the launching of the *Ethiopian Yearbook of International Law*, which bears the name of one of the parties to the dispute in question, constitute an appropriate occasion to reflect again on this case which had a profound influence on the relations of Africa with the ICJ.

The content of the two judgments rendered in this dispute (Sect. 2), the critiques to which they gave rise (Sect. 3), as well as the impact they had on future developments related to the Court (Sect. 4) will be examined in turn.

---

[1] Abi Saab (1996), p. 5.

M.M. Mbengue (✉) • N. Messihi
University of Geneva, Geneva, Switzerland
e-mail: Makane.Mbengue@unige.ch; najib.messihi@graduateinstitute.ch

2 The Judgments of the International Court of Justice in the South West Africa Cases

2.1 Background of the Dispute

On 4 November 1960, Ethiopia and Liberia instituted proceedings before the ICJ to challenge the legality of South Africa's administration of the mandated territory of South West Africa. As former members of the League of Nations, Ethiopia and Liberia were the only Sub-Saharan African states entitled to activate the jurisdictional clause incorporated in Article 7 of the Mandate of 17 December 1920 for German South West Africa (the Mandate), which stipulated that:

> The Mandatory agrees that, if any dispute whatever should arise between the Mandatory and *another Member of the League of Nations* relating to the interpretation or the application of the provisions of the Mandate, such dispute, if it cannot be settled by negotiation, shall be submitted to the Permanent Court of International Justice provided for by Article 14 of the Covenant of the League of Nations (emphasis added).

Although the provision in question referred explicitly to the Permanent Court of International Justice (PCIJ) which had been dissolved in 1946, the referral of the case to the ICJ was appropriate by virtue of Article 37 of its Statute, which states that:

> Whenever a treaty or convention in force provides for reference of a matter to ... the Permanent Court of International Justice, the matter shall, as between the parties to the present Statute, be referred to the International Court of Justice.

This was not the first time that the question of the former German colony of South West Africa was brought before the ICJ. Indeed, throughout the 1950s, upon the request of the United Nations General Assembly, the Court had rendered a series of three advisory opinions in which it emphasised that South West Africa was still a mandated territory, thereby rejecting South Africa's contention that the Mandate had lapsed with the demise of the League of Nations. Consequently, the ICJ considered that as a mandatory power, South Africa was under the legal obligation to comply with the provisions of the Mandate and the Covenant of the League of Nations and to submit to international supervision under the auspices of the UN General Assembly, to whom it had to transmit annual reports and petitions from the inhabitants of the territory.[2]

However, sheltering behind the non-binding character of advisory opinions, South Africa maintained its legal positions with regard to South West Africa and continued to refrain from honouring its obligations under the Mandate. It is this situation that prompted Ethiopia and Liberia, with the support of the Second

---

[2]ICJ, *International Status of South-West Africa*, Advisory Opinion, (1950) ICJ Rep 128; ICJ, *South-West Africa-Voting Procedure*, Advisory Opinion, (1955) ICJ Rep 67; ICJ, *Admissibility of hearings of petitioners by the Committee on South West Africa*, Advisory Opinion, (1956) ICJ Rep 23.

Conference of Independent African States, to institute contentious proceedings against South Africa before the ICJ. The aim of this initiative was to obtain a binding judicial judgment that could be enforced through the application of Article 94 of the UN Charter which confers to the Security Council the power to 'decide upon measures to be taken to give effect to the judgment'.[3]

It is therefore not surprising that in their application, Ethiopia and Liberia primarily asked the ICJ to confirm its previous pronouncements on the survival of the Mandate with all that this implies in terms of obligations and international supervision. Nevertheless, the Court was also invited by Ethiopia and Liberia to go beyond its advisory opinions by finding that South Africa had violated its obligations under the Mandate through, *inter alia*, introducing apartheid, establishing military bases on the territory of South West Africa, and refusing to submit reports and transmit petitions to the United Nations.[4]

Against all expectations, South Africa decided to participate in the proceedings by raising on the 30 November 1961, within the time-limit fixed for the presentation of its first pleading, four preliminary objections. In conformity with Article 63 of its Rules, the ICJ dealt with these objections in a separate phase and issued a judgment on 21 December 1962, in which it rejected all of them by a very narrow majority of eight votes to seven.

2.1.1 The 1962 Judgment

The first preliminary objection filed by South Africa to challenge the jurisdiction of the Court consisted of advancing that the Mandate for South West Africa is not a 'treaty or convention in force' within the meaning of the aforementioned Article 37 of the Statue of the ICJ. This objection was dismissed by the Court, which affirmed that the Mandate in question was an international agreement having the character of a treaty or convention.[5] Recalling its advisory opinion of 1950 concerning the *International Status of South West Africa*, the ICJ added that this agreement, including its jurisdictional clause, was still in force despite the dissolution of the League of Nations. This conclusion was based *inter alia* on Article 80, paragraph 1 of the UN Charter which provides that until the conclusion of trusteeship agreements 'nothing ... shall be construed in or of itself to alter in any manner the rights whatsoever of any States or any peoples or the terms of existing international instruments to which Members of the United Nations may respectively be parties'.[6]

---

[3]Gross (1966), pp. 36 and 39–42.
[4]ICJ, *South West Africa Cases (Ethiopia v. South Africa; Liberia v. South Africa), Preliminary Objections,* Judgment, (1962) ICJ Rep 319, pp. 322–324.
[5]Ibid., pp. 330–332.
[6]Ibid., pp. 332–335.

In its second preliminary objection, South Africa contended that neither of the applicants could be described as 'another member of the League of Nations' as required for *locus standi* by the abovementioned Article 7 of the Mandate. Its position was based on the logical assumption that since the League of Nations had ceased to exist on 19 April 1946, there could no longer exist any members of the League of Nations after this date. To reject this contention, the Court pointed out that the interpretation according to the natural and ordinary meaning of the words employed was not an absolute rule and that no reliance could be placed on it where it resulted in a meaning incompatible with the spirit, purpose and context of the clause or instrument to be interpreted.[7] In this respect, it affirmed that the judicial protection set out in Article 7 was an essential feature of the mandate system and one of the main securities for the performance by mandatory powers of their sacred trust of civilisation. Indeed, the possibility of resorting to the Court contemplated in Article 7 was to serve as a final bulwark of protection against abuse or breaches of the Mandate by the mandatory.[8] Because of the unanimity rule, the mandatory was able to prevent the Council of the League of Nations from adopting any unfavourable and detrimental resolution regarding its administration of the mandated territory. Therefore, the only course left to compel the mandatory to observe its obligations towards the inhabitants of the territory and the international community was to obtain a binding decision by the PCIJ. Since the League and its Council lacked capacity to appear before the Court, the prerogative of instituting proceedings against the mandatory was vested in the other members of the League.[9]

In addition to the fact that such interpretation would safeguard the spirit and the structure of the mandate regime, the Court emphasised that Ethiopia and Liberia should be considered as members of the League within the meaning of Article 7 because of the agreement reached in 1946 to maintain the rights of the members of the League with regard to the different mandates in force. This agreement was evidenced by the content of the dissolution resolution adopted in April 1946, as well as the circumstances and discussions which preceded its adoption.[10]

In its third preliminary objection to the jurisdiction of the Court, South Africa argued that the dispute brought before the Court by Ethiopia and Liberia was not a dispute as envisaged by Article 7 of the Mandate as it did not affect any material interests of the applicant States or their nationals. However, the Court considered that this contention ran counter to the natural and ordinary meaning of the terms of Article 7 whose language was broad, clear and precise. By referring to 'any dispute whatever' relating to the interpretation or the application of the 'provisions' of the Mandate and not to any one particular provision, it was obvious that this article encompassed all types of disputes whether they concern the substantive obligations of the mandatory towards the inhabitants of the territory or towards the other

---

[7]Ibid., p. 336.
[8]Ibid.
[9]Ibid., pp. 337–338.
[10]Ibid., pp. 338–342.

members of the League or to its obligation to submit to the supervision of the latter. Consequently, the Court affirmed that the manifest scope and purport of Article 7 indicates that:

> [T]he Members of the League were understood to have a legal right or interest in the observance by the Mandatory of its obligations both toward the inhabitants of the Mandated Territory, and toward the League of Nations and its Members.[11]

This *dictum* is of the highest importance to understand the controversy induced by the subsequent judgment issued in the second phase of the proceedings which will be analysed below.

Finally, the fourth preliminary objection raised by the respondent consisted in saying that if a dispute existed within the meaning of Article 7, it was not one which could not be settled by negotiation with the applicants. In this respect, South Africa emphasised that neither Ethiopia nor Liberia had made any direct attempts to negotiate a settlement of the dispute with it. However, the ICJ rejected this objection on the basis that the deadlock reached in the collective negotiation carried out in the past within the ambit of the United Nations, as well as the pleadings of the parties before it, compel a conclusion that no reasonable probability existed that further negotiations would lead to a settlement.[12]

By dismissing the four preliminary objections filed by South Africa, the ICJ decided that it had jurisdiction to adjudicate upon the merits of the dispute. The 1962 judgment generated a wave of hope and optimism among African countries. There were no more obstacles that could bar the Court from rendering a binding judgment that would serve as a basis for prompting the decolonisation of South West Africa. However, four years later, in a judgment handed down on 18 July 1966, the Court finally decided by the casting vote of its president to reject Ethiopia and Liberia's claims without really dealing with the substantive merits of the case. It justified its decision on the basis that the applicants had failed to establish any legal right or interest appertaining to them in the subject matter of their claims.

2.1.2 The 1966 Judgment

To reach this conclusion, the ICJ began its reasoning by stating that before addressing the contentions of the applicants with regard to the continuance of the Mandate and the violation of its provisions by South Africa, it had first to deal with a question appertaining to the merits of the case but having an antecedent character, namely that of the legal right or interest of Ethiopia and Liberia in the subject matter of their claims. According to the Court, this question had to be dealt with first as a decision on it might render unnecessary the enquiry into the other aspects of the merits.[13]

---

[11]Ibid., p. 343.
[12]Ibid., pp. 344–346.
[13]ICJ, *South West Africa Cases, Second Phase,* Judgment, (1966) ICJ Rep 6, paras. 4–5.

To make such decision, the Court turned to the structure of the Mandate and explained that its provisions could be split into two categories: the 'conduct' provisions and the 'special interests' provisions. The first of these categories was deemed to designate the articles defining the mandatory's powers and obligations in respect of the inhabitants of the territory and towards the League of Nations and its organs while the second consisted of the articles conferring certain rights in relation to the mandated territory directly upon the members of the League as individual states or in favour of their nationals.[14]

After drawing this distinction, the Court pointed out that the dispute brought before it by Ethiopia and Liberia related exclusively to the 'conduct' provisions of the Mandate. Therefore, to decide whether the applicants had a legal right or interest in the subject-matter of their claims, the ICJ was invited to determine whether any legal right or interest was vested in the members of the League of Nations, individually and each in its own, to call for the carrying out of the mandates as regards their 'conduct' clauses or alternatively whether this function must be regarded as having appertained exclusively to the League itself. Put differently, the question was whether the obligations imposed upon the mandatory by the 'conduct' provisions were owed to the members of the League of Nations individually and separately or to the League as an institution.

To answer this question, the Court analysed the mandate system and paid due attention to the relevant texts and instruments in this respect. It noted for instance that Article 22 of the Covenant stipulated that the tutelage of the peoples of mandated territories should be exercised by the mandatories 'on behalf of the League' and not on behalf of its members in their individual capacities. Thus, the mandatories were considered as agents of the League and not of each and every member of it individually.[15]

In the same vein, the Court pointed out that pursuant to the same article, mandatories were requested to submit annual reports to the Council and to the Permanent Mandates Commission, which were organs of the League of Nations and not to the members of the latter. These reports were to be rendered to the satisfaction of the Council. In fact, individual member states of the League could take part in the administrative process of supervision of the Mandate only through their participation in the activities of the League's organs. They had no right of direct intervention in relation to mandatories.[16]

Furthermore, the Court underlined the fact that while under Article 7, paragraph 1 of the Mandate, the consent of the Council of the League was required for any modification of the terms of the former, it was not stated that the consent of individual members of the League was required in addition to this.[17]

---

[14]Ibid., para. 11.
[15]Ibid., para. 20.
[16]Ibid., para. 25.
[17]Ibid., para. 31.

In view of all these elements, the ICJ concluded that individual members of the League such as Ethiopia and Liberia were not to be regarded as having a separate legal right or interest of their own, respecting the administration of the Mandate. According to the Court, the right to claim the due performance of the Mandate by the mandatory was vested exclusively in the League and was to be exercised solely by its competent organs.[18]

To strengthen this conclusion, the Court also relied on further considerations. In this respect, it explained that the analysis of the genesis of the jurisdictional clause tends to confirm the position of the Court because this provision did not appear in the early drafts of the different mandates and was only included when provisions on the commercial and religious interests of the nationals of the other members of the League were added to the text.[19] According to the Court, the same could be said of the subsequent practice of the League and its members since after the conclusion of the mandates and, until the dissolution of the organisation in question, no member of the League attempted to settle directly with the mandatory any question that did not affect its own interests as a State or those of its nationals. The only case referred to the Permanent Court under a mandate adjudication clause, namely *Mavrommatis Concessions*, concerned 'special interests' provisions and not 'conduct' ones.[20]

Finally, the Court turned once again to the structure of the mandates regime and more specifically to the voting rules within the Council of the League to seek confirmation of its conclusion. It noted that by deliberately deciding that mandatories should be members of the Council for mandate purposes, thereby granting them a right of veto against the decisions related to mandates, the drafters of the League intended to establish a system where the Council as a supervisory body could not impose its views on the mandatory without its consent. The compliance of mandatories with their obligations under the mandates was to be reached by argument, discussion, negotiation and cooperation within the ambit of the League. Therefore, in this context, the Court affirmed that the proposition according to which individual members had a right to refer any matter related to the conduct of the mandates to the PCIJ was misconceived and out of place. In this respect the Court emphasised that this situation was not absurd or unreasonable because 'in the international field, the existence of obligations that cannot in the last resort be enforced by any legal process, has always been the rule rather than the exception, and this was even more the case in 1920 than today'.[21]

The contradiction between the findings of the Court in 1962 and 1966 is blatant and has lead several learned commentators to describe the 1966 judgment as a 'covert reversal' of the 1962 decision.[22] Indeed, while in its decision on preliminary objections, the Court had clearly stated that the applicants were understood to have

---

[18]Ibid., para. 32–33.
[19]Ibid., para. 77–79.
[20]Ibid., para. 84.
[21]Ibid., para. 86.
[22]Falk (1967), p. 11; Anand (1969), p. 138.

a legal right or interest in the observance by the mandatory of its obligations under all the provisions of the Mandate, the Court finally denied the existence of such right or interest concerning what it called the 'conduct' clauses of this instrument. Moreover, if in 1962 the ICJ had qualified the possibility given to the members of the League to institute proceedings against the mandatory as 'an essential feature of the mandates system', it finally considered in 1966 that such direct intervention by member states in the administration of the mandated territory was inconsistent with the spirit of the mandates and the intentions of their drafters.

In fact, this striking reversal could be explained by a series of unforeseeable events which occurred between 1962 and 1966 and which had the effect of modifying the composition of the Court to the detriment of the applicants. As mentioned above, the judgment of 1962 was adopted by 8 votes to 7. However, this narrow majority was subsequently altered by the death of Judge Badawi of Egypt in 1965 and by the illness of Judge Bustamante of Peru which prevented him from participating in the proceedings of the second phase. Moreover, Judge Zafrullah Khan of Pakistan who was likely to uphold the contentions of the applicants had to withdraw from the case upon the request of the then President of the Court because of the fact that he had been asked to sit as an *ad hoc* judge for Ethiopia and Liberia before his election as a member of the ICJ in 1964. Meanwhile, Judge Spender of Australia, who voted against the judgment of 1962, was designated as the President of the Court, a position that enabled him to play a decisive role in the adoption of the judgment of 1966, which was decided by his casting vote. Because of all these events, the minority of 1962 became the majority in 1966 and was able to overrule the judgment rendered by the Court on preliminary objections. In this respect, it is worth noting that the reasoning of the Court in the 1966 judgment is quite similar to the interpretation of the mandates system proposed by Judges Spender and Fitzmaurice in the joint dissenting opinion that they appended to the decision of 1962.[23]

As could have been expected, the judgment of the Court in the second phase of the South West Africa dispute provoked a wide range of reactions that will now be examined.

3 Reaction to the 1966 Judgment

3.1 Political Reactions

Unsurprisingly, the judgment of 1966 was welcomed with outrage and consternation by African States who had hoped the Court would decide differently. These States expressed their deep disappointment and dismay on the occasion of the 21st Session of the UN General Assembly which was held in September of the same

---

[23]ICJ (1962) Rep 465.

year. Indeed, the decision of the Court was described *inter alia* as 'scandalous' by the representative of Guinea,[24] 'grotesque' by the representative of Ghana,[25] 'totally unsound from both the legal and moral standpoints' by the representative of the Central African Republic,[26] 'irresponsible' by the representative of Nigeria,[27] 'a denial of justice' by the representative of Ivory Coast[28] and 'a perversion of justice that brought upon the International Court the greatest opprobrium in its history' by the representative of Liberia.[29] Critical reactions to the 1966 judgment were not limited to African States. Representatives of other third world countries and of many western and eastern States also expressed their strong disapproval of the Court's decision.[30]

The reactions of African States in this respect went, however, far beyond mere statements made within the ambit of the United Nations or in the media. Having understood that the question of South West Africa and of its decolonisation will not be solved by judicial means, they asked for and succeeded in obtaining a UN General Assembly Resolution confirming the illegality of the conduct of South Africa in the territory of South West Africa and revoking the Mandate that had been conferred by the League of Nations in 1920.

Indeed, on 27 October 1966, Resolution 2145 (XXI) was adopted by an overwhelming majority of 114 votes to 2 (South Africa and Portugal) with 3 abstentions (France, United Kingdom and Malawi). In this resolution, after noting that the situation in the mandated territory had seriously deteriorated following the judgment of July 1966, the Assembly declared that 'South Africa has failed to fulfil its obligations in respect of the Mandated Territory and to ensure the moral and material well-being and security of the indigenous inhabitants of South-West Africa, and has, in fact, disavowed the Mandate'.[31] Therefore, it decided that the Mandate conferred upon South Africa 'is ... terminated' and that 'South Africa has no other legal right to administer the Territory and that henceforth South-West Africa comes under the direct responsibility of the United Nations'.[32] The legality of this resolution was subsequently confirmed by the ICJ in its 1971 advisory opinion on *The Legal Consequences of the Continued Presence of South Africa in Namibia*.[33]

---

[24] A/PV 1414.
[25] A/PV 1419.
[26] A/PV 1427.
[27] A/PV 1429.
[28] Ibid.
[29] A/PV 1414.
[30] Fischer (1966), pp. 145–149.
[31] UNGA Res. 2145 (XXI), preamble and para. 3.
[32] Ibid., para 4.
[33] ICJ, *Legal Consequences for States of the Continued Presence of South Africa in Namibia (South West Africa) notwithstanding Security Council Resolution 276 (1970)*, Advisory Opinion, (1971) ICJ Rep 16.

Another concrete response of African States to the 1966 judgment was the modification of the composition of the Court in favour of Africa.[34] Indeed, a few months after this decision, the UN General Assembly and Security Council were called upon to elect five new judges of the ICJ. Therefore, bearing in mind the important role played by the composition of the bench in the outcome of the South West Africa cases, African states insisted that the seat dedicated to the Commonwealth and which was occupied by an Australian judge, be transferred to an African country. Accordingly, the Nigerian candidate Charles Onyeama was finally preferred to the Australian candidate and elected as a Judge. This raised the number of African judges of the Court from one to two.[35]

The years that followed these events were marked by an era of mistrust of African States towards the ICJ. This mistrust took different forms. First, for more than a decade, African States refrained from submitting their disputes to the Court.[36] Indeed, the latter had to wait until 1978 to be called upon to settle a dispute involving African countries.[37] Another expression of the loss of confidence in the ICJ consisted of a slowdown in the filing by African States of declarations recognising the compulsory jurisdiction of the Court.[38] While from the early 1950s to July 1966, eight African nations joined the optional clause system provided for in Article 36 (2) of the Statute, only four of them did so subsequently until the use of the Court by Tunisia and Libya in 1978. After that date, which marked the beginning of a progressive process of reconciliation between Africa and the Court, ten more countries decided to become part of the aforementioned system. Finally, an additional sign of the mistrust of African states towards the ICJ following the 1966 judgment was their reluctance when negotiating treaties to accept the incorporation of adjudication clauses conferring jurisdiction to the Court. For instance, during the Vienna Conference on the Law of Treaties, African States vigorously opposed the proposition advocated by Western States to recognise the compulsory jurisdiction of the ICJ for disputes arising from Part V of the 1969 Vienna Convention on the Law of Treaties, which deals with treaty invalidity and termination.[39] In the same vein, during this period, some African countries like Algeria would systematically make reservations to the compromissory clauses in favour of the ICJ that were included in the treaties to which they were parties.[40]

---

[34]Ajibola (2000), p. 362.

[35]Bastid (1967), p. 582.

[36]Mbengue (2013), p. 170.

[37]ICJ, *Continental Shelf case (Tunisia/Libyan Arab Jamahiria)*. The proceedings were introduced by special agreement on 1 December 1978.

[38]Mahiou (2013), p. 192.

[39]Elias (1971), pp. 397–404.

[40]Mahiou (2013), p. 192 note 12.

3.2 The Reactions of Publicists

As we have seen, the judgment of the Court rendered in the second phase of the South West Africa cases had been the object of strong political reactions from the part of African governments. However, hostile reactions in this respect were not limited to the political sphere. Indeed, the 1966 judgment was also sharply criticised by several prominent and learned international law experts who had questioned its legal validity, persuasiveness and appropriateness. In the introduction to his exhaustive and brilliantly written dissenting opinion, Judge Philip Jessup of the United States of America went as far as stating that he considered the judgment rendered by the Court in the South West Africa cases as 'completely unfounded in law'.[41] In fact, several legal arguments were advanced against the 1966 judgment. For the sake of clarity, these will be assembled and exposed below under three headings.

3.2.1 An Offence of the *res judicata* Principle

Several dissenting judges, as well as qualified commentators, argued that by reversing its 1962 findings on the question of the applicant's standing, the Court has violated the *res judicata* rule which is binding upon it not only as a general principle of law, but also based on Article 60 of its Statute which stipulates that the judgments of the Court are 'final and without appeal'.[42] In this respect, it must be noted however, that in its 1966 judgment, the ICJ had somewhat anticipated and rejected this contention.

Indeed, throughout its reasoning, the Court emphasised that the question of the legal right or interest of the applicants regarding the subject matter of their claims appertained to the merits of the case and was therefore to be distinguished from the preliminary and procedural question of their standing before the Court that had been decided in 1962.[43] In its first judgment, the ICJ confirmed that Ethiopia and Liberia had a right and a sufficient legal interest to invoke the jurisdictional clause of the mandate for they had met all the requirements laid down in this provision.[44] Nevertheless, at the merits phase, the applicants were still required to establish that they had a right or interest in the carrying out of the substantive provisions on which they based their claims.[45] In other words, according to the Court, the 1962 judgment acknowledged that Ethiopia and Liberia had a right or interest to institute proceedings before the Court while the 1966 judgment decided that they lacked

---

[41] ICJ (1966) Rep 325.

[42] ICJ (1966) Rep 331–337 (Jessup), 239–242 (Koretsky), 460 (Nervo) and 490–497 (Mbafeno); Dugard (1966), p. 447; Higgins (1966), p. 582.

[43] ICJ, *South West Africa Cases, Second Phase,* Judgment, (1966) ICJ Rep 6, paras. 4, 58–61.

[44] Ibid.

[45] Ibid.

sufficient interest to obtain the judicial pronouncements and declarations they were seeking from the ICJ. Accordingly, since the Court had ruled on two different questions, the 1966 judgment could not be considered as a reversal of that rendered in 1962.

However, reflecting upon this distinction between two types of legal interest, Judge Jessup affirmed that 'no authority is produced in support of this assertion which suggests a procedure of utter futility'.[46] Similarly, Judge Foster of Senegal stated that this passes his understanding.[47] The Court's position in that respect was moreover qualified as 'juristically untenable and unprecedented' by Wolfgang Friedmann,[48] 'confusing' and 'artificial' by Richard Falk,[49] 'unconvincing' by Georges Abi-Saab[50] and 'baffling' by Rosalyn Higgins.[51]

As noted in the previous part of this paper, the Court had clearly stated in its 1962 judgment that the members of the League 'were understood to have a legal right or interest in the observance by the Mandatory of its obligations both toward the inhabitants of the Mandated Territory, and toward the League of Nations and its Members'. Therefore, it was very difficult to follow the Court in its 1966 assertion that the question of the legal interest of the applicants in the subject matter of their claims was a new one, if only because these claims were actually based on the non-observance by South Africa of its obligations towards the inhabitants and the United Nations under the Mandate.

It is also worth noting in this regard that, contrary to what the Court seemed to suggest in its second judgment, the fact that the above quoted *dictum* appeared in the reasons of the 1962 decision rather than in its operative part is of no relevance concerning the application of the *res judicata* principle.[52] Indeed, from several authorities, Judges Koretsky and Jessup convincingly demonstrated that the finality of the ICJ's judgments does not extend only to their operative parts but also to the reasons on which they are based.[53]

3.2.2 A Misinterpretation of the Mandate

In addition to the considerations related to the *res judicata* principle, critics of the 1966 judgment also contended that, by denying the right or interest of the applicants in the carrying out of the 'conduct' provisions of the Mandate, the Court had misinterpreted the latter. As explained above, to reach this conclusion, the ICJ

---

[46] ICJ (1966) Rep 382.
[47] ICJ (1966) Rep 478.
[48] Friedmann (1967), p. 14.
[49] Falk (1967), p. 7.
[50] Abi Saab (1992), p. 247.
[51] Higgins (1966), p. 581.
[52] ICJ, *South West Africa Cases, Second Phase,* Judgment, (1966) ICJ Rep 6, para. 59.
[53] ICJ (1966) Rep 241 (Koretsky) and 334–335 (Jessup).

analysed the mandate system in light of the substantive provisions of mandate agreements in general, as well as the relevant provisions of the Covenant of the League of Nations. At no time, however, did the Court pay due regard to the adjudication clause of the Mandate for South West Africa. The justification advanced by the Court for not considering Article 7 of the Mandate to find whether the applicants had a legal right or interest in the subject matter of their claims was that 'jurisdictional clauses do not determine whether parties have substantive rights'.[54]

This assertion was challenged by Georges Abi-Saab who convincingly explained that nothing can preclude a compromissory clause from establishing a substantive right, provided that its interpretation clearly leads to such conclusion.[55] In this respect, several dissenting judges and commentators contended that an interpretation of Article 7 of the Mandate in accordance with the natural and ordinary meaning of its terms cannot but evidence the existence of the legal interest of Ethiopia and Liberia in the subject matter of their claims.[56] Indeed, as the Court itself had affirmed in 1962, the language of this provision is broad, clear and precise in this sense as it refers to 'any dispute whatever' relating to the interpretation or the application of the 'provisions' of the Mandate, obviously meaning all the provisions and not only those concerning the 'special interests' of the other members of the League.

Therefore, by deciding upon the legal interest of the applicants in the way it did in 1966, the Court was deemed to have failed to comply with the cardinal principle of treaty interpretation that it had laid down itself in its 1950 advisory opinion on the *Competence of the Assembly regarding admission to the United Nations*:

> The first duty of a tribunal which is called upon to interpret and apply the provisions of a treaty, is to endeavour to give effect to them in their *natural and ordinary meaning* in the context in which they occur.[57]

Moreover, the solution adopted by the Court was also criticised for its inconsistency with a teleological interpretation of the Mandate.[58] This position was based on the idea that it follows from Article 22 of the Covenant of the League that the ultimate purpose of the Mandate was the 'well-being and development' of the inhabitants of the mandated territory as 'a sacred trust of civilization'. Therefore, to give full effect to this purpose, it has been advanced that the Court was supposed to uphold the members of the League of Nations' right to invoke the provisions related to the protection and well-being of the indigenous population. Indeed, by

---

[54] ICJ, *South West Africa Cases, Second Phase*, Judgment, (1966) ICJ Rep 6, paras. 65, 73.

[55] Abi Saab (1967), pp. 144–145.

[56] ICJ (1966) Rep 219–222 (Koo), 248 (Koretsky), 259 (Tanaka) and 499–500 (Mbanefo); Abi Saab (1967), p. 145.

[57] ICJ, *Competence of Assembly regarding admission to the United Nations*, Advisory Opinion, (1950) ICJ Rep 8.

[58] ICJ (1966) Rep 228 (Koo), 258–259 (Tanaka) and 479–480 (Forster).

failing to do so, the ICJ deprived the Mandate from its most effective enforcement mechanism.

The reliance of the Court on the drafting history of the adjudication clause of the Mandate to confirm its interpretation of this instrument was also challenged. In his dissenting opinion appended to the 1966 judgment, Judge Jessup examined thoroughly the *travaux préparatoires* of the mandates and reached a completely different conclusion from that inferred by the Court. He pointed out that earlier drafts of the adjudication clause consisted of two paragraphs: a first paragraph corresponding to Article 7 paragraph 2 of the Mandate and a second one stating that: 'Members of the League may likewise bring any claims on behalf of their nationals for infractions of their rights under this Mandate'. It was therefore possible to infer that disputes over 'conduct provisions' do fall within the scope of the adjudication clause of the Mandate for South West Africa.[59]

Similarly, Judge Jessup also challenged the reference made by the Court to the subsequent practice regarding the resort to the PCIJ for interstate disputes over mandates. He suggested that the scarcity of mandate cases before this court was because of political rather than legal considerations. In support of his contention, Judge Jessup quoted C. Wilfred Jenks who had once stated that:

> Experience has shown that the disadvantages of the existence of divergent views regarding the interpretation of a general international convention of a technical character are rarely regarded by those responsible for the foreign policy of a State as a sufficient reason for accepting the political responsibility involved in instituting contentious proceedings against another State.[60]

Finally, it is worth noting that the interpretation of the Court in 1966 had also been criticised for disregarding the historical background against which mandates were established. Reference was made to the 'wave of idealistic aspiration' that followed the end of the World War, as well as to the 'altruistic outlook of the times' to advocate a notion of legal interest that would go beyond the narrow concept of the individual and material interest of States.[61] In this respect, the Constitution of the ILO, as well as treaties that protect minorities which were concluded shortly before the Mandate, were given as examples to show that the idea of conferring to states a right to institute proceedings against other states, even when their own interests or the interests of their nationals are not at stake, was not unknown or out of place at the time of the establishment of the Mandate.[62]

---

[59] ICJ (1966) Rep 356–373.
[60] ICJ (1966) Rep 408.
[61] ICJ (1966) Rep 373 (Jessup) and 478 (Forster).
[62] ICJ (1966) Rep 377–379 (Jessup); Abi Saab (1967), p. 143.

3.2.3 An Improper Administration of Justice

The way in which the Court conducted the proceedings in the South West Africa cases was also the object of vigorous criticism from legal experts. After its 1962 judgment on preliminary objections, the Court waited more than three and a half years before rendering its judgment on the merits. During this period, two rounds of written pleadings, as well as 99 public sessions of oral hearings, were organised which included, alongside the arguments of agents and counsel of the parties, the testimony of 14 witnesses. However, despite the fact that these proceedings had dealt exclusively with the substantive contentions of the applicants, the Court finally decided after 6 months of deliberations to dismiss the case based on a question of antecedent character, that is to say, the lack of legal interest of Ethiopia and Liberia. The substantive claims of the applicants were therefore not addressed at all in the 1966 judgment.

This led a learned commentator to consider that the Court's decision 'seemed to mock the reality of international adjudication'.[63] Indeed, the parties spent millions of dollars and their counsel hundreds of hours to prepare and expose legal arguments on the merits of the dispute on the firm assumption that the Court was going to pronounce on the substantive contentions of the applicants. At no time during these lengthy proceedings did the Court give an indication to the contrary knowing that a proper administration of justice should have compelled it to do so.

For instance, since it considered that the question of the legal interest of the claimants appertains to the merits of the case, the Court should have joined it to the merits in its 1962 judgment as was provided for in Article 62(5) of the 1946 Rules of Court instead of giving the impression of having settled it.[64] The Court could have also hinted that it remained troubled with the *locus standi* of Ethiopia and Liberia during the oral hearings, notably through the questions of judges.[65] But it failed to do so, thereby preventing the parties from adjusting their strategy and argumentation accordingly. Hence, the parties to the dispute wasted a large amount of time and resources discussing questions that were never addressed by the ICJ.

In the same vein, it was also pointed out that, in its 1966 judgment, the Court had raised *motu proprio* the issue of the lack of interest of the applicants in the subject matter of their claims.[66] Indeed, this argument was not advanced by South Africa in its final submissions. The right of the ICJ to freely choose the legal basis of its decisions was not really questioned in this regard. However, the Court's approach was deemed unfair because the parties had not been able to express their views on the question that constituted the bulk of the ICJ's decision on the merits.[67]

---

[63] Falk (1967), p. 6.
[64] Higgins (1966), pp. 578–579.
[65] Falk (1967), p. 6.
[66] ICJ (1966) Rep 328 (Jessup); Higgins (1966), pp. 581–582.
[67] Favoreu (1966), p. 137.

In view of the elements exposed above and their unsatisfactory character, Richard Falk called in 1967 for judicial reform of the Court.[68] This reform was carried out in the following years, as will be explained below.

4 The Impact of the 1966 Judgement on Future Developments Related to the Court

The 1966 judgment, and the particularly hostile reactions it provoked in the political and legal spheres, had consequences on the work of the Court. Indeed, in the years that followed, the Court drew lessons from this experience by modifying its rules of procedure, as well as its position on the question of *ius standi*.

4.1 The 1972–1978 Amendments to the Rules of Court

As explained earlier, the 1966 judgment was followed by a period of 'mistrust' of African States towards the Court. This mistrust caused a slowdown in the activity of the ICJ, which felt an urgent need to enhance its attractiveness. This was done through a complete revision by the Court of its rules of procedure which led to two series of amendments adopted in 1972 and 1978.

An exhaustive analysis of this substantial reform of the Rules of the ICJ is certainly beyond the scope of the present study. However, it is worth noting that several amendments seem to have been at least partly induced by the 1966 judgment and a result of the criticisms levelled against it. It is precisely these amendments that will be now examined.

One of the main pillars of the 1972–1978 reform consisted of the establishment of new rules concerning *ad hoc* chambers that can be constituted by the Court at the request of the parties to deal with a particular dispute.[69] Pursuant to these new rules, the parties to a dispute were given a decisive influence in the composition of *ad hoc* chambers. Indeed, Article 17 of the new Rules stipulated that 'the President shall ascertain their views regarding the *composition* of the Chamber, and shall report to the Court accordingly'. This provision reflected quite a broad and liberal interpretation of Article 26 (2) of the Statute according to which 'the *number* of judges to constitute such a chamber shall be determined by the Court with the approval of the parties'.

The link between this change and the mistrust of African and Third World countries towards the Court is not hard to establish. By introducing this new rule, the Court was sending an attractive and reassuring signal to these States. They were

---

[68]Falk (1967), p. 19.
[69]See Article 26 (2) of the Statute of the ICJ.

now able to choose among its bench the judges they trusted most to settle their disputes and exclude those they considered unfavourable to their interests. However, somewhat paradoxically, the first case dealt with by an *ad hoc* chamber after the 1972–1978 amendments was the *Gulf of Maine* dispute whose parties, namely the United States and Canada had requested and obtained a chamber exclusively composed of western judges.[70]

Another important novelty regarding *ad hoc* chambers was that set out in Article 17(4), which reads as follows: 'Members of a Chamber formed under this Article who have been replaced ... following the expiration of their terms of office, shall continue to sit in all phases of the case, whatever the stage it has then reached'. This rule of continued participation was conceived as an important guarantee for the parties. It means that the composition of the chamber that considered their wishes will remain unchanged throughout the proceedings.[71] However, one may also add that it operates as a safeguard against contradictory judgments. A contradiction between the decision on preliminary objections and that on merits is less likely to occur in the context of a case settled by an *ad hoc* chamber for these are rendered by the same judges.

As mentioned above, one of the critiques levelled against the conduct of the Court in the South West Africa cases was its failure to indicate to the parties that the question of the legal interest of the applicants had not been settled in 1962 and was still pending before it at the merits stage. This prevented the parties from expressing their views on the issue and led them to dedicate substantial developments to legal questions that finally appeared to be of little relevance. Bearing in mind this criticism, the Court included in its new Rules of Procedure several provisions aiming at avoiding such undesirable situations in the future.

Among these provisions is Article 61 (1) of the Rules which stipulates that: 'The Court may at any time prior to or during the hearing indicate any points or issues to which it would like the parties specially to address themselves, or on which it considers that there has been sufficient argument'. In the same vein one can also quote Article 79 (8) of the Rules which provides that: 'In order to enable the Court to determine its jurisdiction at the preliminary stage of the proceedings, the Court, whenever necessary, may request the parties to argue all questions of law and fact, and to adduce all evidence, which bear on the issue'. These new rules are particularly useful whenever the Court is willing to raise a legal question *motu proprio*.[72]

A further change that is also worth mentioning here is the introduction in Article 79 (9) of the Rules of a requirement that Court's decisions on preliminary objections shall be rendered 'in the form of a judgment'. This could be considered as further evidence of the assertion that the decisions of the ICJ on preliminary objections are *res judicata* since Article 60 of its Statute stipulates that 'the

---

[70]ICJ, *Delimitation of the Maritime Boundary in the Gulf of Maine Area*, Judgment, (1984) ICJ Rep 246.
[71]Guyomar (1973), p. 760; Aréchaga (1973), p. 4.
[72]Guyomar (1973), p. 766.

judgment is final and without appeal'. In this respect, it is worth underlining that the Court relied on this wording in the 2007 *Genocide case* to affirm that no distinction shall be made between judgments on jurisdiction and judgments on the merits when it comes to the application of the *res judicata* principle.[73]

To conclude, it must be noted that one of the most important aspects of the 1972–1978 reform was the elimination of the express authorisation in the rules to join a preliminary objection to the merits. The purpose of this change was to push the Court to settle as far as possible all the preliminary questions in the first phase of the proceedings and to avoid the repetition of the same legal arguments in the merits phase. Instead of joining a preliminary objection to the merits, the Court was invited by the new Rules to declare that the objection at stake 'does not possess an exclusively preliminary character'.[74] One may of course consider that this amendment was of a pure semantic character and that the joining of a preliminary objection to the merits was not really put aside by the reform. However, it was believed that the new formulation would limit and objectivise the discretionary power of the Court to refrain from dealing with an objection at the preliminary phase.[75] Moreover, it was contended that this modification would deter respondents from raising objections that cannot be decided without going into the merits for they would now run the risk of an adverse decision from the Court in this matter.[76]

4.2 Erga omnes *Obligations and* locus standi

As explained earlier, in 1966, the contentions of Ethiopia and Liberia were rejected because the ICJ considered that they had failed to establish the existence of any legal right or interest appertaining to them in the subject-matter of their claims. By this ruling, the Court seemed to suggest that an individual and direct interest was required for standing before it. This was confirmed by the explicit disapproval by the Court of the application of the *actio popularis* principle on the international plane:

> Looked at in another way moreover, the argument [of necessity] amounts to a plea that the Court should allow the equivalent of an "actio popularis", or right resident in any member of a community to take legal action in vindication of a public interest. But although a right of this kind may be known to certain municipal systems of law, it is not known to international law as it stands at present: nor is the Court able to regard it as imported by the "general principles of law" referred to in Article 38, paragraph 1 (c), of its Statute.[77]

---

[73]ICJ, *Application of the Convention on the Prevention and Punishment of the Crime of Genocide (Bosnia and Herzegovina v. Serbia and Montenegro)*, Judgment, (2007) ICJ Rep 43, para. 117.
[74]See article 79 (9) of the Rules of Court.
[75]Kolb (2013), p. 265.
[76]Aréchaga (1973), p. 16.
[77]ICJ, *South West Africa Cases, Second Phase*, Judgment, (1966) ICJ Rep 6, para. 88.

However, 4 years later, in its 1970 judgment rendered in the *Barcelona Traction* case, the ICJ appeared to reverse its narrow approach to the question of the legal interest. Indeed, in an *obiter dictum* that became very famous, the Court recognised the existence of a category of legal obligations, namely the *erga omnes* obligations whose observance concerns all the states of the international community:

> [A]n essential distinction should be drawn between the obligations of a State towards the international community as a whole, and those arising vis-à-vis another State ... By their very nature the former are the concern of all States. In view of the importance of the rights involved, all States can be held to have *a legal interest* in their protection; they are obligations *erga omnes*.[78]

This dictum has been interpreted as a rectification by the Court itself, whose composition had in the meantime changed, of its 1966 judgment in the *South West Africa* cases.[79] It appears that it was included in the 1970 decision upon the request of Judge Lachs who had been inspired in this regard by the ideas expressed by Judge Jessup in his 1966 dissenting opinion.[80] This explanation is quite convincing since the developments made by the Court on *erga omnes* obligations were of no relevance for the settlement of the dispute between Belgium and Spain. It is also further confirmed by the fact that the Court had included protection from racial discrimination in its list of examples of *erga omnes* obligations. By doing so, the ICJ seemed to indicate that if the *South West Africa* cases were brought before it again, it would have to uphold the legal interest of the applicants in the subject matter of their claims, for *apartheid* amounts to a breach of an *erga omnes* rule.

Indeed, the logical conclusion to be drawn from the above quoted ruling was that by stating that all states have a 'legal interest' in the protection of the rights involved in *erga omnes* obligations, the Court confirmed that all states have standing to invoke the breach of such obligations by other states before it. However, another paragraph included in the same decision cast some doubt on this assertion:

> [O]n the universal level, the instruments which embody human rights do not confer on States the capacity to protect the victims of infringements of such rights irrespective of their nationality. It is therefore still on the regional level that a solution to this problem has had to be sought; thus, within the Council of Europe, of which Spain is not a member, the problem of admissibility encountered by the claim in the present case has been resolved by the European Convention on Human Rights, which entitles each State which is a party to the Convention to lodge a complaint against any other contracting State for violation of the Convention, irrespective of the nationality of the victim.

Indeed, this paragraph seemed to imply that except in some regional systems, a nationality link between the victims of violations of *erga omnes* obligations and the

---

[78]ICJ, *Barcelona Traction, Light and Power Company, Limited,* Judgment, (1970) ICJ Rep 3, para 33.
[79]Voeffray (2004), p. 75.
[80]Ibid.

applicant States is still required to establish the standing of the latter.[81] In the following years, several cases involving this category of obligations were brought before the Court. However, they did not contribute to clarifying the relation between the *erga omnes* nature of a rule and the *ius standi* of states intending to invoke it.

For instance, in the *Nuclear Tests* cases, Australia and New Zealand based their standing, *inter alia*, on the existence of an alleged *erga omnes* rule prohibiting atmospheric nuclear tests. However, the Court did not pronounce on the matter since it decided that the claim of the applicants had no object.[82] In the *East Timor* case, the Court emphasised that 'the *erga omnes* character of a norm and the rule of consent to jurisdiction are two different things', meaning by that that the mere fact that rights and obligations *erga omnes* may be at issue in a dispute would not give the Court jurisdiction to entertain that dispute.[83] Nevertheless, this assertion did not answer the question whether, provided that the Court has jurisdiction, the fact that rules invoked by the applicants are *erga omnes* suffices to confer them *locus standi*.

A first turning point in that respect was the adoption in 2001 by the International Law Commission (ILC) of its 'Draft Articles on Responsibility of States for Internationally Wrongful Acts'. Indeed, this authoritative text which codified to a large extent the rules of state responsibility contains an article on the 'invocation of responsibility by a State other than an injured State,' which reads as follows:

> Any State other than an injured State is entitled to invoke the responsibility of another State in accordance with paragraph 2 if:
>
> (a) the obligation breached is owed to a group of States including that State, and is established for the protection of a collective interest of the group; or
>
> (b) the obligation breached is owed to the international community as a whole.[84]

This provision distinguishes between two types of *erga omnes* obligations: the *erga omnes partes* obligations (paragraph a) and the *erga omnes* obligations *tout court* (paragraph b). Interestingly, in its official commentary to this article, the ILC gave Article 22 of the Covenant of the League along with Mandate agreements as examples of provisions established for the protection of a collective interest of a group of States within the meaning of paragraph (a).[85] It also added that the above quoted Article 48 constitutes 'a deliberate departure' from the 1966 judgment of the ICJ in the South West Africa cases.[86] It follows from this last assertion that, for

---

[81] Ibid., pp. 76–78.
[82] ICJ, *Nuclear Tests (Australia v. France)*, Judgment, (1974) ICJ Rep 273; ICJ, *Nuclear Tests (New Zealand v. France)*, Judgment, (1974) ICJ Rep 457.
[83] ICJ, *East Timor (Portugal v. Australia)*, Judgment, (1995) ICJ Rep 90, para. 29.
[84] Article 48 (1).
[85] Yearbook of the ILC (2001), Vol. II, p. 127, note 725.
[86] Ibid.

the ILC, a breach of an *erga omnes* obligation should be able to serve as a basis for the establishment of the *locus standi* of a state which is not directly affected by the breach in question.

This view was finally endorsed and confirmed by the ICJ in the 2012 *Questions Relating to the Obligation to Prosecute or Extradite* case involving Belgium and Senegal. In this case, Senegal challenged the admissibility of Belgium's claims by arguing that the latter was not entitled to invoke its international responsibility for the alleged breach of its obligation under the Torture Convention to either prosecute or extradite Hissène Habré.[87] To substantiate this contention, Senegal advanced that 'none of the alleged victims of the acts said to be attributable to Mr. Habré were of Belgian nationality at the time when the acts were committed'.[88]

However, the Court rejected the Senegalese objections. To do so, it explained that it follows from the object and purpose of the Torture Convention, which is to make more effective the struggle against torture throughout the world, that States parties to this Convention have a common interest in the compliance by any State party with its obligation to prosecute or extradite the persons responsible for acts of torture. This was deemed true regardless of the nationality of the offender or the victims, or of the place where the alleged offences occurred. Consequently, the Court affirmed that these obligations may be defined as *erga omnes partes* for they are owed by any State party to all the other States parties to the Convention.[89] According to the Court, this qualification implied the entitlement of each State party to the Convention to make a claim concerning the cessation of an alleged breach of these obligations by another State party.[90] Therefore, it concluded that Belgium had standing to invoke the responsibility of Senegal in the present case.[91]

In view of the evolution exposed above, one can assume that if the South West Africa cases were brought before the ICJ today, the Court would render a different decision. It would certainly consider that the Mandate derived from Article 22 of the Covenant was established to protect a common interest of all the members of the League, namely the well-being and the development of the indigenous inhabitants which forms a sacred trust of civilisation. Drawing upon this finding, it would undoubtedly assert that the obligations allegedly breached by South Africa are of an *erga omnes partes* character and that, therefore, Ethiopia and Liberia as former members of the League have standing to invoke the responsibility of the respondent before it.

---

[87] ICJ, *Questions relating to the Obligation to Prosecute or Extradite (Belgium v. Senegal)*, Judgment, (2012) ICJ Rep 422, para. 64.
[88] Ibid.
[89] Ibid., para. 68.
[90] Ibid., para. 69.
[91] Ibid., para. 70.

5 Conclusion

Fifty years later, it can be affirmed without much hesitation that the ICJ has managed to overcome the crisis that followed its 1966 judgment in the South West Africa cases. African States have become 'good clients' of the Court to which they refer, fairly regularly, a large variety of disputes: maritime and territorial boundaries, criminal cooperation, use of force, state responsibility, human rights, etc.[92] From a technical point of view, as explained above, the Court has abandoned its narrow conception of *locus standi* which had prevented it from dealing in a satisfactory manner with the claims of Ethiopia and Liberia. Does all this mean however that nothing remains from the South West Africa cases today? The answer is negative. What remains is this tendency of the Court to hide behind technicalities to avoid taking a stand on highly political and sensitive issues. Indeed, if the Court resorted in 1966 to an artificial distinction between two types of legal interest to eschew the question of the legality of the application of apartheid in South West Africa, it used similar strategies in much more recent cases. For instance, in 2010, it managed to abstain from pronouncing on the legal status of Kosovo by distinguishing the declaration of independence from the question of statehood.[93] In the same vein, in 2012, the Court drew upon the classical distinction between substantive and procedural rules to refrain from enhancing the effectiveness of *jus cogens* norms.[94] Judicial caution and conservatism are still characteristic features of the case law of the ICJ.

References

Abi Saab G (1967) Les exceptions préliminaires dans la procédure de la Cour internationale. Pedone 279
Abi Saab G (1992) De l'évolution de la Cour internationale: réflexions sur quelques tendances récentes. In: Kohen M, Jesko Langer M (eds) (2013) Le développement du droit international, réflexions d'un demi-siècle. Presses Universitaires de France, pp 243–263
Abi Saab G (1996) The international court as a world court. In: Lowe V, Fitzmaurice M (eds) Fifty years of the International Court of Justice: essays in honour of Sir Robert Jennings. Cambridge University Press, pp 3–16
Ajibola P (2000) Africa and the International Court of Justice. In: Armas Barrea C et al (eds) Liber Amicorum in Memoriam of Judge José Maria Ruda. Kluwer Law International, pp 353–366
Anand R (1969) Studies in international adjudication. Vikas Publications, India, p 298
Bastid S (1967) L'affaire du Sud-Ouest africain devant la Cour internationale de justice. Journal du droit international 94:571–583

---

[92]Pellet (2013), pp. 284–285.

[93]ICJ, *Accordance with International Law of the Unilateral Declaration of Independence in Respect of Kosovo*, Advisory Opinion, (2010) ICJ Rep 403.

[94]ICJ, *Jurisdictional Immunities of the State (Germany v. Italy: Greece intervening)*, Judgment, (2012) ICJ Rep 99.

Dugard J (1966) The South West Africa cases, second phase, 1966. S Afr Law J 83:429–460
Elias T (1971) Problems concerning the validity of treaties, vol 134. Collected Courses of the Hague Academy of International Law, pp 333–412
Falk R (1967) The South West Africa cases: an appraisal. Int Organ 21(1):1–23
Favoreu L (1966) L'arrêt de la Cour Internationale de Justice dans les affaires du Sud-Ouest africain. Annuaire français du droit international 12:123–143
Fischer G (1966) Les réactions devant l'arrêt de la Cour internationale de Justice concernant le Sud-Ouest Africain. Annuaire français de droit international 12:144–154
Friedmann W (1967) The jurisprudential implications of the South West Africa case. Columbia J Transnat Law 6(1):1–16
Gross E (1966) The South West Africa case: what happened? Foreign Aff 45(1):36–48
Guyomar G (1973) La révision du règlement de la Cour internationale de justice. Revue générale de droit international public 77(3):751–773
Higgins R (1966) The International Court and South West Africa: the implications of the judgment. Int Aff 42(4):573–599
Jiménez de Aréchaga E (1973) The amendments to the rules of procedure of the International Court of Justice. Am J Int Law 67(1):1–22
Kolb R (2013) La Cour internationale de Justice. Pedone 1358
Mahiou A (2013) L'Afrique et la CIJ: un bref aperçu de la pratique. In: Kamga M, Mbengue M (eds) Mélanges en l'honneur de Raymond Ranjeva. Pedone, pp 191–203
Mbengue M (2013) African perspectives on inter-state litigation. In: Klein N (ed) Litigating international law disputes. Cambridge University Press, pp 166–189
Pellet A (2013) Remarques cursive sur les contentieux "africains" devant la CIJ. In: Kamga M, Mbengue M (eds) Mélanges en l'honneur de Raymond Ranjeva. Pedone, pp 277–295
Voeffray F (2004) L'*actio popularis* ou la défense de l'intérêt collectif devant les juridictions internationales. Presses Universitaires de France 403

Makane Moïse Mbengue is an associate professor at the University of Geneva Law School and an affiliated professor at Sciences Po Paris (School of Law). He acts as a professor for regional courses in international law organised by the United Nations Office of Legal Affairs (OLA), and as counsel for states before the International Court of Justice, and has acted as a legal advisor for the World Bank and the Senegal River Organization, as well as a legal expert for the Secretariat of the Nile Basin Initiative, the International Labour Organization (ILO), the Swiss Federal Office of Public Health, the World Health Organization (WHO) and the International Institute for Sustainable Development (IISD).

Najib Messihi is a PhD candidate at the Graduate Institute of International and Development Studies and a teaching and research assistant at the University of Geneva Law School. He also acts as a lecturer at Sciences Po Paris (Middle Eastern and Mediterranean Undergraduate College) where he teaches an introduction to public international law.

Decolonisation as the Source of the Concepts of *Jus Cogens* and Obligations *Erga Omnes*

Jean Allain

Abstract The scholarly consensus is that *jus cogens* emerged from the work of the UN International Law Commission on invalidation of treaties, and the International Court of Justice developed the concept of obligations *erga omnes* in its wake.

This study challenges that perspective by demonstrating that these concepts were developed to accommodate Newly Independent States during the decolonisation process. It takes issue with the recognised starting point of the development of *jus cogens* in the literature: the deeply problematic piece written by Verdross; and demonstrates that leading jurists of the 1960s recognised that *jus cogens* was "a political concession to the New States" rather than a technical imperative of the law of treaties.

The study considered the evolution of the litigation regarding Namibia before the International Court of Justice, demonstrating the communal interest which Ethiopia and Liberia sought to engage, so as to end the racist regime which South Africa instituted within its Mandate for South West Africa. The ultimate outcome, manifest in the *dicta* of the *Barcelona Traction* case, was to escape that specific litigation and transform the very fabric of international law, embedding a communal interest beyond the bilateralism of *jus publicum Europeaum*.

The author invites scholars to look anew to the sources of this communitarian interest and points to the writing of Judge Alejandro Alvarez as one possible staring point.

1 Introduction

The Inaugural volume of the *Ethiopian Yearbook of International Law* falls on the 50th anniversary of the so-called 'disaster of 1966': the determination by the International Court of Justice that Ethiopia and Liberia, which had championed the cause of the people of what is today Namibia, did not have a legal interest in

---

J. Allain (✉)
Centre for Human Rights, Faculty of Law, University of Pretoria, Pretoria, South Africa

Faculty of Law, Monash University, Melbourne, VIC, Australia
e-mail: jean.allain@monash.edu

challenging the racist manner in which South Africa administered its Mandate for South West Africa. Much has transpired over the last half-century to rectify the wrong of 1966; but no substantive element of international law is more important and has garnered more attention than the recognition that beyond the interests of individual States, there exists certain interests of the international community as a whole. Those interests, most readily expressed through the concepts of the norm of *jus cogens* and obligations *erga omnes*, were conceptualised and developed within the crucible of the decolonisation process of the latter-half of the twentieth century which brought, in its wake, the destruction of the ideological foundations of European *qua* Western international law.

Set out in the 1970 *Barcelona Traction* case, the International Court of Justice sounded the death-knell for *jus publicum Europeaum* masquerading as international law where, as late as 1955, Georg Schwarzenberger sought to maintain the dichotomy between 'civilised nations' and their 'other': those 'barbaric' lands open to European appropriation as *res nullius*.[1] While Western scholars have been quick to point to the inability of the New International Economic Order or the Nyerere Doctrine to take hold as being indicative of the failure of Newly Independent States having a lasting influence on the evolution of international law, this study puts another perspective forward.[2] That, in fact, the legacy of the decolonisation process in international law should be recognised as moving away from the European-based bilateralism of yesteryear and ushering in a recognition that there are communal interests which transcend those of any given State. In the vanguard of what was to become, for the first time in history, a truly *international* law—applicable to all peoples and spanning the four corners of the globe—was Ethiopia which spearheaded the need to recognise that a larger, communal, interest was required to ensure an effective international legal order. As a result, the legacy which decolonisation leaves to international law is its two most engaging concepts: *jus cogens* and obligations *erga omnes*.

2 Historical Antecedence to *South West Africa* Case

Under the 1919 Treaty of Versailles, Germany was forced to renounce the rights to its overseas possessions including what is today Namibia, that is: South-West Africa. That territory was placed under the League of Nations' international regime—the Mandate System—wherein colonial power was effectively transferred from the vanquished to the victors of the First World War; in this case to "His British Majesty to be exercised on his behalf by the Government of the Union of South Africa".[3] Under the pretext of Europe's 'civilising mission', the Mandate

---

[1] Schwarzenberger (1955), p. 220.
[2] For consideration of the Nyerere Doctrine, see Yusuf (2014), pp. 116–118 and 132–139; and for the New International Economic Order, see Rajagopal (2003), pp. 73–94.
[3] Preamble, The Mandate for South West Africa, as reproduced in Dugard (1973), p. 72.

System, under Article 22 of the Covenant of the League of Nations, deemed that such territories, "which are inhabited by peoples not yet able to stand by themselves under the strenuous conditions of the modern world" should be entrusted to "advanced nations" as tutelage based on "the principle that the well-being and development of such peoples form a sacred trust of civilisation".

As early as the 1945 San Francisco Conference, which negotiated the substance of the Charter of the United Nations, South Africa gave notice of its intention to incorporate South-West Africa into its Union. Having governed the territory throughout the League era with the aim of dependency and making it an integral part of the Union, the South African Representative in San Francisco reserved his country's right as to the future status of South-West Africa, stating that there "is no prospect of the Territory ever existing as a separate State, and the ultimate objective of the mandatory principle is therefore impossible to achieve".[4]

While the Charter of the United Nations was silent as to the status of the Mandates, it was assumed that Mandatories would place their territory under the newly established trusteeship regime as set out in Chapters XII and XIII of the Charter. While the Union did not make of South-West Africa a UN Trust, it did originally allow the United Nations to have oversight by providing the Organisation with reports on the Union's administration of the territory in line with its previous obligations under the Covenant of the League of Nations. Thereafter, the Union of South Africa moved to have its incorporation of South-West Africa sanctioned by the United Nations General Assembly. Much to its dismay, the General Assembly rejected this proposal, instead recommending to the Union of South Africa that it place the territory under the international trusteeship regime established by the United Nations Charter and to negotiate with it the future status of South-West Africa.[5]

In 1949, the Government of the Union of South Africa effectively annexed South-West Africa; the previous year having notified the United Nations that it would no longer report to it on matters related to this Mandate.[6] The response of the United Nations General Assembly was to seek legal clarity on the matter by submitting a request for an advisory opinion to the International Court of Justice as to "the international status of the Territory of South Africa and what are the international obligations of the Union of South Africa arising therefrom".[7]

In its Opinion, delivered on 11 July 1950, the International Court of Justice determined that: the Union of South Africa continued to have obligations as Mandatory Power as envisioned by the Covenant of the League of Nations, including the requirement to report; that the United Nations had assumed the supervisory function originally vested with the League of Nations; and, that original references to the Permanent Court of International Justice were to be replaced by reference to the International Court of Justice, as a means of dispute settlement. The

---

[4]Dugard (1973), pp. 89–90.
[5]UNGA (1946) Resolution.
[6]Dugard (1973), pp. 119–120.
[7]UNGA (1949) Resolution.

International Court of Justice was unanimous in determining that the Union of South Africa could not unilaterally "modify the international status of the Territory of South-West Africa"; finding instead that the competence to determine lay with the Union, in conjunction "with the consent of the United Nations". Finally, by a vote of eight to six, the International Court concluded the United Nations Charter does "not impose on the Union of South Africa a legal obligation to place the Territory under the Trusteeship System".[8]

Within that Opinion would be sown the seeds of public interest which Ethiopia in partnership with Liberia, sought to bear fruit in making its application 10 years later to the International Court of Justice in their contentious case against South Africa. In his 1950 Dissenting Opinion, Judge Alejandro Alvarez stated that a transformation of international law was required; one which necessitated a 'new international law', whose purpose it was to bring about "international social justice". And to that end, the purpose of this new international law "must lay stress on the notion of *obligation* of States, not only between themselves, but also *toward the international community*".[9]

For its part, the Union of South Africa refused to abide by the Advisory Opinion. As a result, the positions of the sides hardened, with South Africa refusing to co-operate and the United Nations' newly established Committee on South West Africa which acted, for all intents and purposes, as the former League of Nations' Permanent Mandates Commission had in regard to the Mandate for South West Africa. While the Union of South Africa sought solace in the support offered by France, the United Kingdom and the United States of America, as the three remaining Principal Allied and Associated Powers which had agreed to the original Mandate; the majority of the Members of the United Nations held firm in their determination that settlement of the issue had to pass through the Organisation. As a result of the solidifying of positions, the Committee's considerations hit a number of procedural hurdles which ultimately were addressed by further advisory opinions of the International Court of Justice. In 1955, the United Nations General Assembly requested an opinion as to the correct voting procedure required to consider the Committee's reports and petitions; and, in 1956, on the legality of granting oral hearings to petitioners before the Committee on South West Africa.[10]

For its part, the Committee on South West Africa laid out the situation in the Territory of South West Africa, which may also be read as an indictment of European colonialism writ large at its sharpest end—what would come to be known as—apartheid:

> The life on the Territory continues to present two distinct and separate aspects. On the one hand, the Committee has been able to report the continued free political activity of the 'European' section of the population, the influential role which it plays in the institutions of

---

[8]ICJ, *International Status of South-West Africa*, Advisory Opinion, (1950), ICJ Rep 143 and 144.
[9]*Id.*, 175 and 176. Emphasis added.
[10]See ICJ, *Voting Procedure on Questions relating to Reports and Petitions concerning the Territory of South-West Africa*, Advisory Opinion, (1955); and ICJ, *Admissibility of Hearing of Petitions by the Committee on South-West Africa*, Advisory Opinion (Dissenting Opinion), (1956).

government, and the further expansion and prosperity of the mining, agricultural and commercial enterprises which it owns or controls [...] On the other hand, the Committee has shown that the vast majority of the population, classified as 'Non-European', continues to be deprived on racial grounds of a voice in the administration of the Territory and of opportunities to rise freely, according to merit, in the economic and social structure of the Territory. [...] By means of discriminatory legislative and administrative acts, authority and opportunity are retained as a matter of policy in the hands of the 'European' population, while the 'Non-European' majority is confined to reserves except to the extent that its manpower is needed in the 'European' economy in the form of unskilled labour and under strict regulation.[11]

With an impasse looming, the United Nations moved on a number of fronts, one of which would ultimately lead Ethiopia to the gates of the Peace Palace in The Hague and its application instituting contentious proceedings against the Union of South Africa before the International Court of Justice.[12] In 1957, the General Assembly requested the Committee on South West Africa study "what legal action is open [...] to ensure that the Union of South Africa fulfils the obligation assumed by it under the Mandate".[13] In its Special Report, the Committee on South West Africa noted once again the possibility of requesting an advisory opinion, but also explored the possibility of calling on the contentious proceedings of the International Court of Justice. This possibility flowed from the original compromissory clause found in Article 7 of the Mandate for South West Africa, which proscribed submission to the Permanent Court of International Justice—and by extension, its successor the International Court of Justice—as the ultimate fora for dispute settlement. Foreshadowing the evolution of the 'international community', the Special Report asked whether "a Member of the United Nations is entitled to institute contentious proceedings in order to enforce a right enjoyed by it as a member of one of the United Nations organs, or in order to enforce a right enjoyed by the organ of which it is a member".[14]

The final consideration which the Special Report turned to in developing a suite of possible legal actions which might be utilised to ensure that the Union of South Africa fulfilled its mandatory powers was in regard to former Members of the League of Nations. The Committee recognised that while the International Court of Justice had not engaged with the possibility of United Nations Members bringing contentious proceedings before the Court, "it would seem that at least some former Members of the League of Nations certainly enjoy that right". By this it meant, specifically those States—notably Ethiopia and Liberia amongst others—which had been Members of the League of Nations at its final dissolution and which were now Members of the United Nations. From these considerations, the

---

[11]UNGA (1958b), pp. 28–29.

[12]The General Assembly also established a Good Offices Committee on South West Africa, which failed in its mission. See Article 80, United Nations, Repertory of Practice of United Nations Organs, 2016, paras. 83 and 93; and UNGA (1958a) Resolution.

[13]UNGA (1957) Resolution.

[14]*Id.*

Committee drew the conclusion that "there would appear to be no legal bar to the General Assembly drawing the attention of such former Members of the League of Nations to article 7 of the Mandate", in bringing a claim before the International Court of Justice.[15]

This call to invoke the contentious jurisdiction of the International Court of Justice was heard at the historic Conference of Independent Africa States at the Ethiopian Parliament in Addis Ababa in June 1960. While the Ethiopian Delegation sought to call on the United Nations to declare South West Africa independent "without waiting any longer for the lengthy and complicated procedures of the Trusteeship system"; the delegation of South African observers—that is: those involved in the struggle against apartheid, including the African National Congress—"asked Independent African States 'to take the case of the Mandate to the International Court of Justice for compulsory jurisdiction, as provided in Article 7'".[16] To that end, on 24 June 1960, the Plenary Session of the Conference of Independent African States adopted the following Resolution on the Question of South-West Africa, which stated, in part, "that the international obligations of the Union of South Africa concerning the Territory of South-West Africa should be submitted to the International Court of Justice for adjudication"; while noting "that the Governments of Ethiopia and of Liberia have signified their intention to institute such a proceeding".[17]

Upon returning to the forum of the United Nations, the Representative of Ethiopia, Mr Hailemariam, as a Member of the Committee on South West Africa, noted that "his delegation had drafted an additional paragraph" to be added to the Annual Report of the Committee which in substance would state that the "Committee should welcome the resolution passed at Addis Ababa and strongly recommend that the General Assembly should support it as a first practical step to ensure the legal status of the Mandated Territory in accordance with international law and the spirit of the Mandate".[18] To that end, the following paragraph was included in the 1960 Report of the Committee on South West Africa:

> The Committee recognizes the importance of the constructive intention expressed in the Second Conference of Independent African States held in Addis Ababa which is in conformity with General Assembly Resolution 1361 (XIV) dealing with the legal action open to Member States to institute judicial proceedings. The Committee wishes to commend this intention on the part of the Governments of Ethiopia and Liberia to the General Assembly as one of the practical approaches for the implementation of resolution 1361 (XIV).[19]

---

[15] *Id.*, pp. 5 and 6.

[16] Speeches at the Plenary Sessions, Conference of Independent African States in Addis Ababa, June 14–24, 1960, Pankhurst (1960), pp. 295 and 305.

[17] Resolution on the Question of South-West Africa, Resolutions of the Plenary Session of the Second Conference of Independent African States, held in Addis Ababa, adopted on June 24, 1960, as found in Sylvia Pankhurst (1960), p. 315.

[18] UNGA I (1960), p. 3.

[19] UNGA II (1960), para. 27.

While our attention now turns to the proceeding before the International Court of Justice, it might be noted that the Union of South Africa sought to silence the political organs of the United Nations by pleading *sub judice*, that is: the "not taking of any action likely to hinder, embarrass or prejudice the exercise of judicial functions", to no avail.[20] During deliberations within the UN General Assembly, this position was deemed "untenable" as, *inter alia*, the Union had failed to indicate whether "it would accept any judgment which the International Court might give"; having contested "the International Court's jurisdiction to hear the case brought against South Africa by Ethiopia and Liberia".[21]

2.1 The South West Africa *Case: A Lack of Communal Interest*

In initiating the proceedings of the *South West Africa* case, Liberia partnered with Ethiopia in bring a claim to the International Court of Justices as against the Union of South Africa. That said, Liberia was a junior partner in respect of the substance of the legal proceedings. This was most evident in the application instituting proceedings before the International Court. Ethiopia having set out its justifications for bring the claim forward; Liberia's own Application read that the "text of the Application filed by the Government of Liberia is the same as the Application filed by the Government of Ethiopia, except for the following differences: [...]".[22]

On 4 November 1960, Ato Haddis Alemayehou, the Minister of State in the Ministry of Foreign Affairs of Ethiopia applied to institute proceedings on behalf of his Government before the International Court of Justice against the Government of the Union of South Africa.[23] The dispute was not solely whether South Africa was administering the Mandate properly, rather Ethiopia and Liberia also noted, more generally that "the subject of the dispute is the continued existence of the Mandate for South Africa".[24] In other words, the need for South Africa to vacate the Mandate and allow what would become Namibia to gain its independence. Beyond this general cause justifying their Applications, the African States set out seventeen factual examples upon which it deemed South Africa was in violation of the original Mandate and the Covenant of the League of Nations' requirement as to a 'sacred trust of civilization'.

The examples put forward in the Application were a further indictment of the racist policies of the Union of South Africa, wherein it "by law and in practice,

---

[20] UN (1961), p. 456.

[21] UN (1962), p. 443.

[22] ICJ, *South West Africa (Liberia v South Africa)*, Application Instituting Proceedings by the Government of Liberia, (1960) ICJ Rep 26.

[23] *Id.*, p. 18.

[24] *Id.*, p. 4.

distinguishes as to race, color, national and tribal origin", it being understood that this "official practice is referred to as *apartheid*". "The Union", Ethiopia and Liberia accused, "has adopted and applied legislation, regulations, proclamations and administrative decrees which are by their terms and in their application arbitrary, unreasonable, unjust, and detrimental to human dignity". This included "racial discrimination in the education system", segregation of residential areas, denial to all but 'European' of the ability to join a trade union or take on specific roles, including police officers, managers, engineers, or surveyors. 'Natives' were required to have passes to travel "beyond the confines of particular location, reserve, farm", etc. The Union has also appropriated to itself the power of the Governor-General to "whenever he deems it expedient in the general public interest, order the removal of any tribe or portion thereof or any native from any place".[25]

As the 'disaster of 1966' turned on standing and the legal interest in bringing a claim before the International Court of Justice, emphasis will now quickly turn to the jurisdiction phase to consider the emergence of the argument which would evolve to end the case before it was considered on the merits.[26] While the Government of the South Africa set out four preliminary objections as to the jurisdiction of the Court; these were rejected by the International Court of Justice in its Judgment on Preliminary Objections of 21 December 1962, thus moving the case to the merits phase.[27] Yet, it is worth considering the third of those preliminary objections as it speaks to the interest which Ethiopia might have in bringing a claim forward. More precisely, the International Court considered the argument that the dispute between the Parties "does not affect any material interests of the Applicant [State or its] nationals". In considering the compromissory clause found at Article 7 of the Mandate for South Africa, the Court determined that "the language used is broad, clear and precise", allowing for "any dispute whatever" to be brought as against the Mandatory State by any Member of the League of Nations.

The Judgment on Preliminary Objections revealed the Court to be divided having voted by the narrowest of majorities—eight to seven—in favour; with five dissenting and three separate opinions proffered. With regard to those dissenting opinions, it was the rationale found in the Dissenting Opinion of the President Winiarski which came the closest to dealing with the issue which would ultimately cause the case to collapse in 1966, through the Court's determination that Ethiopia had "no legal right or interest [...] in the subject matter" of the case.[28] President Winiarski from Poland noted that there were two questions at play, the first that an interim phase existing between jurisdiction and merits, wherein "the question of admissibility is one which comes after that of jurisdiction"; and second "involves both substantive and procedural law: it is the question of whether the Court has

---

[25]*Id.*, pp. 6–12.
[26]Abi-Saab (1996), p. 5.
[27]ICJ, *South West Africa (Ethiopia v South Africa)*, Judgment, (1962) ICJ Rep 11-12.
[28]ICJ, *South West Africa (Ethiopia v South Africa)*, Judgment, (1966) ICJ Rep 49.

jurisdiction to hear a case in which [Ethiopia or Liberia has] no individual legal interest".[29] Turning to the supervision of the Mandate and "disagreement on a point of law or fact" as between the Parties, the President noted that reference had "been made in this connection to an institution under Roman penal law known as '*actio popularis*' which, however seems alien to the modern legal systems of the 1919–1920 and to international law". Basing himself on a reading specific to the Mandate system, President Winiarski wrote that the Principal Allied and Associated Powers were resistant to such a system. As such:

> It is difficult to believe that they should have, as Mandatories, accepted the heavy new burden of judicial accountability, with all its unforeseeable implications, towards any Member of the League which might take exception to their administration of the Mandate. This *actio popularis* would have been such a novelty in international relations, going far beyond the novelty of the Mandates system itself in its implications that, if the drafters of these instruments had all agreed on the self-imposition of such a responsibility, they would not have failed to say so explicitly [...].[30]

In the Dissenting Opinion of Judge Morelli, which appears to be a prototype of the Judgment delivered in 1966, he writes: "the Court cannot exercise its function in contentious proceedings, by giving a decision on the merits, unless a dispute genuinely exists between the parties". For Judge Morelli of Italy, no dispute existed as Ethiopia, being a member of the United Nations, simply "took up a position from the viewpoint of the Organization".[31]

Despite the dissenting opinions, the Court determined "that it has jurisdiction to adjudicate upon the merits of the dispute". Yet, before turning to consider the merits phase and the Judgment of 1966, it should be noted that the composition of the International Court of Justice fundamentally changed between its judgments of 1962 and 1966, as a result of a number of factors. As the Judgment in the preliminary phase had been determined by eight votes to seven, the make-up of the Court was to be fundamental to any future outcome. First, the regular three-year cycle of judicial elections meant that Judges Alfaro and Moreno Quintana who had been with the majority and Judge Basdevant who had dissented in 1962, were no longer on the Court. Further, it is clear that the disqualification of newly appointed Judge Sir Muhammad Zafrulla Khan—who had been approached to act as Judge Ad Hoc in the 1962 case by the Applicants—was not voluntary but came about as a result of pressure brought to bear by the President of the Court, Sir Percy Spender.[32] Finally, Judge Bustamante y Rivero was too ill to participate in the decision and Judge Badawi died, meaning that the Court lost two more judges who formed part of the majority in the 1962 jurisdiction phase Judgment.[33] In the end, fourteen judges including the judges *ad hoc* considered the second phase of *South West Africa Case*.

---

[29]ICJ, *South West Africa (Ethiopia v South Africa)*, Judgment, (1962), ICJ Rep 134.
[30]*Id.*, p. 138.
[31]ICJ, *South West Africa (Ethiopia v South Africa)*, Judgment, (1962), ICJ Rep 256.
[32]Kattan (2015), p. 346.
[33]*Id.*, p. 345.

While the 1962 Judgment (Preliminary Objections) was determined by the narrowest of majorities, the 1966 Judgment (Second Phase) was decided by an even slimmer margin: the votes having been equally split, the Court's decision came at the hands of the President, Sir Percy Spender, who exercised a casting vote. While the International Court of Justice confirmed that, in 1962, it had rejected the Union of South Africa's preliminary objections and "found that it had 'jurisdiction to adjudicate upon the merits of the dispute'" it went on to say in its 1966 Judgment, having considered the pleadings and arguments of both Ethiopia and Liberia, as well as South Africa, that "there was one matter that appertained to the merits of the case but which had an antecedent character, namely the question of the Applicants' standing in the present phase of the proceedings". That is, the question "of their legal right or interest regarding the subject-matter of their claim, as set out in their final submissions.[34] As the International Court of Justice went on to say, "the question which now arises for decision by the Court is whether any legal right or interest exists" in the dispute as regards Ethiopia or Liberia. To which the Court added: "if the answer to be given to this question should have the effect that [Ethiopia and Liberia] cannot be regarded as possessing the legal right or interest claimed, it would follow that even if the various allegations of contraventions of the Mandate for South West Africa on the part of the Respondent were established, they would still not be entitled to the pronouncements and declarations" the Applicants had asked the Court to make.[35]

As neither of the Parties had argued the rationale which the International Court of Justice ultimately came to *motu proprio*, the Court sought to consider, rather incredibly, what the Parties might have argued had South Africa raised the issue of legal standing. Having framed its argumentation so as to develop the outcome it wanted, the majority of the International Court of Justice in the Second Phase of the *South West Africa* determined that "the argument amounts to a plea that the Court should allow the equivalent of an '*actio popularis*', or right resident in any member of a community to take legal action in vindication of a public interest. But although a right of this kind may be known to certain municipal systems of law, it is not known to international law".[36] Thus, the International Court of Justice determined, by the casting vote of President Sir Percy Spender of Australia, that Ethiopia and Liberia "cannot be considered to have established any legal right or interest appertaining to them in the subject-matter of the present claims, and that accordingly, the Court must decline to give effect to them".[37] Fundamental critiques of the majority's determination were manifest in the dissenting opinions which emerged, not least from the Judge Jessup of the United States of America, who quite succinctly noted that the Judgment was "completely unfounded in law".[38] As

---

[34]ICJ, *South West Africa (Ethiopia v South Africa)*, Judgment, (1966) ICJ Rep 18.
[35]*Id.*, p. 20.
[36]*Id.*, p. 45.
[37]*Id.*, p. 49.
[38]*Id.*, p. 325.

regards whether Ethiopia and Liberia had standing in the public interest, Judge Tanaka of Japan stating that "each State may possess a legal interest in the observance of the obligations by other States".[39]

It fell to Judge Padilla Nervo from Mexico to project the fall-out of the 1966 Judgment in the *South West Africa* case. As he noted, under the growing tide of decolonisation, manifest in the activities of the political organs of the United Nations, times where changing: "Whatever conclusions one might draw from these activities, it is evident that their far-reaching significance is the fact that the struggle towards ending colonialism and racism in Africa, and everywhere, is the overwhelming will of the international community of our days". "From those activities and under the impact of political factors", Judge Padilla Nervo continued, "new legal norms or standards emerge".[40] That predicted fall-out was "sharp and immediate". Ernest Gross, the Agent for Ethiopia called it an "abortion of the judicial process", and Taieb Slim of Tunisia stated before the United Nations General Assembly that:

> Created two decades ago, the International Court of Justice represented the world as it existed after the last war. Today, it only represents a somewhat unclear and tarnished picture of a world that has become emancipated; that comprises new nations which enrich it. As composed at present, the Court is unable to fulfil its essential functions. Legal concepts have evolved in the world taking into account progress achieved. But the International Court, through its defaults, seems to excuse political practices such as *apartheid*, which has been condemned by all nations.[41]

More impressive than the rhetorical anger was the action of the General Assembly. On 27 October 1966, the Assembly reaffirmed the "inalienable right of the people of South West Africa to freedom and independence", including the "inalienable right of self-determination" and "condemned the policies of apartheid and racial discrimination practised by the Government of South Africa in South West Africa as constituting a crime against humanity". And with this, the UN General Assembly:

> *Decides* that the Mandate conferred upon His Britannic Majesty to be exercised on his behalf by the Government of the Union of South Africa is therefore terminated, that South Africa has no other right to administer the Territory and that henceforth South West Africa comes under the direct responsibility of the United Nations.[42]

From this point onwards, the issue of South West Africa becomes less important to this study. As a result, a rather cryptic consideration is now presented of the end game which resulted in the independence of Namibia in 1990.

Just over a month after 1966 Advisory Opinion, an armed struggle in South West Africa commenced. It having been noted by a leading figure in South West Africa

---

[39]*Id.*, p. 251.

[40]*Id.*, pp. 468-467.

[41]Anand (1969), pp. 144–145. Recently James Crawford has written that "the fallout from the judgement was severe and deserved". See Crawford (2013), p. 536.

[42]UNGA (1966).

that "in fact, the decision of the International Court of Justice has had one positive result: It has underlined, for the people of South-West Africa, that a direct confrontation with the government of South Africa may be inevitable".[43] By 1970, the United Nations Security Council called on States to end economic dealings in South African occupied Namibia.[44] In June 1971, an International Court of Justice with five new judges and Sir Muhammad Zafrulla Khan presiding, delivered a further Advisory Opinion related to the *Legal Consequences for States of the Continued Presence of South Africa in Namibia* in which it found South Africa's hold on Namibia illegal, and determined that States had an obligation to refrain from any act and in particular any dealings with the Government of South Africa implying recognition [...] of such presence".[45] In 1988, under growing international isolation and sanctions, and with participation in wars both in Namibia and Angola, the now Republic of South Africa agreed to leave Namibia. On 21 March 1990, the Republic of Namibia declared itself independent.

3 Verdross as the Problematic Source of Communal Interests

The fallout over the determination of the Court in the *South West Africa* case would ultimately lead to the International Court of Justice recognising a communal interest beyond the bilateralism which was the heart of the *jus publicum Europeaum* through its 1970 Judgment in the *Barcelona Traction* case. To contextualise how the International Court was able to move to this ultimate determination, attention must first turn to the development of the concept of *jus cogens* at the international level.

While international jurists are quick to find the sources of the norms of *jus cogens* and obligations *erga omnes* in the development of work of the United Nations International Law Commission on the law of treaties, one should rather broaden the perspective from this myopic technical understanding of the emergence of the community interests which came to be recognised during the latter-half of the twentieth century, by asking what were the main currents of international relations which had the International Law Commission working feverishly, codifying fundamental areas of international law when no such law reform commission existed during the League of Nations era. The answer, when put this way is self-evident: the decolonisation process. The existential questions raised during the 50th anniversary

---

[43]Jarirtundu Kozonguizi, former President of the South West African National Union as quoted in Dugard (1973), p. 377.
[44]UNSC (1970).
[45]ICJ, *Legal Consequences for States of the Continued Presence of South Africa in Namibia (South West Africa) notwithstanding Security Council Resolution 276 (1970)*, Advisory Opinion, (1971) ICJ Rep 58.

celebrations of the UN International Law Commission bring the issue into sharp relief.[46] During its 'golden age' of the 1950s and 1960s, the Commission had codified the fundamental tenets of international law, including the law of treaties, diplomatic and consular relations, and the three law of the sea conventions; but why?[47] In the context of the decolonisation process, wherein Newly Independent States questioned the very nature of international law and whether they should be bound by the obligations forged by European States during their epoch of conquests, the International Law Commission brought forth an opportunity for representatives of these newly independent States to be integrated into the process of law-making and have their States participate in the formation of international law through its codification and progressive development.[48]

As regards the process of bringing to life the concept of a public interest, English–language jurist often turn to the writings of Alfred von Verdross as the source of the concept of *jus cogens* at the international level.[49] Yet, to consider Verdross' 1937 article, which appeared in the *American Journal of International Law*, is to recognise to what extent this piece, as a starting point for the development of a concept of a common interest of the international society is deeply problematic, and yet wilfully venerated by Western scholars as the beginning of the evolution of the international conception of *jus cogens*.

Verdross, for his part, entered into the discussion of *jus cogens* by reference to a Report on the Law of Treaties prepared in 1935 under the auspices of the Harvard Research in International Law cluster. That study, published in the same volume of the *American Journal of International Law*, did not consider treaties which might conflict with general international law.[50] Verdross engaged this lacuna in his exploration by studying the "compulsory norms concerning the contents of international treaties" and making the distinction between those which result from "compulsory norms of customary international law" and "those which constitute *jus cogens*". In considering examples of the former, Verdross provided first, an unproblematic situation of two States concluding a treaty purporting to exclude a third from the high seas. Unproblematic in that he recognised that this "would be in contradiction to a compulsory principle of general international law". Yet, his second example negated the notion of an international community rightly understood. That is, Verdross is captured by the height of the European colonial project so that, in developing his argument, he points to the *right* of colonial conquest. He wrote: "International Law authorises states to occupy and to annex *terra nullius*. In

---

[46]UN (1998), p. 183; and, more generally, Pellet (1998), pp. 583–612.

[47]See Daudet (2000), p. 114.

[48]See Abi-Saab (1963), p. 10; where he states: "codification can serve as a means of consolidating customary international law. The participation of the new states in such an endeavour would reduce psychologically their distrust of customary international law, and would give them a part in the elaboration of its written version".

[49]See, for instance, Tomuschat (2015), p. 14.

[50]Verdross (1937), p. 571.

consequence, an international treaty by which two states would bind themselves to prevent other states from making such acquisition of territory would be violative of general international law".[51] How can this statement be reconciled with the notion of the interests of an international community? The answer is not hard to discern for those with a modicum of knowledge of the precepts of international law during the first half of the twentieth century. Verdross' international law was a deeply Eurocentric international law centred on its exclusive application to 'civilised nations', a term often referred to in his considerations.[52]

Thus, for Verdross, the concept of *jus cogens* consisted of "the general principle prohibiting states from concluding treaties *contra bonos mores*. This prohibition, common to the juridical orders of all civilized states, is the consequence of the fact that every juridical order regulates the rational and moral coexistence of the member of a community". Verdross continued, "No juridical order can, therefore, admit treaties between juridical subjects, which are obviously in contradiction to the ethics of a certain community".[53] Yet, as has just been pointed out, the community which Verdross spoke of—the community encompassing the globe and regulating 'the rational and moral coexistence of the members of that community'—did not preclude the ability to conquer, to 'occupy and to annex *terra nullius*', rather it promoted it as a right. "This principle": that of not admitting treaties that contradict the ethics of the community, Verdross determined "is valid also in international law because the general principles of law recognized by civilized nations are also biding between the states".[54]

It is from this basis that Verdross developed an argument which speaks to treaties being void as against general international law, as against the norm of *jus cogens*:

> In order to advance the solution of our problem, it is necessary to see what treaties are regarded as being *contra bonos mores* by the law of civilized nations. To this problem the decisions of the courts of civilized nations give an unequivocal answer. The analysis of these decisions show that everywhere such treaties are regarded as being *contra bonos mores* which *restrict the liberty of one contracting party in an excessive or unworthy manner or which endanger its most important rights.*
>
> This and similar formulas prove that the law of civilized states starts with the idea which demands the establishment of a juridical order guaranteeing the rational and moral coexistence of the members. It follows that all those *norms* of treaties which are incompatible with this goal of all positive law – a goal which is implicitly presupposed – must be regarded as void.[55]

Considered from this perspective, and despite the paradigm of civilisation in which it was couched, the solution which Verdross proposed in regard to treaties in

---

[51]*Id.*, p. 572.

[52]See Anghie (2007), pp. 84–87; and more generally, Gong (1984).

[53]Verdross (1937), p. 572.

[54]*Id.*, p. 573.

[55]*Id.*, p. 574. Emphasis in the original.

conflict with general international law is indeed the source of the appearance of the *jus cogens* within positive international law. Yet, what Verdross was proposing in this regard was a technical solution to a technical problem flowing from the application of treaties.

If one follows this narrative, the conceptualisation of *jus cogens* is a natural development over the period of the mid-twentieth century by Western jurists focused on dealing with the issue of the operation of treaties. However, this is a matter of perspective, built on the weight of Western scholarship which, repeated enough, accepts as received wisdom the trajectory of Verdross, through the work of the rapporteurs of the International Law Commission—Lauterpacht, Fitzmaurice, and Waldock—to inclusion of the concept of *jus cogens* within the 1969 Vienna Convention on the Law of Treaties.[56]

However, another perspective is possible.

4 Decolonisation as the Source of *Jus Cogens*

The starting point for another perspective of the source of *jus cogens* might be to seek to understand whose interests were being served by the introduction of a communal element to international law through, in the first instance, this concept of *jus cogens*. Apparently, it was not Western States. At the 1969 Vienna Conference, the proposed inclusion of the concept of *jus cogens* created a split: "Western States disagreed with the provision, whereas it found much support with African, Asian, and Southern American States".[57] As the decolonisation process had changed the balance of numbers in favour of newly independent States, a French delegate to the Vienna Conference expressed the fear that if the article related to invalidation of treaties "was interpreted to mean that a majority could bring into existence peremptory norms that would be valid *erga omnes*, then the result would be to create an international source of law subject to no control and lacking all responsibility. The result would be to deprive States of one of their essential

---

[56]During 1950s and 1960s, with momentum of the decolonisation process only starting to gain pace, it was impossible for jurists from Africa or within other colonial settings to impact on the technical evolution of *jus cogens* within the International Law Commission. With this in mind, it should come as no surprise that there was little to no literature emerging from colonial states on the issue of *jus cogens* before independence.

In a geography survey of writings on *jus cogens* in 1974, it was noted that: "the opinions on the subject prevailing in Africa, Asia, and Latin America cannot be ascertained with much precision. By the time the ILC began the discussion on *jus cogens* there was virtually no literature from these continents, touching specifically upon the subject. As for more recent literature (after 1965), this author is aware of about a dozen publications by authors from Africa, Asia and Latin America, which are directly relevant to the subject. Insofar as this material allows for generalization, one may note a strong support for the concept of *jus cogens after* its having been introduced by the ILC". Sztucki (1974), p. 93. Emphasis in the original.

[57]Villiger (2009), p. 667.

prerogatives, since to compel them to accept norms established without their consent and against their will infringed their sovereign equality".[58]

At a 1965 Conference organised by the Carnegie Endowment for International Peace, meant to facilitate dialogue during the deep-freeze of the Cold War, the proceedings "brought together twenty scholars from East and West", leaders in the field of international law. During those deliberations, in seeking to set out an agenda for discussion, the Swiss jurist, Paul Guggenheim, considered that *jus cogens* should be a point of discussion. Thus, Guggenheim acknowledged the discussions taking place within the International Law Commission in regard to the law of treaties, but believed that the momentum for its consideration lied elsewhere:

> *Professor GUGGENHEIM* thought that the concept of *jus cogens* had been introduced by the ILC to facilitate the access of new States to customary international law rules. His own opinion was that it was a political concession to the new States.[59]

While no other participant challenged this assertion; Hans Blix and Igor Lukashuk did accept the premise and, as the Summary Record indicated, engaged with it:

> *Dr BLIX* said the choice of accepting customary law, including *jus cogens* or standing outside the international community was a problem connected with new States. It was not enough, in his view, that they accepted the rule *pacta sunt servanda*, which was a rule of *jus cogens*. They would also have to accept other rules which did not constitute *jus cogens*.

> *Professor LUKASHUK* said that with regard to rules which were not *jus cogens*, new States were free to accept or reject them but that their choice would have to be dictated by the practical consequences of their action.[60]

While this might be a short peg upon which to hang the argument that the decolonisation process is the source which drove the introduction of the concept of *jus cogens* onto the international agenda; 2 years later, Guggenheim's words were once more invoked, this time, as a result of his suggestion that the issue of *jus cogens* be the basis of further discussion.

Thus, a 1967 Conference entitled *The Concept of Jus Cogens in Public International Law* hosted by the Carnegie Endowment which brought together a blue-ribbon panel of international legal scholars from beyond the Cold War paradigm was convened to consider *jus cogens* in depth. Georges Abi-Saab acting as the Rapporteur of the Conference, reported that it was the participants sense that "to the extent that *jus cogens* imposes limitations on the freedom of action of the powerful, wealthy and old established States who [sic] muster the greater bargaining power on the international scene, it extends a valuable protection to the newer and weaker States".[61]

---

[58] UN (1969), p. 95. The concerns of Western States were address through the compromised provisions of Article 66(a) which created compulsory jurisdiction in regard to disputes arising from the possible invalidation of a treaty as a result of *jus cogens*.

[59] Carnegie Endowment for International Peace (1965), p. 17.

[60] *Id.*, p. 22.

[61] Abi-Saab (1967), p. 14.

Abi-Saab's reporting resulting, in large part, from the lead taken by Erik Suy who brought this issue to the table, stated that "it emerged that one of the fundamental problems of contemporary international law was to what extent the recently independent States are bound by existing international law, and more precisely, whether there exists in international law peremptory norms binding the subjects of international law absolutely and from which derogation is not possible". Later, Suy elaborated on these previous considerations, and repeated once more the words of Guggenheim, stating that: "if [...] the International Law Commission had proposed the concept of *jus cogens* it was in order to facilitate the access of new States to customary international law. In his view, it was a political concession to the new States".[62]

Let us pause to let this previous statement sink it. Thus, according to Guggenheim and Suy, *jus cogens* was not lifted to the international plane so as to address a technical issue around invalidation of treaties; instead this was a pretext allowing it to emerge. Rather, the source of *jus cogens*, internationally, lay in questions being raised by Newly Independent States as to their being bound by customary norms of international law developed during the epoch of *jus publicum Europeaum*. Here then, the peg upon which the argument is hung (as to the decolonisation process being the source of *jus cogens*) lengthens. It might be noted that no objections by the participants were made to Suy's invocation of Guggenheim's words—who, it may be said, were many of the leading international jurists of the era—including those who had been, or were then, Members of International Law Commission.[63] Instead, these considerations were the basis of the discussion which ensued. Vratislav Pechota from Czechoslovakia, added the following to the substantive considerations: "it would be inconceivable to admit that these [New] States could consider themselves as not bound by at least certain fundamental rules. New States would only be free to accept or reject dispositive rules".[64] Taking these considerations in mind, Suy stated his belief that the narrow conception of *jus cogens* related to invalidation of treaties within the International Law Commission no longer held; that is: "the traditional framework of application of *jus cogens* was broken". He continued:

> The concept of *jus cogens* has always been discussed in relation to the law of treaties, although its significance was much wider. It has taken the emergence of new States and the ensuring problem of their attitude towards international law in order to reveal the true effects of the notion of *jus cogens* or a truly universal public policy; namely, the limitation on the sovereign will of States through their submission to principles necessary for the peaceful co-existence of all States whatever their social, ideological and legal system. It is the idea of a legal order common to all members of the community of States which is about to take shape.[65]

---

[62] Suy (1967), p. 17.

[63] Members or former Members of the International Law Commission in attendance at the 1965 and/or 1967 Carnegie Conferences were Ionasco, Ruda, Tunkin and Ustor.

[64] Suy (1967), p. 59.

[65] *Id.*, p. 59. See also mention within the "Summary Record of the Discussion on the Concept of *Jus Cogens* in Public International Law", *id.*, at p. 107 (Amerasinghe).

Professor Suy, who would later become the Legal Counsel of the United Nations (1974–1983), was true to his word in speaking of *jus cogens* having broken out of its traditional understanding associated with the work of the International Law Commission on the law of treaties by setting out a definition in which he sought to capture its wider, communal, essence of *jus cogens*:

> it is the body of those general rules of law whose non-observance may affect the very essence of the legal system to which they belong to such an extent that they subjects of law may not, under pain of absolute nullity, depart from them in virtue of particular agreements. The rules of *jus dispositivum*, are valid only in so far as there are no rules freely chosen by the Parties. Thus, the *jus cogens* restricts the freedom of Parties; its rules are absolutely binding.[66]

Having set out the evolution of the positive law of the notion of *jus cogens* within the law of treaties, and shown that the concept of *jus cogens* itself was developed not to address the technical question of invalidation of treaties, but rather introduced within the crucible of decolonisation to provide a core of norms which governed all States both old and new; attention now turns to the development of obligations *erga omnes*.

5 Decolonisation as the Source of Obligations *Erga Omnes*

It will be recalled that there had been a split at the 1969 Vienna Conference between Western States, and the rest of the international community over the introduction of provisions related to *jus cogens* into the proposed Convention on the Law of Treaties. As this had been the most controversial element of the negotiation in Vienna, it has been argued by James Crawford that the International Court of Justice introduced the concept of obligations *erga omnes*, so as to avoid having to use the term *jus cogens* (re: peremptory norms):

> What happened between 1966 and 1970 was nothing other than the adoption of the Vienna Convention, by a majority of 79 to 1 (France) with 19 abstentions. Although a number of other issues had been controversial, the most controversial was the issue of peremptory norms and the related question of dispute settlement. Indeed the package deal which allowed the Convention to be concluded provided, exceptionally, for dispute settlement in respect to disputes concerning peremptory norms: Article 66 (a). For the Court to have used the language of Article 53 of the Vienna Convention, the year after its adoption and at a time when its entry into force could not be assumed was evidently a leap too far. So instead of a leap we got a concept.[67]

That concept—obligations *erga omnes*—was introduced in what may be regarded as the most famous *dictum* of the International Court of Justice wherein,

---

[66]Suy (1967), p. 18.
[67]Crawford (2006), 2007, pp. 410–411.

in the words of Crawford, the Court "was in effect apologizing for getting it wrong in 1966".[68] And yet, the pronouncement in the *Barcelona Traction* case, couched as it was in general terms, did much more than that, as it effectively slipped the confines prescribed by Article 59 of the Statute of the International Court of Justice, that its decisions have "no binding force except between the parties and in respect of that particular case". Instead, the *dictum* embedded the very concept of obligations *erga omnes* into the fabric of international law. In so doing, it took the issue of public interest beyond the realm of jurisdiction and *locus standi* which was at play in the *South West Africa* case and instead broadened the very nature of international law from its bilateralism under the *jus publicum Europeaum* to a multilateralism that recognised interests for the 'international community as a whole'.

Where, in regard to the development of *jus cogens* on the international plane, the ability to speak to its source as being tied to—and a result of—the decolonisation process is a plausible argument, though one clouded by the positivist, technical, evolution within the law of treaties; the same cannot be said of obligations *erga omnes*. Its *dénouement* was a result of the actions precipice by Newly Independent States, and ultimately on their behalf by Ethiopia and Liberia, promoting the public interest in regard to the people of Namibia at the International Court of Justice. What did the International Court of Justice in fact, say in the *Barcelona Traction* case?

On 5 February 1970, the International Court of Justice provided Judgment on the merits phase of the *Case concerning the Barcelona Traction, Light and Power Company, Limited*. The case revolved around a claim by Belgium touching on the bankruptcy, in Spain, of Barcelona Traction, a company which was, however, incorporated in Canada. While Belgium sought to invoke diplomatic protection over its nationals who were shareholders to guard their interests in the lost venture, the Court determined that Belgium lacked standing to exercise such protection.[69] It was in this case that the International Court of Justice found voice to speak to its Judgment of 1966, though it will be recalled that by this time the International Court of Justice had a different bench than that which sat in judgment in 1966.

As for the pronouncement in the *Barcelona Traction* case, the International Court stated in the following paragraphs *obiter dicta*, first with reference to obligations afforded to foreigners:

> 33. When a State admits into its territory foreign investments or foreign nationals, whether natural or juristic persons, it is bound to extend to them the protection of the law and assumes obligations concerning the treatment to be afforded them. These obligations, however, are neither absolute nor unqualified. [...]

The Court then continued:

> [...] In particular, an essential distinction should be drawn between the obligations of a State towards the international community as a whole, and those arising vis-à-vis another

---

[68]*Id.*, p. 410.

[69]ICJ, *Case concerning the Barcelona Traction, Light and Power Company, Limited*, Judgement, (1970).

State in the field of diplomatic protection. By their very nature the former are the concern of all States. In view of the importance of the rights involved, all States can be held to have a legal interest in their protection; they are obligations *erga omnes*.

34. Such obligations derive, for example, in contemporary international law, from the outlawing of acts of aggression, and of genocide, as also from the principles and rules concerning the basic rights of the human person, including protection from slavery and racial discrimination. Some of the corresponding rights of protection have entered into the body of general international law (*Reservations to the Convention on the Prevention and Punishment of the Crime of Genocide*, Advisory Opinion, I.C.J. Reports 1951, p. 23); others are conferred by international instruments of a universal or quasi-universal character. [...]

The apology, which was this *dictum* of the International Court of Justice, was a reflection of the decolonisation process which transpired throughout the 1960s and would continue unabated through much of the 1970s and beyond, as it touched on the fundamental tenants of the project which was the *jus publicum Europeaum*; and in so doing, brought this epoch-long chapter to a close. The imposition, globally, of the European conception of international law over other vying international laws from the fifteenth century onwards was by force of arms.[70] *Barcelona Traction* was a recognition afforded to newly-independent States that this conquest was no more. That the darkest pages of Western Civilisation—the industrialisation of slavery and the ideology of racial superiority—were specifically delegitimised; and if ever and wherever they were to rear their ugly heads once more, it would be deemed a concern of the international community as a whole.

The establishment of obligations *erga omnes* by the International Court of Justice in 1970 was given further substance by its operationalisation within the 2001 Articles on State Responsibility. In so doing, the Commission noted that a *jus cogens* norm and an obligation *erga omnes*, "are aspects of a single basic idea" and where a distinction was to be made, it was as follows:

While peremptory norms of general international law focus on the scope and priority to be given to a certain number of fundamental obligations, the focus of obligations to the international community as a whole is essentially on the legal interest of all States in compliance — i.e. in terms of the present articles, in being entitled to invoke the responsibility of any State in breach.[71]

As was noted by the International Law Commission in its Commentary to those Articles: "the Court's statement clearly indicates that for the purposes of State responsibility, certain obligations are owed to the international community as a whole, and that by reason of "the importance of the rights involved, all States have a legal interest in their protection".[72] To that end, the Commission introduced within the Articles on State Responsibility the provision of Article 48(1)(b), which "intends to give effect to the statement by the ICJ in the *Barcelona Traction* case" by establishing that "each State is entitled, as a member of the international

---

[70] See generally Onuma (2010).
[71] ILC (2001), pp. 111–112.
[72] *Id.*, p. 111.

community as a whole, to invoke the responsibility of another State for breaches of such obligations". And these obligations "are by definition collective obligations protecting interests of the international community as such".[73]

In broad terms, the Articles on State Responsibility determine that third States may invoke obligations *erga omnes*, calling on a State in breach to cease the wrongful act, provide assurances and guarantees of non-repetition, and address reparations *vis* the aggrieved party. In essence, where there are obligations *erga omnes* owed, a third party is in the same position as an injured State where an 'ordinary' wrongful act which had transpired. The same that is, but for the proviso in regard to 'serious' breaches of the norm of *jus cogens*. This is so, as the Articles on State Responsibility deem that where there is "a serious breach by a State of an obligation arising under a peremptory norm of general international law", States have a further obligation, to: "cooperate to bring to an end through lawful means" such a breach.[74]

As Crawford, the Rapporteur who navigated the stagnant draft Articles on State Responsibility out of their doldrums, noted 10 years after their acceptance by the UN General Assembly: "The ILC Articles on State Responsibility [...] give teeth to the communitarian norms with the potential to serve as a corrective tool for compliance with norms in the interest of all".[75] In 2005, the Institute of International Law—*Institut de Droit International*—set out the norm of obligation *erga omnes*, in the following terms, placing emphasis on its communitarian value: "an obligation *erga omnes* is [...] an obligation under general international law that a State owes in any given case to the international community, *in view of its common values and its concern for compliance,* so that a breach of that obligation enables all States to take action.[76]

6 The Communal Vision of Judge Alejandro Alvarez

Thus, if it is correct to say that the legacy which decolonisation has provided for international law is, among other things, the two concepts just considered, that of *jus cogens* and obligations *erga omnes*; then we should also seek to recognise that the underpinning development of these communal interests should not manifest itself by venerating the anti-communitarian ideas of Verdross, steeped as he was in justifications of *terra nullius* and application of general principles of law recognised by civilised nations. Rather, the theoretical ideas should speak to a bigger vision than that of treaty invalidation: one already pointed to, from a jurist who was

---

[73]*Id.*, p. 127.

[74]See generally Articles 40 and 41 of the 2001 Articles on State Responsibility.

[75]Crawford (2011), p. 240.

[76]Article 1(a), *Obligations and Rights Erga Omnes in International Law*, Institute of International Law, 2005.

immersed in the traditions of the first major decolonisation process—the Bolivarian revolutions of Latin America—Judge Alejandro Alvarez of Chile.[77]

More than any other judge to sit on the International Court of Justice, Judge Alvarez had a distinct vision of international law which infused all his writings. He recognised the era he was living through was transforming the international society and spoke of the need to, not so much establish but rather, recognise the existence of a 'New International Law'. The move from the 'old order,' that of *jus publicum Europeaum*, to a 'new order' was self-evident, a product of the "cataclysmic" changes brought on by the European *qua* World Wars of the first half of the Twentieth Century.[78] While Alvarez considered various elements—economic, political, psychological, sociological, etc.—in seeking to demonstrate the changes which transpired, he saw, amongst other connections which were being forged internationally, the requirement for a communal interest to emerge. Although couched in his own terminology, Alvarez saw the bilateralism of the past giving way to what he termed the 'social interdependence' of an 'international society': "The *regime of social interdependence* creates", Alvarez would write in later years, "a general interest superior to the particular interests of each of the members of the society; a general interest previously almost unknown and which must be taken account of in a large manner within the *New International Law*".[79]

Having been elected to the International Court of Justice in 1946, Judge Alvarez utilised his individual opinions to set out the vision he had previously developed—and would continue to develop after leaving the bench in 1955. In the first Advisory Opinion of the new Court, the 1948 *Conditions of Admission* case, Judge Alvarez spoke on the transformation of international relations creating communal interests:

> This society comprises all States throughout the world, without there being any need for consent on their part or on that of other States; it has aims and interests of its own; States no longer have an absolute sovereignty but are interdependent; they have not only rights, but also duties towards each other *and towards this society*.[80]

It would then fall to the 1950 *International Status of South-West Africa* case, where Judge Alvarez would project into the future a new legal order that went beyond the interests of any given individual States and instead established interests in the common good:

> The purposes of the new international law, based on social interdependence differ from those of classical international law: they are to harmonize the rights of States, to promote co-operation between them and to give ample room to common interests; its purpose is also to favour cultural and social progress. In short, its purpose is to bring about what may be called international social justice.

---

[77]On Latin American emancipation see Alejandro Alvarez, *Le Droit International Américain*, 1910, pp. 23–36.

[78]Alvarez (1959), pp. 11–33.

[79]*Id.*, p. 605. Emphasis in the original.

[80]ICJ, *Conditions of Admission of a State to Membership in the United Nations (Article 4 of the Charter)*, Advisory Opinion, (1948), ICJ Rep 68. Emphasis added.

To achieve these purposes this law must lay stress on the notion of *obligation of States, not only between themselves, but also toward the international community*.[81]

Here then, through the words of Judge Alvarez we witness the emergence of the concept of a communal interest before the deliberations on the law of treaties started in earnest, or for that matter, before the decolonisation process. Emphasis having be placed for so long on the emergence of the concept of *jus cogens* through its technical development by the International Law Commission, that little recognition has been given to Alvarez and his vision of a new international law which conceptualised an interest beyond the bilateralism of *jus publicum Europeaum* and conceived of an international order which included communal interest.

7 Conclusion

The *Ethiopian Yearbook of International Law* provides a forum for a different perspective on international law. The perspective brought forward here is that *jus publicum Europeaum* was put to an end during the decolonisation process of the latter half of the twentieth century by the development of communitarian conception of international law. The source of the concepts of *jus cogens* and obligation *erga omnes* were thus conceived within the crucible of decolonisation. The consideration of the cases related to Namibia by the International Court of Justice reminds us of the sharp end of the European conception of international law manifest in the apartheid regime of South Africa. Through the initiating of proceedings before the International Court of Justice by Ethiopia and Liberia much more was gained than had been anticipated. The end result, set out in the 1970 *Barcelona Traction* case was no less than the end of *jus publicum Europeaum*. In this manner, decolonisation did much more than influence international law: it reconceptualised it.

As the engine that pushed the International Law Commission to develop the conception of *jus cogens* within the law of treaties; and the International Court of Justice to establish obligations *erga omnes*, the decolonisation process can be seen in a new light. In the first instance, it breaks the link to Verdross as the deeply unsatisfactory starting point of an emerging conception of a communal interest. In so doing, it allows us to look anew and to widen our perspective beyond invalidation of treaties to seek out those who had a vision of the future which others then operationalised. What this study has put forward is that Alejandro Alvarez provided one such vision. Although Alvarez's 'New International Law' never materialised, and Judge Alvarez was not able to influence the International Court of Justice to take on his meta-narrative; he was nevertheless at the epicentre of international law during the first 10 years of the existence of the International Court of Justice and did

---

[81] ICJ, Judge Alvarez, *International Status of South West Africa*, Advisory Opinion, (1950) ICJ Rep 177. Emphasis added.

speak to the need to reconceptualise international law to include, amongst other elements, a communal interest.

References

Abi-Saab G (1963) In: Carnegie Endowment for International Peace, the newly independent states in international law. Carnegie Endowment for International Peace, Geneva
Abi-Saab G (1967) Introduction. In: Carnegie Endowment for International Peace, the concept of *jus cogens* in public international law: papers and proceedings. Carnegie Endowment for International Peace, Geneva
Abi-Saab G (1996) The International Court as a world court. In: Lowe V, Fitzmaurice M (eds) Fifty years of the International Court of Justice: essays in honour of Sir Robert Jennings. Cambridge University Press, Cambridge
Alvarez A (1959) *Le Droit International Nouveau*. Librairie Pédone, Paris
Anand RP (1969) Studies in international adjudication. Oceana Publications, Dobbs Ferry
Anghie A (2007) Imperialism, sovereignty and the making of international law. Cambridge University Press, Cambridge
Carnegie Endowment for International Peace (1965) The process of change in international law. Carnegie Endowment for International Peace, Geneva
Crawford J (2007) Multilateral rights and obligations in international law, vol 319. Collected Course of The Hague Academy of International Law, Brill, Leiden, pp 325–482
Crawford J (2011) Responsibility for breaches of communitarian norms: an appraisal of Article 48 of the ILC articles on the responsibility of states of states for wrongful acts. In: Fastenrath U, Geiger R, Khan DE, Paulus A, Schorlemer S, Vedder C (eds) From bilateralism to community interest: essays in honour of Judge Bruno Simma. Oxford University Press, Oxford
Crawford J (2013) Dreamers of the Day: Australia and the International Court of Justice. Melb J Int Law 14:520–549
Daudet Y (2000) *Sujets futurs et problèmes du processus légisatif international*. In: United Nations, The International Law Commission fifty years after: an evaluation. United Nations, New York, pp 113–121
Dugard J (ed) (1973) The South West Africa/Namibia Dispute. University of California Press, Berkeley
GA (1946) Resolution (14 December 1946). UN Doc A/RES/65
GA (1949) Resolution (6 December 1949). UN Doc A/RES/338
GA (1957) Resolution (26 February 1957). UN Doc A/RES/11/1060
GA (1958a) Resolution (30 October 1958). UN Doc A/RES/9/1243
GA (1958b) Report of the Committee on South West Africa (1 January 1958). UN Doc A/3906
GA (1966) Resolution (27 October 1966). UN Doc A/RES/21/2145
GA I (1960) Committee on South West Africa (22 July 1960). UN Doc A/AC.73/SR.140
GA II (1960) Report of the Committee on South West Africa (1 January 1960). UN Doc A/4464, 1960
Gong G (1984) The standard of 'Civilization' in international society. Oxford University Press, Oxford
ILC (2001) Yearbook of the International Law Commission. UN Doc. A/CN.4/SER.A/2001/Add.1 (Part 2)
Kattan V (2015) Decolonizing the International Court of Justice: the experience of Judge Sir Mahammad Zafulla Khan in the South West Africa cases. Asian J Int Law 5:310–355
Onuma Y (2010) A transcivilizational perspective on international law. Brill, Leiden
Pankhurst S (ed) Ethiopia Observer (August 1960) IV:9

Pellet A (1998) *La Commission du Droit international, pour quoi faire?* In: Boutros-Ghali B (ed) *Amicorum Discipulorumque Liber – Paix, développement, démocratie*. Bruylant, Brussels, pp 583–612

Rajagopal B (2003) International law from below: development, social movements and third world resistance. Cambridge University Press, Cambridge

SC (1970) Resolution (29 July 1970). UN Doc S/RES/284

Schwarzenberger G (1955) The standard of civilisation in international law. Curr Leg Probl 17:212–234

Suy E (1967) The concept of *jus cogens* in public international law. In: Carnegie Endowment for International Peace, the concept of *jus cogens* in public international law: papers and proceedings. Carnegie Endowment for International Peace, Geneva

Sztucki J (1974) *Jus cogens* and the Vienna Convention on the Law of Treaties: a critical appraisal. Springer, Berlin

Tomuschat C (2015) The Security Council and *jus cogens*. In: Cannizzaro E (ed) The present and future of *jus cogens*. Sapienza Università Editrice, Rome

UN (1961) Yearbook of the United Nations. United Nations, New York

UN (1962) Yearbook of the United Nations. United Nations, New York

UN (1969) Conference on the Law of Treaties (1 January 1970). UN Doc. A/CONF. 39/SR.19

UN (1998) The International Law Commission fifty years after: a evaluation. United Nations, New York

Verdross A (1937) Forbidden treaties in international law. Am J Int Law 31:571–577

Villiger M (2009) Commentary on the 1969 Vienna Convention on the Law of Treaties. Brill, Leiden

Yusuf A (2014) Pan-Africanism and international law. Brill, Leiden

Allain also holds an Extraordinary Chair within the Centre for Human Rights, Faculty of Law, and University of Pretoria, South Africa.

The Place of International Law in the Ethiopian Legal System

Getachew A. Woldemariam

Abstract Until this day, no scholarly research has squarely dealt with the process of reception of international law into Ethiopia's domestic legal system and its status and relationship with domestic laws. Some works have addressed the position of international human rights treaties in the Ethiopian legal order. However, the vexing issues that need clarification are: the process of reception of treaties and non-treaty sources of international law into the Ethiopian legal system; whether there are requirements to be met for the direct application of ratified treaties by Ethiopian courts and other state organs; the hierarchical relations between international law applicable to Ethiopia and its national laws; and the division of treaty-making power within the country's federal legal system. This article addresses these critical legal issues.

1 Introduction

Ethiopia has been an active international player since the end of the nineteenth century. It was a member of the League of Nations and it participated in the drawing up of the United Nations Charter, the Universal Declaration of Human Rights (UDHR) and the Convention on the Prevention and Punishment of the Crime of Genocide which it ratified on 1 July 1949. Ethiopia is party[1] to most of the major international and regional human rights treaties including the Convention against Torture, and other Cruel, Inhuman or Degrading Treatment or Punishment[2]; the International Convention on the Elimination of All Forms of Racial Discrimination[3]; the Convention on the Elimination of All Forms of Discrimination Against Women[4]; the Convention on the Rights of the Child[5]; the International Convention

---

[1] See <https://treaties.un.org/Pages/Treaties.aspx?id=4> (accessed 20 October 2016).
[2] Opened for signature 10 December 1984, 1465 UNTS 85 (entered into force 26 June 1987).
[3] Opened for signature 21 December 1965, 660 UNTS 195 (entered into force 4 January 1969).
[4] Opened for signature 18 December 1979, 1249 UNTS 13 (entered into force 3 December 1981).
[5] Opened for signature 20 November 1989, 1577 UNTS 3 (entered into force 2 September 1990).

G.A. Woldemariam (✉)
School of Law, Addis Ababa University, Addis Ababa, Ethiopia
e-mail: Getachew.assefa@aau.edu.et

© Springer International Publishing AG 2017
Z. Yihdego et al. (eds.), *Ethiopian Yearbook of International Law 2016*, Ethiopian Yearbook of International Law 2016, DOI 10.1007/978-3-319-55898-1_4

on the Protection of the Rights of All Migrant Workers and Members of their Families[6]; the Convention on the Rights of Persons with Disabilities[7]; the African Charter on Human and Peoples' Rights[8]; and the African Charter on the Rights and Welfare of the Child.[9]

Ethiopia's overall political system has dramatically changed over the course of the twentieth century. From the tenth century B.C.[10] up until 1974, Ethiopia had a monarchical system of government, its last monarch being the well-known Emperor Haile Selassie I (r. 1930–1974). Haile Selassie's government was brought down by a military coup led and controlled by Colonel Mengistu Hailemariam (r. 1974–1991). Mengistu Hailemariam's regime subscribed to the socialist ideology and attempts were made to overhaul the state structure and its laws in tune with Marxism-Leninism. Finally, in 1991, the Coordinating Committee of the Armed Forces, Police and Territorial Army (the Derg) was removed from power by the Ethiopian Peoples' Revolutionary Democratic Front (EPRDF), which has been in power since 1991. The EPRDF installed a federal state structure by restructuring the country along ethno-linguistic lines based on the Constitution of Ethiopia in 1995 ('the 1995 Constitution').

Throughout the transformative changes in the political system that occurred in the twentieth century, it is fair to say that Ethiopia's stance in relation to international law remained steady. As this paper will show, all governments of Ethiopia, past and present, have followed similar approaches to incorporating international law into domestic law. However, as will be discussed in the paper, the 1955 Constitution of Ethiopia under Emperor Haile Selassie was unique in explicitly according supremacy to ratified treaties along with the Constitution.

Some research has been undertaken to attempt to clarify the position of international human rights treaties in the Ethiopian legal order.[11] However, comprehensive studies that have dealt with the process of reception of all sources of international law, as well as their status and relations with national laws of Ethiopia, have so far not been undertaken. This paper attempts to fill this gap. It tries to clarify the overall place of international law in the country's legal system.

The paper is organized as follows.

The next section discusses the inter-play between sources of international law and domestic law in Ethiopia. Section 3 focuses on treaties to which Ethiopia is a party and outlines the status they have within the Ethiopian legal system up until the 1995 Constitution. Section 4 addresses the process of reception of treaties into the

---

[6]Opened for signature 18 December 1990, 2220 UNTS 3 (entered into force 1 July 2003).

[7]Opened for signature 13 December 2006, UN Doc A/61/611 (entered into force 3 May 2008).

[8]Opened for signature 28 June 1981, OAU Doc CAB/LEG/67/3, rev. 5, 21 ILM 58 (entered into force 21 October 1986).

[9]Opened for signature 11 July 1990, OAU Doc CAB/LEG/24.9/49 (entered into force 29 November 1999).

[10]Marcus (2002), pp. 7–8.

[11]*See,* e.g., Bulto (2009), Assefa (2001), and Idris (2000).

Ethiopian legal system in the current constitutional order. It will also clarify whether there are requirements to be met for ratified treaties to be directly applied by Ethiopian courts and other state organs. Section 5 deals with the hierarchy of sources between international law applicable to Ethiopia and its national laws. Section 6 covers the judicial and quasi-judicial enforcement of international law in Ethiopia. Section 7 addresses the treaty-making power within the context of the federal state structure to examine the role of the constituent units in matters of foreign relations. Finally, Sect. 8 makes concluding remarks.

2 International Law and the Domestic Laws of Ethiopia

Ethiopia's existence as a state dates back more than three millennia although it has been known under different names and has been comprised of varied territories in the East African sub-region.[12] Its external relations accordingly also date back centuries. In the nineteenth century, for instance, various Ethiopian monarchs and some of its prominent regional lords concluded treaties with European nations, such as the UK and Italy.[13]

As will be shown in the next section, past Ethiopian constitutions, as well as the current one, mention only international agreements[14] and do not include other sources of international law, namely, international custom, general principles of law,[15] and international soft laws. The Constitution's silence however does not affect Ethiopia's obligations emanating from these non-treaty sources of international law on the international plane. But certainly, this gives rise to the question of the domestic effect of non-treaty sources of international law in the country.[16]

The 1995 Ethiopian Constitution predominantly uses the term 'international agreements,' mentioning this term in ten instances. In Article 2, the Constitution stipulates that Ethiopia's international boundaries shall be determined by international agreements. Article 9(4), which is the main provision integrating treaty-based international law into the country's body of laws, states that "all international agreements ratified by Ethiopia are [an] integral part of the law of the land". Article 28 of the Constitution declares that the prosecution of crimes against humanity "(...) so defined by international agreements ratified by Ethiopia and by other laws

---

[12] *See* Marcus (2002).

[13] *See* Wondimagegnehu (1989), p. 91.

[14] The Ethiopian Constitution uses the term "international agreement" and not "treaty". But it is clear from the Constitution that the term "international agreement" refers to all kinds of treaties whatever the particular designation.

[15] Art. 38, Statute of the International Court of Justice. The Statute also recognizes judicial decisions and teachings of most highly qualified publicists as subsidiary means for the determination of rules of law: *ibid.*

[16] *See,* below, Sect. 4.

of Ethiopia, such as genocide, summary executions, forcible disappearances or torture shall not be barred by statute of limitation".

The fourth reference to international agreements made by the Constitution is in relation to citizenship: "Ethiopian nationality may be conferred upon foreigners in accordance with law enacted and procedures established consistent with international agreements ratified by Ethiopia."[17] Article 43, which deals with the right to sustainable development states: "all international agreements and relations concluded, established or conducted by the State shall protect and ensure Ethiopia's right to sustainable development." Article 51(8) deals with the powers and functions assigned to the national government and declares that the power to negotiate and ratify international agreements belongs to the federal government. Article 55 (12) further specifies treaty-making procedure by stipulating that the federal legislature—the House of Peoples' Representatives—"[ratifies] international agreements concluded by the Executive." The term "international agreement" is also mentioned under Article 71(2) of the Constitution, which deals with the powers and functions of the President of the Republic. Accordingly, "[the President] shall proclaim in the Negarit Gazeta[18] laws and international agreements approved by the House of Peoples' Representatives in accordance with the Constitution." The last two references to international agreements are made in Articles 86(3) and 86(4) where it is stated, respectively, that the principles of external relations of the country include ensuring that "international agreements promote the interests of Ethiopia" and "[observing] international agreements which ensure respect for Ethiopia's sovereignty and are not contrary to the interests of its Peoples."

The only instance where the Constitution makes reference to the terms 'international covenants', 'international instruments' and the Universal Declaration of Human Rights is in Article 13(2) in relation to the interpretation of the Bill of Rights, ordaining that the fundamental rights and freedoms specified in the Bill of Rights of the Constitution be "interpreted in a manner conforming to the principles of the Universal Declaration of Human Rights,[19] International Covenants on Human Rights and international instruments adopted by Ethiopia". I will return to the discussion of the implication of the provisions of Article 13(2) on the hierarchical relations between the Constitution and sub-constitutional domestic laws on the one hand and international law applicable to Ethiopia on the other.[20]

As far as the Constitution is concerned, the earlier noted references to sources of international law are the only constitutional stipulations connecting domestic

---

[17] *Ibid*, Art. 33(4).

[18] Negarit Gazeta is the official law gazette of the federal government first established in 1942. In 1995, it was re-established as "Federal Negarit Gazeta". Each of the regional states has its own law gazette.

[19] It is interesting to note however that the Amharic (and governing) version of Article 13(2) does not make reference to the Universal Declaration of Human Rights. Instead, it contains in its place what can be roughly translated as "international human rights laws" creating redundancy with subsequent reference in the same Article to "international human rights treaties".

[20] *See* below, Sect. 5.

Ethiopian law and international law. The Constitution's reference to "international instruments" in Article 13(2), in my view, embraces both treaty law and soft law instruments. In any case, however, the Constitution leaves unanswered the question of whether other sources of international law, such as international custom and general principles of law form an integral part of the law of Ethiopia.

Unlike the Constitution, the Criminal Code of Ethiopia makes many references to non-treaty sources of international law in relation to the criminalization and punishment of certain conduct. Thus, Article 17 of the Code states that a crime against international law, an international crime specified in Ethiopian legislation, or an international treaty or a convention which Ethiopia has ratified committed outside of Ethiopia could be subject to a trial in Ethiopia unless a final judgement has been given after being tried in a foreign country. The broad reference to crimes against "international law" and "international crime" in Article 17 applies to any acts criminalized by any one of the sources of international law. This shows that sources of international law other than treaties are made part of the Ethiopian criminal law.

The Criminal Code also provides that a subordinate shall be criminally liable if he knows that an order given by a superior was against 'international law', again making a general reference to international law.[21] Reference is also made to 'principles of international law' and 'public international law' in relation to the criminalization of violations of territorial and political sovereignty of foreign states in Articles 242 and 263 of the Criminal Code respectively. The Criminal Code also makes crimes against civilian population including the maltreatment of, or dereliction of duty towards, the wounded, sick, or prisoners of war and the denial of justice to a civilian, a wounded person, a prisoner of war or an internee committed in violation of the rules of public international law punishable.[22]

The foregoing discussion on the relevant provisions of the Criminal Code reveals that in so far as criminal matters are concerned non-treaty sources are generally an integral part of Ethiopian law.[23] As such, criminal law related non-treaty sources of international law have direct domestic effect in Ethiopia. They can be invoked by litigants before the courts and interpreted by the judiciary.

Unlike the Criminal Code, other sources of law including the Constitution do not make any mention of the non-treaty sources of international law. This, in fact, is the case in many other jurisdictions around the world.[24] Because of this, several authors including Bulto argue that the lack of formal reference to customary international law by the Ethiopian Constitution is non-consequential because the former is binding on all states irrespective of the states' consent and without the need for

---

[21] Article 74, 2004 Criminal Code of Ethiopia.

[22] *Ibid*, Articles 270, 279–280.

[23] I should like to mention here that genocide and crimes against humanity have been incorporated directly into the Criminal Code: *see* Articles 269–270.

[24] Shelton (2011), p. 13.

an enabling domestic law.[25] Bulto further argues that customary international law cannot be set aside by a conflicting domestic law, including the Constitution.[26] This conclusion may be correct insofar as Ethiopia's obligations on the international plane are concerned. But this does not automatically settle the place of international customary law in the domestic legal order. The domestic application of all sources of international law is determined by the domestic legal system of individual states.[27]

Although many legal systems do not formally ascertain the place of customary international law on the domestic plane, it is common to integrate customary international law through judicial practice. For example, in common law systems, e.g. in the United Kingdom, customary international law that does not conflict with domestic legislation has long been held by courts to automatically form part of the common law.[28] In Canada, if it is not possible to harmoniously interpret international custom with domestic legislation, domestic law prevails.[29] In the United States, the federal courts do not incorporate customary international human rights law into domestic law without clear congressional authority.[30] Some other countries like Italy give custom prevalence over domestic legislation but not over the constitution and treaties.[31]

3 Treaties in the Domestic Legal System of Ethiopia: An Historical Overview

Ethiopia's formal relationship with other nations had taken an institutional shape several years after Emperor Menelik II's (r. 1889–1913) consolidation of power over all parts of the present-day Ethiopia during the first decade of the twentieth

---

[25] Bulto (2009), p. 154.

[26] Shelton (2011), p. 13. Bulto's view that all rights contained in the UDHR have obtained *jus cogens* status is not well supported. This at least is not borne out by the constitutional practices of nations. For example, Courts of nations like Hungary, Canada, US, Czech, Russia, UK and Argentina have recognized this norm in relation to few matters such as genocide and crimes against humanity: *see* Shelton (2011), p. 7. Some US federal courts of appeals have, under the Alien Tort Statute, recognized customary international human rights law prohibitions on torture, summary executions or murder, causing disappearances, prolonged arbitrary detention, and may be inhuman and degrading treatment, in addition to prohibitions on genocide and slavery. A violation of free speech, however, "does not rise to the level of such universally-recognized rights and so does not constitute a part of the 'law of nations'": Christenson (1995/96), p. 235.

[27] Shelton (2011), p. 5.

[28] *Ibid*, p. 13.

[29] *Ibid*, p. 7.

[30] Christenson (1995/96), p. 234.

[31] Shelton (2011), p. 7.

century.[32] At the end of 1907, Emperor Menelik opened the first ministerial offices in the history of the nation. Until this point, the Emperor, at least in theory, had undertaken all the responsibilities of the government in his personal capacity because any delegation of authority was believed to be antithetical to the idea of the king as the emissary of the Divine on earth combining the functions of all governmental powers in his person.[33] With Menelik II's rule this changed and in 1907 a proclamation[34] that established certain ministries was passed.

This law bestowed treaty-making powers on some of the ministers, such as the Minister of Foreign Affairs and Commerce, and the Minister of Health.[35] While the Emperor reserved the power to conclude basic treaties and the power to choose his plenipotentiaries for himself, the Minister of Foreign Affairs and Commerce was given the power to submit proposals to the Emperor on basic political treaties, and to conclude treaties that addressed postal, telegraphic and telephonic devices, treaties of war victims, and treaties for the extradition of foreigners—whether for political or other offences—in consultation with the foreign national's consular representative.[36] Further, other ministers such as the Minister of Health also had the power to make treaties in their areas of competence.[37]

The centralization of treaty-making power in regards to so-called 'basic treaties' was a deliberate design by Emperor Menelik under whose leadership the unification of the country's administration was completed. His rule as the King of Kings[38] was preceded by a time in which regional rulers (including Emperor Menelik himself during his time as the King of Shewa Province whilst Emperor Yohannes IV (r. 1872–1889) was the King of Kings of Ethiopia) were engaged in concluding various kinds of treaties with foreign powers. Menelik was also keen to impress upon the rest of the world that Ethiopia is a modern, sovereign and independent state that speaks in unison to the outside world.[39]

Further, the Emperor had quite a clear idea of the consequences of treaties-gone-wrong from his experience with the Italians in relation to the 1889 Treaty of

---

[32]Emperor Menelik II completed his expansion into the present-day Southern, South-Western and Eastern parts of Ethiopia by about 1907: Marcus (1975), pp. 64–76.

[33]Woldemeskel (1970), p. 52.

[34]A Parliamentary statute in Ethiopia is referred to (in English) as "proclamation". This comes from the Amharic term "Awaj" which connotes the act of making an announcement. Before the advent of the print-media, laws and other announcements made by the king and his officials were communicated to the public by designated personnel who beat-up a traditional drum (called "Negarit") and announced the terms of the law moving from place to place.

[35]Woldemeskel (1970), pp. 175–177.

[36]*Ibid.*

[37]*Ibid.*

[38]The notion 'King of Kings' connotes that the Emperor of Ethiopia is superior to the various regional rulers who were designated as Kings, such as the King of Gojjam Province, the King of Shewa, the King of Wollo, etc.

[39]*See* Marcus (2005).

Wuchalle that sparked the Italio-Ethiopian war at Adwa in 1896.[40] Indeed, Ethiopia's experience with treaties and international agreements particularly with the dominant colonial powers in Africa—Britain, France and Italy—in the nineteenth and early twentieth centuries was full of reminders that the terms and stipulations in treaties depict international power politics. It suffices to mention the pressure exerted by the British on Ethiopia's Empress Zewditu (r. 1916–1930) to sign what was known as the "Lake Tana Concession" allowing the British to construct a dam on Lake Tana of Ethiopia for the benefit of its colonial interests in Egypt and the Sudan as an example.[41] Iadarola writes that "both Major Hugh Dobbs, the British minister in Addis Ababa, and his successor, Claud Russell, [in the 1920s] spoke strongly to Empress [Zewditu]... and threatened the intervention of European powers if she refused to concede to their wishes".[42]

In any case, Ethiopia remained steady in its pursuit of equal standing within the international community. In 1923, it was admitted to the League of Nations, one of the major treaty acts undertaken before the coming into force of its first written Constitution in 1931. The 1931 Constitution appeared to give sole power to make treaties to the Emperor who, by the terms of the same Constitution, was both the Head of State and Government. The Constitution provides that "[t]he Emperor has legally the right to negotiate and sign all kinds of treaties" and "[t]he right of declaring war and of concluding peace."[43] By an Imperial Order passed in 1943 (Order No. 1/1943), the Minister of Foreign Affairs was granted the power to negotiate matters of mutual interest on behalf of the Ethiopian Government with other states. It was not clear whether Parliament had any power in the process of integrating international treaties into domestic law. But Article 34 of the Constitution stated that "no law may be put into force without being discussed by the Chambers..." It can be argued that, as was the case with any other law, Parliament had the power to "discuss," but not to ratify or accede to, the treaties signed by the Emperor before they entered into force for Ethiopia.

The 1955 Revised Constitution of Ethiopia, which replaced the 1931 Constitution, contained much clearer provisions on treaty-making power compared with its predecessor. This Constitution, like its precursor, gave the Emperor the sole power over all foreign relations, as well as giving him the power to settle disputes with foreign powers by means of adjudication and other peaceful means; and to provide for and agree to measures of cooperation with foreign powers for the realization of the ends of security and common defence; and to ratify treaties.[44] Article 30 of the Constitution provides, inter alia, that

---

[40] The Italian version of Article 17 of this treaty required that Ethiopia forge relations with other nations through Italy as an agent while the Amharic version stated that Ethiopia could use Italian services if it so wished: Zewde (2002), pp. 74–75.

[41] See Iadarola (1975).

[42] Ibid, p. 613.

[43] 1931 Constitution of Ethiopia, Arts. 12, 14.

[44] Art. 30, 1955 Constitution of Ethiopia.

[the Emperor] alone, has the right to ratify, on behalf of Ethiopia, treaties and other international agreements and to determine which treaties and international agreements shall be subject to ratification before becoming binding upon the Empire...

The Constitution therefore clearly determined not only that the Emperor (the executive) was given the sole power to make treaties but also that he determined which treaties needed ratification before they came into force.

But the Constitution also provided for robust Parliamentary involvement in regards to treaty making. Although the Constitution gave the Emperor the power to determine treaties to be subjected to ratification and identify those that did not require ratification, it put some limitation on the Emperor's power in this matter. Thus, Article 30 further provides that:

> all treaties of peace and all treaties and international agreements involving a modification of the territory of the empire, or of sovereignty or jurisdiction over any part of such territory, or laying a burden on Ethiopian subjects personally, or modifying legislation in existence, or requiring expenditures of state funds, or involving loans or monopolies, shall, before becoming binding upon the Empire and the inhabitants thereof, be laid before Parliament, and if both Houses of Parliament[45] approve the same in accordance with the provisions of Articles 88-90 inclusive[46] of this Constitution, shall then be submitted to the Emperor for ratification.

The above stipulation determined at once that treaties and international agreements dealing with the above matters could not have come into force without ratification by the Emperor and that they were required to be laid before Parliament and get their approval before making their way to the Emperor for ratification. Subsequent legislation added detail to these constitutional provisions on treaty-making power, most notably in Imperial Order No. 46/1966 by which the Emperor delegated the power to make certain kinds of treaties to some ministers. Accordingly, the Ministers of Foreign Affairs, Finance, and Planning and Development were given the power to negotiate and conclude international treaties, agreements and arrangements in their spheres of operation.

Based on the above constitutional legal framework, Ethiopia's imperial regime played an active part in the development of international treaties and conventions including in the drafting and signing of the Vienna Convention on the Law of Treaties.[47] In 1974, the operation of the 1955 Constitution was suspended when the Emperor was deposed by a coup d'état which installed a military government commonly known as the Derg (r. 1974–1991). One of the early laws enacted by the Derg, Proclamation No. 2/1974, provided for the making of treaties in a detailed manner which seem to be copied from Article 30 of the 1955 Constitution, except of course for the ratifying and deliberative bodies. The Proclamation provided that the Provisional Military Administrative Council, the governing body of the Derg, had

---

[45] The Constitution established a bicameral Parliament comprising the Senate and the Chamber of Deputies (Art. 76).

[46] Articles 88–90 dealt with the Parliamentary law-making process.

[47] <https://treaties.un.org/Pages/ViewDetailsIII.aspx?src=TREATY&mtdsg_no=XXIII-1&chapter=23&Temp=mtdsg3&clang=_en> (accessed 7 December 2016).

the power to ratify treaties and to determine the treaties to be subjected to ratification before becoming binding upon the state. It also stated that all treaties of peace and all treaties and international agreements involving a modification of the territory of the state or of sovereignty or jurisdiction over any part of such territory or laying a burden on Ethiopian subjects, or modifying legislation in existence or involving loans or monopolies should first be deliberated upon by the Council of Ministers before ratification by the Provisional Military Administrative Council. This proclamation was overridden by Proclamation No. 110/1974, which provided for more generally worded provisions on treaty making leading to less clarity overall. It stated that the Congress of Provisional Military Administrative Council had the power and responsibility to ratify basic economic and political, defence and joint defence treaties and international agreements. It left issues such as the meaning of basic economic and political treaties open.

The military government undertook both executive and legislative functions without constituting a body that went by the name Parliament until after the effectivity of the 1987 Constitution of the People's Democratic Republic of Ethiopia by which the military government transformed itself into a 'civilian' administration while retaining Colonel Mengistu Haile-Mariam, the Chairman of the Derg and, since 1977, the Head of State and Government, as its new President. Under the Constitution, the executive was comprised of the Presidency and the Cabinet consisting of a Prime Minister, Deputy Prime Minister and other minsters while the legislature was a unicameral chamber known as the "National Shengo" with the Council of State as its standing body.

Under the 1987 Constitution, the President was given the power to "conclude" treaties on behalf of Ethiopia and establish diplomatic missions and appoint diplomatic representatives. The National Shengo was given the power to determine the state of peace and war while its standing body, the Council of State, was given the power to ratify and block the ratification of treaties. These general stipulations in the 1987 Constitution were further elaborated by a subsequent proclamation entitled "Treaty-Making Procedure Proclamation" (No. 25/1988).

Proclamation No. 25/1988 provided important details on the division of duties between the various organs of state in regards to treaty making power and the processes involved. The law provided that The Prime Minister and the Minister of Foreign Affairs could enter into treaties on behalf of Ethiopia upon delegation by the President. Other government officials had the power to negotiate and conclude treaties upon producing "full powers", i.e., an accreditation document. Procedurally this law prescribed that proposals for the negotiation, conclusion of and accession to treaties were to be submitted to the Council of Ministers by the Ministry or other government office concerned in consultation with the Ministry of Foreign Affairs. However, in the case of treaties concluded by ministers and other government officials with their foreign counterparts, in matters of technical cooperation within their competence or regarding treaties whose sole purpose was to implement prior basic treaties, the Council of Ministers would authorize negotiation and conclusion of, or accession to, such treaties.

The 1987 Constitution was tacitly abrogated when the Derg was toppled militarily by the Ethiopian Peoples' Revolutionary Democratic Front (EPRDF) in 1991. The EPRDF and its allies formed a transitional government which adopted what was known as the "Transitional Period Charter" that served as an interim Constitution for the transitional period that lasted until August 21, 1995.[48] The Charter stated that Ethiopia abides by all international agreements that respect the sovereignty of Ethiopia and are not contrary to the interests of the people. It further gave the Council of Representatives, the legislature of the transitional government, the authority to ratify international agreements.

4 Treaty-Making Power and Process in the Current Constitutional Order

National systems diverge as regards the approaches they use to incorporate treaties into domestic law. One of the major points of difference is on whether treaties are brought into domestic effect by the acts of the executive organ alone or whether they require the approval of the legislature. As Shelton observes the practice in most states is that the head of state or government concludes treaties which must then be approved by one or both chambers of the Parliament before a formal act of ratification.[49] The domestication process and requirement also diverge based on the subject-matter of the treaties. For example, many states within the EU system require approval by a supermajority in Parliament in regards to treaties that involve a transfer of governmental powers to international institutions.[50] Certain types of treaties (that go better with the name "agreements" or "executive agreements") come into domestic effect by the acts of the executive without going through the formal process of ratification. Such is the case with the US, Germany, Poland, Argentina, Austria and Venezuela where members of the executive can (by the constitutional stipulation or through court-sanctioned practices) bring executive agreements into domestic effect.[51]

As noted in the previous section, Ethiopia's past constitutions and laws also clearly attached different requirements to the incorporation of treaties into the domestic legal system based on the subject matter of the treaties.[52] But neither the 1995 Constitution nor any primary legislation made under its authority has clearly ordained distinctions among treaties in regards to the power and process by which they are made. The Constitution however leaves no doubt that the House of Peoples' Representatives (HoPR), the law-making House of the bicameral federal Parliament, has the power to "ratify international agreements concluded by the

---

[48] *See* Article 3, Proclamation No. 2/1995.
[49] Shelton (2011), p. 8.
[50] *Ibid.*
[51] *Ibid*, p. 9.
[52] *See*, above, notes 45–46 and the accompanying text.

executive."[53] This constitutional stipulation raises an important question of whether all international agreements Ethiopia concludes through the executive need to be subjected to legislative ratification before they become effective at the domestic level or, in other words, whether the federal executive can bring treaties into domestic effect without the legislature's approval?

As earlier noted, the Constitution, in addressing the powers and functions of the HoPR, states that the latter ratifies international agreements concluded by the executive. Article 51, in enumerating the federal (i.e. the national) government's competence, provides that the federal government has the exclusive power to negotiate and ratify international agreements. What is more, Article 9(4) of the Constitution declares that "all international agreements ratified by Ethiopia are an integral part of the law of the land". The *a contrario* reading of the provisions of Article 9(4) renders a literal meaning that international agreements not ratified by Ethiopia, i.e. not subjected to the approval of the HoPR in the sense of the Constitution's Article 55(12), cannot be an integral part of the law of the land. In relation to the executive, the overall effect of the constitutional passages noted seems to be that the executive cannot on its own enter into treaties that bind Ethiopia, and that its tasks are limited only to the negotiation and conclusion of treaties that come into effect only after ratification by the HoPR.

The cumulative effect of these constitutional stipulations is that all kinds of treaties or international agreements Ethiopia enters into can only be brought into domestic effect upon ratification by the HoPR. The federal executive's power in relation to treaties is constitutionally limited to the negotiation and signing of treaties. The Ethiopian Constitution does not clearly exempt any type of treaties from ratification, as for example is the case with the German[54] and South African[55] Constitutions. This rule however does not preclude the possibility of the HoPR authorizing the executive through law, to bring into effect certain kinds of treaties that may fall within the remit of the executive power. This, for example, has been the case with the United States' constitutional practice. The US Constitution empowers the nation's President to make treaties by and with the advice and consent of the Senate.[56] The Constitution does not envisage treaties being concluded without the advice and consent of the Senate. However, the great majority of international agreements that the United States enters into are not treaties but executive agreements—agreements entered into by the executive branch that are not submitted to the Senate for its advice and consent. Congress generally requires notification on the conclusion of such an agreement.[57]

---

[53] Article 55(12), Ethiopian Constitution.

[54] Art. 59, German Basic Law.

[55] Section 231, South African Constitution.

[56] Article 2, Section 2.

[57] There are three types of legal executive agreements: (1) congressional-executive agreements, agreements entered into by the executive which Congress has previously or retroactively authorized; (2) executive agreements made pursuant to an earlier treaty, in which the agreement is authorized by a ratified treaty; and (3) sole executive agreements, in which an agreement is made pursuant to the President's constitutional authority without further congressional authorization: *see* Garcia (2013).

This could as well be the case in Ethiopia. The Constitution envisages that the Prime Minister can be entrusted with responsibilities by law.[58] This legal bestowal of responsibility may include the power to enter into treaties in relation to certain matters that are necessary to implement executive powers. Similarly, the Constitution provides that the Council of Ministers may be given responsibilities by the HoPR other than the ones enumerated in the Constitution.[59] These are sufficient constitutional bases for the legislature to authorise the executive to make treaties in matters falling under its general or departmental competences.

The practice in place conforms to the approach I espouse here. The law that defines the powers and functions of the executive department (i.e. the ministries) of the federal government, Proclamation No. 916/2015, states that each ministry is given the power in its areas of jurisdiction to enter into international agreements in accordance with the law.[60] This recognizes the impossibility for the HoPR to deal with each and every international agreement. But, at the same time, it is imperative to keep in mind that the bestowal on the executive of a treaty-making power needs to consider the nature and importance of the subject-matters of the treaties. This, for example, was clearly dealt with in the 1955 Constitution of Ethiopia wherein "all treaties of peace and all treaties and international agreements involving a modification of the territory of the empire, or of sovereignty or jurisdiction over any part of such territory, or laying a burden on Ethiopian subjects personally, or modifying legislation in existence, or requiring expenditures of state funds, or involving loans or monopolies" were required to be approved by the legislature before ratification by the Emperor.[61] Hence, the argument here is that Article 55(12) of the Ethiopian Constitution needs to be given the meaning so that the executive can bring into legal effect without HoPR's approval treaties on subject-matters falling within its general or departmental competence.

In terms of the process of making of treaties in Ethiopia, this is done primarily by or under the direction of the executive, and may follow two different paths. The first is that Ethiopia participates in the process of treaty-making at the international level right from the negotiation and drafting stages all the way to the adoption by signature of the treaties drafted and finally to ratification by the HoPR. The second path is through acceding to an existing treaty adopted by other countries. In the case of the former, the Ministry of Foreign Affairs is given the power and the duty, in consultation with the concerned organs, to negotiate and sign the treaties in question, except insofar as such power is specifically given by law to other departments.[62] In the latter's case, i.e. the ratification of treaties already adopted and opened for signature and ratification, the Ministry of Foreign Affairs or any other concerned government organ marks the need for ratification of the treaty in

---

[58] Article 74(12).
[59] Article 77(12).
[60] Article 10(1) (f), Proclamation No. 916/2015.
[61] Article 30, 1955 Constitution of Ethiopia.
[62] *Ibid*, Article 15(3).

question before the Council of Ministers with its reasons and justifications. Then the Council of Ministers, if in agreement, approves the request to become party to the treaty and instructs the ministry in question on the next steps. Following this, the concerned ministry fulfils all the necessary requirements and reintroduces the treaty in question to the Council of Ministers for deliberation on its contents. When the Council adopts the treaty, it passes it on to the HoPR for ratification. Hence, in both cases of treaty-making just described, the approval of the Council of Ministers and the Prime Minister must be obtained before the process is initiated. After the ratification by the HoPR,[63] the Ministry of Foreign Affairs is responsible for all the formalities involved in the ratification process.[64] This includes the preparation of a ratification instrument in Amharic and English, which are then signed by the Prime Minister and submitted to the designated repository of the treaty in question.

4.1 Automatic or Legislative Incorporation?

Another issue, which is of overarching importance in treaty-making, is the mechanism of incorporating treaties into the domestic legal system. The question here is whether treaties obtain domestic effect automatically upon ratification or whether they need some form of publication via or incorporation into domestic legislation in addition to ratification. By and large, different legal systems have adopted two approaches in regards to this matter: the monist and the dualist approach.[65] In some legal systems like the UK, Germany, Ireland, Sweden, Norway and also South Africa, which fall within the dualist camp, ratified treaties can have domestic effect only after incorporation by Parliamentary legislation whereas in the US, Greece, Bulgaria and Serbia, ratified treaties are automatically applicable on the domestic plane without any further action.[66] Of course, there is variation within states that subscribe to the same theoretical camp. For example, as de Wet observes, South Africa utilizes four different approaches for the incorporation of treaty law into its domestic law.[67] The first one is considering the pre-existing legislation sufficient to domestically fulfil the international obligation contracted by the treaty in question. Second is the embodiment of the provisions of the treaty in question

---

[63]The process of consideration of the treaty for ratification by the HoPR follows its normal law making procedure: Arts. 49, 170-71, HoPR Rules of Procedure and Members' Code of Conduct Regulations No. 3/2006.

[64]Article 15(3), Proclamation No. 916/2015.

[65]In simple terms "monism" assumes that international law and national law form part of the same legal system and holds that international law is "the law of the land" while "dualism" assumes, in contrast, that "international law and national law are entirely separate branches of law" and that the former must be incorporated or transformed into domestic law to have effect domestically: Wolfrum et al. (2015), p. 3; Hestermeyer (2015), p. 449.

[66]Shelton (2011), p. 8; Phooko (2014), pp. 07-408; Sweet and Keller (2008), p. 686.

[67]de Wet (2015), pp. 31–32.

into an Act of the nation's Parliament. The third approach is appending the treaty being domesticated as a schedule to a Parliamentary statute. Finally, an Act of Parliament "may grant the executive the power to bring a treaty into effect in municipal law by means of proclamation or notice in the Government Gazette."[68]

An examination of the Ethiopian legal order reveals that neither the Constitution nor any sub-constitutional law unequivocally settles how treaties are domesticated. As earlier noted, Article 9(4) of the Ethiopian Constitution provides that all international agreements ratified by Ethiopia are an integral part of the law of Ethiopia. A somewhat related provision in Article 71 of the Constitution states that the President's powers and functions include that "he shall proclaim in the [law gazette] laws and international agreements approved by the House of Peoples' Representatives in accordance with the Constitution". Some authors hold that by virtue of Article 71 of the Constitution, treaties ratified by the HoPR can come into domestic effect only upon proclamation or publication in the federal government's official law gazette.[69]

Other authors espouse an opposite view regarding the publication requirement. Basing their argument chiefly on Article 9(4) noted earlier and the absence of any other contrary stipulation in the Constitution on the matter, they argue that ratification by the HoPR brings treaties into domestic effect, whether or not they are published in the official law gazette.[70] I, too, hold the view that publication is not a necessary precondition for a ratified treaty to take domestic effect. I offer three arguments for holding this position. First, as is clear by now, treaties are ratified by the HoPR (the legislature) based on its regular law-making procedure, thus allowing the treaties to obtain a stamp of approval from the federal lawmaker in the same manner as other federal laws. Second, publication of laws, even of the Constitution, does not seem to be a validity requirement in the Ethiopian legal dispensation. Nowhere does the Constitution mention of the need for its publication as a requirement for its entry into force. This can be contrasted with publication requirements explicitly set forth in many foreign constitutions in regards to both the constitutions themselves and parliamentary legislation. The 2010 Kenyan Constitution thus provides: "This Constitution shall come into force on its *promulgation* by the President or on the expiry of a period of fourteen days from the date of the *publication* in the *Gazette* of the final result of the referendum ratifying this Constitution, whichever is the earlier"[71] (emphasis added). Likewise, the 1996 South African Constitution contains specific provisions regarding the need for

---

[68]*Ibid*, p. 32.

[69]Idris (2000), pp. 125–126. Idris in fact argues that publication can occur in three different ways: publication of the whole treaty content in the federal Negarit Gazeta, the law gazette; cross referencing the content of the treaty in proclamation that heralds the ratification of the treaty; or incorporating the content of the treaty in a domestic legislation: *ibid*.

[70]*See* Amare (1998) and Assefa (2001).

[71]Article 263.

proclamation of the Constitution by the Republic's President for its effectivity.[72] The 1978 Spanish Constitution also stipulates that "[it] shall become effective on the day of the publication 'in the Official State Gazette'".[73] On the contrary, the Ethiopian Constitution does not say anything in regards to its publication.

Similarly, as I have also argued elsewhere,[74] a close scrutiny of the relevant provisions of the Ethiopian Constitution reveals that the Constitution does not make publication or promulgation a precondition for the validity of ordinary domestic laws. Article 57 of the Constitution reads: "Laws deliberated upon and passed by the House shall be submitted to the Nation's President for signature. The President shall sign a law submitted to him within fifteen days. If the President does not sign the law within fifteen days *it shall take effect without his signature*" (emphasis added). The provision in quote does not make any reference to the need for publication but only to the law's taking effect with or without the signature of the President. It is my contention that if publication were a validity requirement, it would have been explicitly stated in the Constitution or in any other law of the country which so far is not the case.[75] In legal systems where laws take effect only upon publication, explicit stipulations are made to that effect.[76] Finally, the practice in Ethiopia with respect to ratified treaties demonstrates that publication is not a requirement for a treaty law to enter into force domestically. It is well known that in Ethiopia, texts of ratified treaties, including all human rights treaties to which Ethiopia is a party,[77] are not published in the official law gazette.[78] But both the international community and, importantly, the Ethiopian government consider the

---

[72]Section 243.

[73]Final Provision.

[74]Assefa (2009), p. 168.

[75]The most relevant domestic law, other than the Constitution, where such a requirement could have been set forth is the "Federal Negarit Gazeta" establishment Proclamation (No. 3/1995). Article 2(2) states: "All laws of the Federal Government shall be published in the Federal Negarit Gazeta" while Article 2(3) provides: "All Federal or Regional legislative, executive and judicial organs as well as any natural or juridical person shall take judicial notice of Laws published in the Federal Negarit Gazeta". What the former signifies is that the Federal Negarit Gazeta is the only official law gazette of the federal government while the latter obligates state organs, as well as natural or juridical persons, to accept laws published in the Federal Negarit Gazeta as legally binding without requiring any further proof to that effect. In both cases, publication of a law has not been made a (pre)condition for the law's entry into force.

[76]See, e.g., section 81, South African Constitution; Article 15(3), Russian Constitution; Article 116, Kenyan Constitution; Article 88, Dutch Constitution; Article 81(2), the German Basic Law.

[77]Above n 1 and accompanying text.

[78]Following ratification by the HoPR, in most cases (not in all cases) a one-page notice of ratification of any given treaty is published in the Federal Negarit Gazeta. The contents of the treaties are not published in any form. An example is Proclamation No. 10/1992 titled "the Convention on the Rights of the Child Ratification Proclamation" which as noted is a one-page proclamation that stated the fact of Ethiopia's ratification of the said Convention on the date specified in the Proclamation. I should hasten to note here that even such notices of ratification have not been published in the case of treaties such as the two Covenants of 1966 and the Convention against Torture, and other Cruel, Inhuman or Degrading Treatment or Punishment.

country bound by the treaties. As the discussion under Sect. 6 below will show, Ethiopian courts have applied human rights treaties such as the International Covenant on Civil and Political Rights (ICCPR) to disputes before them. The fact the ICCPR has not been published in the official law gazette of the country has never been brought up—by the courts or the parties—in the proceedings to challenge its domestic legal force.

4.2 The Self-Executing/Non-Self-Executing Nature of Treaties

A closely related notion that is usually invoked as affecting the domestic effect of ratified treaties is the (non-) self-executing nature of treaties. A treaty is said to be self-executing if it is capable of judicial enforcement without an intervening legislative or executive act being required.[79] If not, a treaty is non-self-executing. Again, legal systems have adopted divergent approaches in relation to adjudging treaties in either way. The US Senate and courts have categorically treated virtually all human rights treaties as non-self-executing thereby making their domestic enforcement subject to implementing legislation.[80] In South Africa, section 231 (4) of the Constitution states that self-executing provisions of treaties approved by the Parliament could directly become law without the need to be enacted by the national legislation. Again, although the Ethiopian Constitution is not clearly forthcoming on this matter, one can draw a conclusion from the provisions of Article 9(4) that, under normal circumstances, ratified treaties are presumed to be self-executing. This conclusion is strengthened by the fact that ratification of most human rights treaties by Ethiopia has not been accompanied by any declarations that categorized any number of the provisions of any of these treaties as non-self-executing.

4.3 The Termination of Treaties

The Ethiopian Constitution does not regulate the denunciation or termination of treaties. In fact, it is interesting to note that of the four past constitutions (of 1931, 1955, 1987 and the 1991 Transitional Charter) of Ethiopia, only the 1987 Constitution explicitly dealt with the issue of denunciation of treaties by, as noted earlier, giving the Council of State—the body in charge of ratification of treaties—the power to denounce treaties if the need arose. Since Ethiopia is not party to the Vienna Convention on the Law of Treaties, the terms of this Treaty on termination

---

[79]Shelton (2011), p. 11.
[80]Bradley and Goldsmith (2000), p. 399.

are not directly applicable to it unless it is established that the relevant terms of the Treaty form part of customary international law.

In any case, however, if the mechanism of termination or denunciation (or withdrawal) of a treaty is specified in the treaty in question, Ethiopia has to abide by that provision for it has accepted the whole content of the treaty during ratification, unless of course it has made a reservation or any other interpretive declaration with regard to the provisions governing termination of or withdrawal from the treaty. If the treaty does not govern its termination, then it seems to me that the HoPR has the authority to approve the termination of treaties. This is because the HoPR ratifies all treaties and the act of termination is an act equivalent to ratification which therefore has to be done by the HoPR.

5 The Hierarchical Relationship Between International Law and Domestic Law in Ethiopia

The past Ethiopian constitutions had divergent stands on the question of the hierarchy of treaties. The 1931 and 1987 Constitutions made no reference to the status of treaties. However, the 1955 Imperial Constitution had unequivocally spoken about the status of treaties in the domestic legal order by using wording that closely resembled that of the US Constitution. It stated that "[the 1955 Constitution], together with those international treaties, conventions and obligations to which Ethiopia shall be party, shall be the supreme law of the Empire (....)."[81] The 1991 Charter, the interim Constitution of the Transitional Government of Ethiopia which served from 1991 to 1995, is especially noteworthy for its incorporation of the whole of the UDHR as binding domestic law. Its Article 1, thus, declared: "Based on the Universal Declaration of Human Rights of the United Nations ... individual human rights shall be respected fully and without any limitations whatsoever ..." The Charter, however, was not clearly forthcoming in regards to the status of other ratified treaties vis-à-vis the Charter itself or other domestic laws.

It has been noted earlier that the 1995 Constitution of Ethiopia does not recognize non-treaty sources of international law.[82] Thus, we cannot talk about the status of these sources of international law in the Ethiopian domestic legal setting from the point of view of the Constitution. In regards to treaties, however, having declared that ratified treaties form an integral part of the law of the land, the Constitution fails to clearly pronounce the place such treaties occupy in the country's hierarchy of norms. As a result, the status ratified treaties hold vis-à-vis the Constitution and other laws of the country is one of the highly debatable legal questions in the Ethiopian legal order today.

---

[81] Article 122.

[82] *See* n 15 above and accompanying text.

By a broad categorization, there are two camps espousing divergent views on the status of ratified treaties within the Ethiopian legal order. The first view holds that ratified treaties in general have equal normative status with the Constitution while ratified human rights treaties are superior to or at least on par with the Ethiopian Constitution.[83] Regarding the status of ratified treaties vis-à-vis domestic primary laws, their view is that treaties override sub-constitutional laws, including federal proclamations.[84] The authors in the second camp, on the other hand, espouse that, on the domestic plane, treaties are on par with federal proclamations and are subordinate to the Constitution.[85] Thus, according to this view, conflict between treaties and primary legislation would be resolved by resorting to the principle of *lex posterior derogate legi priori*.

The authors in the first camp rely on the understanding of some monist theorists who assert that international law and national law are not only part of the same system of norms but also that international law is superior to domestic law.[86] Bulto, for example, has argued that domestic law remains authoritative and valid so long as it conforms to international law in the absence of which domestic law becomes null and void resulting in international law's direct effect in domestic sphere.[87] He characterized the views in the second camp, which he dubbed as erroneous,[88] as emanating from the influence of the dualist theoretical position on the relationship between international law and national law.[89]

The views held by Bulto and others who say treaties, on the domestic plane, are on par with or even superior to the Ethiopian Constitution are not grounded in the textual reading of the Ethiopian Constitution and are oblivious to its drafting history. Furthermore, their views fail to grasp the important practical difference between international law's force on the international plane and its implementation domestically by courts and other domestic organs. Indubitably, a state's breach of its treaty obligations—whether because of its contrary domestic law or for any other reason—results in the violation of international law leading to an international accountability of that state. However, the domestic application of treaties is determined by domestic legal systems. As Wolfrum observes, it is quite possible that the international application and domestic application of a treaty may not match, i.e. "even though a state is bound by a rule of international law", that same rule

---

[83]Bulto (2009), pp. 250, 252–253; Idris (2000), p. 138.

[84]*Ibid*, p. 148.

[85]Haile (2005), pp. 27–28; Assefa (2001), p. 257.

[86]Sloss (2011), p. 2.

[87]Bulto (2009), p. 135.

[88]*Ibid*, p. 133.

[89]In fact, as Professor Sloss succinctly explains, monism and dualism are not much about the hierarchical relations between national law and international law. According to him, "dualist states are states in which...all treaties require implementing legislation to have domestic legal force. Monist states are states in which some treaties have the status of law in the domestic legal system, even in the absence of implementing legislation": Sloss (2011), pp. 2–3.

may not "be applied as binding law by organs of that state".[90] Accordingly, in dualist states such as Australia, Canada, Denmark, Germany, India, Israel, the United Kingdom and some Nordic states, treaties can have domestic effect only if the legislature incorporates the treaties into domestic law via legislation.[91] This means that although these states are bound internationally by the treaties, their national courts cannot apply these treaties to settle cases brought before them unless their respective legislatures bring these treaties into domestic effect through legislation.[92]

Likewise, the rank of ratified treaties within a state's hierarchy of norms is also determined by its domestic constitutional system. Thus, for the dualist states, since treaties obtain domestic force through incorporation normally by laws passed by legislatures,[93] they often have the rank of Parliamentary statutes. As such therefore in the above-named dualist states (and others with similar orientation), treaties occupy a statutory rank in their respective legal systems and, in principle, the *lex posteriori* rule applies in the event of conflict between a treaty and a statute later in time.[94] In South Africa, some treaties can even rank below parliamentary statutes "depending on the manner of [their] incorporation".[95] As Erika de Wet observes "while a treaty enacted into law by an Act of Parliament will enjoy the same status as other Parliamentary Acts, a treaty enacted into law through subordinate legislation (for example, a ministerial proclamation in the Government Gazette), will be on par with other subordinate legislation".[96] When it comes to the monist states, variability exists among the states in regards to the hierarchical status they accord to ratified treaties. For example, in Austria, Egypt and the US, treaties have the rank of statutes.[97] This is also the case in Ireland.[98] Certain treaties rank higher than statutes and below constitutions in France, Japan, Mexico and Poland.[99] The Netherlands puts international treaties above its domestic laws.[100]

The above examples show that diversity abounds in relation to the domestic rank and application of treaties. Ethiopia's constitutional dispensation forms part of this spectrum of approaches and, contrary to what some authors[101] tend to believe, the mere departure of domestic law from international law cannot *ipso facto* render the domestic law in question null and void. If that was the case, we would have

---

[90]Wolfrum et al. (2015), p. 3.
[91]*Ibid.*
[92]*Ibid*, p. 4.
[93]Dinokopila (2015), p. 476.
[94]Wolfrum et al. (2015), p. 14; Sweet and Keller (2008), p. 685.
[95]de Wet (2015), p. 33.
[96]*Ibid.*
[97]Sloss (2011), p. 8.
[98]Sweet and Keller (2008), p. 685.
[99]Sloss (2011), p. 8.
[100]Shelton (2011), p. 5.
[101]*See*, e.g., Bulto (2009).

domestic laws of many nations of the world as dead letters in our hands. True, legal systems that accord treaties statutory status (or even a status above statutes but below their constitutions) recognize the special nature of treaties and their origin in public international law and have developed practices by which domestic laws are interpreted consistently with their international commitments. For example, in the UK, a typical dualist state, courts presume when interpreting statutes that the British Parliament did not intend to violate the country's international obligations.[102] In relation to the European Convention on Human Rights, the Human Rights Act instructs UK courts to interpret domestic legislation 'so far as it is possible to do so' in a manner compatible with the European Convention.[103]

Similarly, in *Whitney v. Robertson* the US Supreme Court ruled that when a statute and treaty relate to the same subject, the courts will always endeavour to construe the two so as to give effect to both, if that can be done without violating the language of either; but, if the two are inconsistent, the one last in date will control the other.[104] In Germany, the Constitutional Court reiterated in its 2004 decision that the European Convention and its Protocols have the status of federal German statutes while at the same time declaring that the Convention is *lex specialis* and that all provisions in the German legal order have to be construed in accordance with the ECHR so as to avoid any conflict.[105] In 1998, in Bangalore, India, British Commonwealth judges adopted the "Bangalore Principles" agreeing that it is the "vital" duty of the judiciary "to interpret and apply national constitutions and ... legislation in harmony with international human rights codes and customary international law and to develop the common law in the light of the values and principles enshrined in international human rights law".[106]

Israeli courts often resort to international law to substantiate constitutional rights.[107] Australian courts are also increasingly becoming willing to examine the international law of fundamental rights as offering a contextual consideration to inform the judicial decision-makers about the way in which they should interpret the contested national constitutional provision.[108] Also, the Swedish Constitution states that all Swedish laws shall be interpreted and applied in light of international treaties.[109] In its 1989 decision (in *Slaight Communications v. Davidson*), the Canadian Supreme Court declared that it could refer to international law, both treaty and custom, to determine the substance of constitutional rights.[110] The

---

[102]Shelton (2011), p. 19.

[103]Section 3, UK Human Rights Act (1998).

[104]*Whitney v. Robertson*, 124 U.S. 190 (1888).

[105]Press Release No. 92/2004, 19 October 2004, Press Office, Federal German Constitutional Court.

[106]Cited in Shelton (2011), p. 15, n 61.

[107]Shelton (2011), p. 19.

[108]Kirby (2010), p. 172.

[109]Sweet and Keller (2008), p. 684.

[110]Sandholtz (2015), p. 599.

Supreme Court of India clearly stated that it places reliance on international commitments for the purpose of construing the nature and ambit of rights guarantees in the Constitution while in Bangladesh treaty law can "be used to interpret fundamental rights in the constitution and to develop common law on the matter.[111] Courts of many other countries of both monist and dualist orientations, such as Austria, the Netherlands, Nigeria and Poland, use treaties and other international instruments as guides, or aids, in the interpretation of domestic laws.[112]

The discussion in the preceding paragraphs clearly shows that while treaties are given statutory ranks in many legal systems, because of their origins in international law, states have considered treaties as *lex specialis* and developed practices that require domestic laws to be interpreted as far as possible consistently with treaty commitments, or at least that treaty provisions would serve as aide or guides to the interpretation of statutory or constitutional rules. This in my view also shows that the positions held by authors like Bulto that under no circumstances can the domestic application of treaties be set aside or overridden by the operation of domestic law is not well supported by legal practices around the world.

Turning to the hierarchical status of treaties (including human rights treaties) in the Ethiopian legal system, the main bases for my analysis are the text of the Ethiopian Constitution, the practice of the Ethiopian government and the *travaux préparatoires* of the Constitution. Unfortunately, so far, no judicial or quasi-judicial body has dealt with the issue of hierarchical rank of treaties in any manner and therefore no domestic jurisprudence has developed in the area.

To start with the text, the Ethiopian Constitution does not clearly settle the hierarchical status of ratified treaties in the Ethiopian legal system. But, the most relevant provisions of the Constitution on the subject are contained in Article 9(1) and 9(4), and Article 13(2). In Article 9(4) the Constitution states: "All international agreements ratified by Ethiopia are an integral part of the law of the land". The Amharic version connotes in a similar manner but perhaps more clearly that treaties ratified by Ethiopia are part and parcel of the law of the country. This stipulation meshes ratified treaties of all sorts with the body of Ethiopian law. But Article 9 (1) has already singled out the Constitution as *"the supreme law of the land"*[113] (emphasis added) leaving no doubt that it alone is "the" supreme law. When treaties are made an integral part of the law of the land, it is clear that all "law of the land" that comprise federal, as well as state laws of various sources and hierarchies, cannot be supreme law of the land. Thus, the wording that treaties are integral part of the law of the land must connote that they are part of the body of laws to which the Constitution is declared supreme. This understanding is confirmed by scholars.[114]

---

[111] *Ibid.*

[112] *Ibid*, pp. 598–599.

[113] Article 9(1) of the Constitution in whole reads: "The Constitution is the supreme law of the land. Any law, customary practice or a decision of an organ of state or a public official which contravenes this Constitution shall be of no effect".

[114] *See*, e.g., Haile (2005).

Some scholars like Bulto, as noted earlier, particularly rely on Article 13(2) of the Constitution to argue that international human rights treaties are accorded equal status or are even considered superior to the federal Constitution. This Article reads: "The fundamental rights and freedoms specified in this [Bill of Rights] Chapter shall be interpreted in a manner conforming to the principles of the Universal Declaration of Human Rights, International Covenants on Human Rights and international instruments adopted by Ethiopia". So the question is whether this stipulation is determinative of the hierarchical relations between the domestic laws of Ethiopia, including the Constitution, and human rights treaties.

It may be useful to look into some comparative constitutions here. Almost identical stipulation exists in the 1978 Spanish Constitution. Article 10(2) of that Constitution reads: "The principles relating to the fundamental rights and liberties recognised by the Constitution shall be interpreted in conformity with the Universal Declaration of Human Rights and the international treaties and agreements thereon ratified by Spain." Nevertheless, this provision has not become the basis for the determination of the hierarchical relations between Spanish domestic laws and ratified treaties. That issue is regulated by a separate provision in the Constitution, Article 95, which states that "the conclusion of any international treaty containing stipulations contrary to the Constitution shall require prior constitutional amendment". This is understood and so declared by the Spanish Constitutional Court to underscore that the Spanish Constitution takes precedence over international rules and that treaties including the European Convention on Human Rights rank below the Constitution.[115] The value attached to the provisions of Article 10(2) cited earlier is to ensure the indirect application of the rights enshrined in the Spanish Constitution. Thus, ratified treaties and the UDHR are made the most important source of reference in the interpretation of rights and freedoms recognized by the Constitution, obligating national courts and all other national authorities to follow the case law of treaty enforcement bodies like the European Court of Human Rights.[116]

We find related provisions in the South African Constitution which states that 'when interpreting the Bill of Rights, a court, tribunal or forum (...) must consider international law'.[117] The South African Constitutional Court in *S v Makwanyane*[118] said that by virtue of this constitutional stipulation, international law and the jurisprudence of international and regional bodies provide guidance to the correct interpretation of particular provisions of the Bill of Rights, as well as a framework within which its provisions can be evaluated and understood. This constitutional stipulation has not been taken to be in any way determinative of the hierarchical relations between international law and the domestic law of

---

[115] Soriano (2008), p. 403.

[116] *Ibid*, p. 404.

[117] *South African* Constitution, Art. 39(1)(b).

[118] *S v Makwanyane* 1995 (3) SA 391 (CC), [36]-[37], cited in Currie and de Waal (2005), p. 159.

South Africa and it has already been noted that in South Africa treaties may rank below statutes.[119]

In a similar fashion Article 13(2) of the Ethiopian Constitution should be understood to ensure the indirect application of the treaties and instruments enlisted in it by requiring national courts and all other national authorities to interpret the constitutional rights consistently with these instruments, and not as a marker of the domestic hierarchical position of treaties. In fact, it must be noted that Article 13 (2) enlists both binding and non-binding instruments (or those that are amenable to ratification such as ICCPR and ICESCR, and those that are not such as the UDHR). This shows that its primary concern is to provide for the interpretation and enforcement of the constitutional rights and not the hierarchical relationship between these rights and those contained in the international instruments mentioned in Article 13 (2).

This understanding is supported by the drafting history of the Constitution and the official position of the Ethiopian government. During the deliberations on the original draft of the Constitution, it was argued that international instruments shall be used as interpretative guidelines for the provisions already in the Constitution without having the status to override or be equal with the Constitution itself.[120] Proclamation No. 251/2001, a law regulating the powers and functions of the House of the Federation, a body in charge of the interpretation of the federal Constitution, is reflective of the Ethiopian government's position.[121] According to this proclamation, the House is empowered to review the constitutionality of international agreements ratified by Ethiopia.[122]

The foregoing discussion sets out the hierarchical position of ratified treaties vis-à-vis the Ethiopian Constitution but does not resolve the question of the hierarchical relations between ratified treaties and other laws of the country, mainly federal statutes or proclamations. The three likely scenarios are for the treaties to be superior to proclamations and below the Constitution; be of the same hierarchical status with proclamations or be of lower hierarchy than proclamations. Of these possibilities, the one that puts ratified treaties at the same level as federal proclamations has drawn greater "consensus of the dominant literature."[123]

I have already argued that Article 9(1) of the Constitution, its drafting history and government practice, establish the supremacy of the Constitution. It has also been pointed out that Article 9(4) declares that ratified treaties are an integral part of the law of the country. The Constitution further subjects all kinds of treaties to the

---

[119] Above, n 95 and accompanying text.

[120] See *Minutes of the Ethiopian Constituent Assembly*, vol. 2 (December 1994), pp. 65–70.

[121] Articles 62(1), 83–84 of the Constitution provide that the House of the Federation interprets the Constitution and settles all constitutional disputes aided by the Council of Constitutional Inquiry organized as per Article 82 of the Constitution.

[122] This is apparent from the reading of Article 2(2) of Proclamation No. 251/2001 in conjunction with other relevant provisions of the Constitution.

[123] Bulto (2009), p. 133.

ratification or approval of the federal law-maker, the House of Peoples' Representatives.[124] The Process of ratification, including the scrutiny of treaties proposed for ratification and the decision-making on whether to accept or reject a proposed treaty, are all done in accordance with the HoPR's legislative rules and procedures.[125] Finally, as it is the case for federal proclamations, ratified treaties are also required to be proclaimed in the official law gazette by the President of the Republic (and as I argued earlier, publication is not a validity requirement in both cases).[126] All of these put together are indicative of the hierarchical parity between federal proclamations and ratified treaties making the *lex posteriori* principle applicable in times of conflict.

But it is interesting to note that the official position of the Ethiopian government, at least as far as it can be gleaned from the Core Document of its periodic reports to the UN Treaty Bodies,[127] is that by virtue of Article 13(2) of the Constitution, earlier referred to, ratified human rights treaties have a higher status than ordinary legislation, including proclamations.[128] Although in my view this does not clearly emerge from the textual reading of the relevant provisions of the Constitution, it can be taken as a positive interpretation of the Constitution through political practice and it is a welcome development.

In any case, however, even if the dominant position regarding the hierarchical relationship between treaties and proclamations is one in which the latter trumps the former, courts and other domestic authorities have to consider the international law origins of treaties and must adopt interpretive approaches by which domestic laws, including the Constitution, are consistently interpreted with Ethiopia's treaty commitments. As earlier noted, such an interpretive approach is made a requirement by the Ethiopian Constitution in regards to its Bill of Rights.[129] It could be logically derived from this that other domestic laws of the country dealing with fundamental rights and freedoms should as well be interpreted consistently with the principles of international human rights instruments adopted by Ethiopia.[130] It is also upon the legislature to harmonize domestic laws when they stand in conflict with the country's treaty commitments so that Ethiopia does not violate international law, which it willingly abided by.

---

[124] Articles 55(12), 71(2), Ethiopian Constitution.

[125] Above, n 63 and accompanying text.

[126] Article 71(2), Ethiopian Constitution.

[127] UN Doc HRI/CORE/ETH/2008 (6 February 2009).

[128] *Ibid*, [123].

[129] Article 13(2), Ethiopian Constitution. This constitutional requirement of "consistent interpretation" of course needs to consider other more specific requirements and principles in the Constitution like the ones in Article 43(3) (requiring that international agreements Ethiopia enters into protect its right to sustainable development) and Article 86(4) (declaring that Ethiopia observes international agreements that ensure its sovereignty and are not contrary to the interests of its people). I am grateful to Professor Melaku G. Desta for pointing this out to me.

[130] Abebe (2012), p. 66.

6 Judicial and Quasi-Judicial Enforcement of International Law in Ethiopia

It has been noted[131] that the Criminal Code of the country makes reference to non-treaty sources of international law and makes criminal conduct under public international law or international custom punishable. But in other areas of the law, including in the Ethiopian Constitution, non-treaty sources have not been formally received into the country's legal system. This makes both their status and enforceability on the domestic plane unclear. Of course it can be argued that to the extent that customary international law or general principles of law pertaining to human rights are incorporated into the Constitution and other laws of the country, these sources of international law are indirectly applicable in the country.

In any case, the judicial and quasi-judicial enforcement of international human rights treaties applicable to Ethiopia is guided and regulated by the federal Constitution. The Bill of Rights, comprising of Articles 13–44 of the Constitution, begins with the declaration of the scope of application and the interpretation of its rights provisions. As regards the scope, it provides that 'all federal and state legislative, executive and judicial organs at all levels shall have the responsibility and duty to respect and enforce the provisions of [the Bill of Rights]'.[132] The bills of rights of the constitutions of the member states of the Ethiopian federation—which by and large are replicas of the federal Constitution—contain similar provisions that impose duties and responsibilities on all state organs to respect and enforce the provisions of the respective bills of rights.[133]

Article 13(2) of the Constitution makes it mandatory that the interpretation of the provisions of the federal Bill of Rights be undertaken in a manner conforming to the principles contained in human rights treaties and other human rights instruments (including the UDHR) adopted by Ethiopia. As it is clear from the wording of this provision, it is not only treaties that can be used as sources of interpretation, non-treaty instruments can also be put to that use. Identical stipulations also exist in the Bills of Rights of the members of the Federation. These interpretative requirements are also included in relevant federal and regional statutes that provide further details on the interpretation of these fundamental rights. For example, Article 7(2) of Proclamation No. 251/2001 instructs the House of the Federation—the interpreter of the Constitution—in the following manner: "Where the Constitutional case submitted to the House pertains to the fundamental rights and freedoms enshrined in the

---

[131] Above n 21–23 and accompanying text.

[132] See *Ethiopian* Constitution, Art. 13(1). We find similar declarations in other federal systems like Germany, the USA and Switzerland: *see* Fercot (2008). Such a declaration of national applicability is also part of the Canadian Constitution: *Canadian Charter of Rights and Freedoms*, s 32.

[133] E.g., Art. 13(1) of *Constitution of Amhara National Regional State* (Ethiopia), reads: 'All legislative, executive and judicial organs of the national regional state at all levels shall have the responsibility and duty to respect and enforce the provisions of [the State's Bill of Rights]'.

Constitution, the interpretation shall be made in a manner conforming to the principles of the Universal Declaration of Human Rights, International Covenants on Human Rights and International instruments adopted by Ethiopia."

The full implications of the interpretative requirement in Article 13(2) of the Federal Constitution and its mirror provisions in state and federal laws have not been authoritatively settled yet. But in my view courts and others that are subject to Article 13(2) requirements are obliged not only to conform to the wording of the treaties in question but also to the jurisprudence and authoritative comments of international and regional bodies that oversee the implementation of these treaties. Ethiopian courts, the House of the Federation and other relevant national organs are advised particularly to pay serious attention to the case law and other authoritative pronouncements of the African Commission on Human and Peoples' Rights which has the jurisdiction to hear individual complaints from Ethiopia by virtue of Ethiopia's accession to this Charter.[134]

The Bill of Rights of the Ethiopian Constitution contains a catalogue of rights drawn from a variety of international human rights instruments, including the UDHR, the International Covenant on Civil and Political Rights (ICCPR), the International Covenant on Economic, Social and Cultural Rights, the Convention on the Elimination of All Forms of Discrimination Against Women, and the Convention on the Rights of the Child. Thus, given the constitutional requirement to interpret the provisions of the Bill of Rights consistently with the principles of international human rights instruments adopted by Ethiopia, the international human rights instruments are indirectly applied through the application of the constitutional rights.

The provisions of ratified treaties can also be directly applied by domestic courts and other organs like the Council of Constitutional Inquiry and the House of the Federation. This is because, by virtue of Article 9(4) of the Constitution, treaties form part of the law of the country upon ratification without any further actions which gives Ethiopia a monist feature. The federal legislature in recognition of the direct applicability of international treaties has clearly empowered federal courts to settle disputes that come before them by using international treaties along with the Constitution and other domestic laws.[135]

The practice of direct application of international human rights treaties by judicial and quasi-judicial organs in Ethiopia so far has not developed well as it is clear from the dearth of cases decided relying on human rights treaties. However, there are some noteworthy positive developments as well. An important case that was decided by the Cassation Bench of the federal Supreme Court of Ethiopia is *Tsedale Demissie v. Kifle Demissie*.[136] Decisions given by the Cassation Bench such as *Tsedale Demissie* are noteworthy because the interpretive decisions of the

---

[134] It is interesting to note that Ethiopia has shut off most avenues for individuals having access to human rights treaty bodies by failing to ratify optional protocols or making necessary declarations.

[135] Articles 3, 6, Proclamation No. 25/1995.

[136] Federal Cassation File No. 23632 (2006).

Bench handed down by a panel of five or more judges are binding on all lower federal courts and all state courts.[137]

Tsedale Demissie was a case involving a custody battle between a paternal aunt and the father of a 12-year-old child whose mother had passed away. The facts of the case show that the child's aunt challenged a custody right awarded to the father of the child by court saying that she cared for the child for more than ten years while the father had not cared for the child at all.[138] Lower courts followed the literal provisions of the law, awarding custody to the father as the surviving parent. The lower courts decided the case based on the Family Code of the Southern Nations, Nationalities and Peoples State of Ethiopia where the parties to the case were domiciled. The Code in question does not explicitly embrace the principle of the "best interests" of the child as a guiding principle in the determination of child-related disputes. The Cassation Bench reversed the lower courts' verdicts on the case relying directly on the UN Convention on the Rights of the Child. The Bench stated that the Convention has become part of the law of the country by virtue of Article 9(4) of the federal Constitution.

In another case, *Tesfaye Tumro v. Federal Anti-Corruption Commission*,[139] the Cassation Bench directly invoked Article 15(1) of the International Covenant on Civil and Political Rights along with the Constitution and the Criminal Code. In the case, Mr. Tesfaye Tumro was accused by the Federal Anti-Corruption Commission of committing a corruption crime in the years between 2000 and 2004 based on the 2004 Criminal Code that came into force in April 2005. The Cassation Bench applied the principle of non-retroactivity of criminal law, enshrined in Article 22 of the federal Constitution, the ICCPR (Article 15) and the Criminal Code (Article 5). The Bench relied on the English version of the Covenant and stated that it is directly applicable as it is ratified by Ethiopia.

The last example of a direct application of international human rights treaties, in this case the ICCPR and the African Charter on Human and Peoples' Rights, is from the opinions of the Council of Constitutional Inquiry (CCI), the expert body that aids the House of the Federation in the interpretation of the Constitution.[140] In the *Federal Anti-Corruption Commission v. Tilahun Abay et al.*,[141] the defendants brought a case challenging the constitutionality of a federal law[142] that denied bail rights to persons accused of committing a corruption crime to the CCI and asked the CCI to interpret the constitution. The defendants argued that based on the Ethiopian Constitution Article 19(6) and the ICCPR Article 9(3), that a law that

---

[137] Article 2(1), Proclamation No. 454/2005.

[138] Assefa (2009), pp. 162–163.

[139] Federal Cassation File No. 73514 (2013).

[140] As per Article 84(1) of the Constitution, the CCI has the power to investigate constitutional disputes based on cases submitted to it and should it find the need to interpret the Constitution, it makes recommendations on the same to the House of the Federation. See also Articles 84(2)-(3) of the Constitution.

[141] Unpublished opinion of the CCI, reproduced in the *Journal of Ethiopian Law*, vol. 23, No. 2 (2010), pp. 146–153.

[142] Proclamation No. 236/2001.

legalizes a blanket denial of bail should be quashed as unconstitutional. The Council analysed at some length the provisions of the ICCPR and of the African Charter dealing with the right to liberty along with the provisions relating to bail rights. The Council also cited the General Comments of the Human Rights Committee on the protection against arbitrary arrest in the ICCPR. Finally, although the Council did not find the law unconstitutional, it engaged in the analysis and interpretation of ratified human rights treaties underscoring their direct application to individual cases in Ethiopia.

7 Federalism and Treaty-Making Competence in Ethiopia

Given the defining tenet of federalism as the exercise of power on citizens and territories of a nation by national and sub-national governments based on the constitutional division of powers, the powers of the respective governments in relation to foreign policy in general and treaty-making in particular need to be regulated. Federations exhibit differences regarding, for example, the involvement of sub-national units in foreign affairs, including treaty-making, as well as in how they deal with treaties that encroach upon the jurisdictions assigned to the sub-national units by the federal constitution.

In most federations issues of foreign affairs including treaty-making power are placed under the exclusive competence of the federal government.[143] These include the US, Australia and Russia.[144] Also, in South Africa, the provinces in principle have no competence to enter into treaties.[145] Ethiopia also falls within this camp. In the US, as determined by the US Supreme Court in *Missouri v Holland*[146] in 1920, the federal government has legislative competence to implement all treaties even those whose subject matter falls within state jurisdiction with the consequence of invalidation of any conflicting state law.[147]

Some other federal systems formally grant various roles to the competent organs in their constituent 'states'. For example, the Austrian Constitution (Article 16(1)) provides that "in matters within their own spheres of competence the Länder can conclude treaties with states, or their constituent states, bordering on Austria". However, the Constitution requires the Governor of the said Länder to inform the Federal Government (which shall act through the President of the Republic) before the initiation of negotiations about such a treaty, and to obtain the approval of the

---

[143]Shelton (2011), p. 21.

[144]*Ibid*, p. 8; de Wet (2015), p.

[145]de Wet (2015), p. 30.

[146]252 U.S.416 (1920).

[147]However, this case law may be changing in the US where some are arguing for restricting the national government's exclusive power of treaty-making to only matters falling under its constitutional competence: *see: Bond v US 134* S. Ct. 2077 (2014).

Federal Government before its conclusion.[148] The Constitution further provides that treaties concluded by a Land in accordance with Article 16(1) cited above can be revoked upon request by the Federal Government.

In the case of Germany, granting the power to conduct relations with foreign states to the national government, the Basic Law also stipulates that the national government shall consult a Land, in a timely fashion, before concluding a treaty that affects its special circumstances.[149] The Basic Law provides that the Lander may conclude treaties with foreign states in the area of their legislative competence with the consent of the national government.[150] In practice, the national government and the Länder have reached an agreement about the matter, which provides, amongst others, that the national government shall reach agreement with the Länder before concluding agreements in areas of exclusive competence of the Länder.[151]

In Canada, the national government lacks legislative competence to implement treaties whose subject matter falls within provincial jurisdiction.[152] The Canadian Constitution is not specific about the scope and breadth of the national government's treaty-making and implementation powers. But the Privy Council in 1937 in the *Labour Conventions*[153] case (involving the federal government's legislation implementing an ILO Convention ratified by Canada) decided that the national government cannot enact an implementing legislation if the matter relates to an exclusive jurisdiction of the provinces implying that in such cases the two orders of government must consult for the implementation of Canada's international obligations.[154] The practice in Canada now is that the national government enters into treaties that require the implementation of legislation by the provinces after it secures the agreement of the provinces to pass the implementing legislation.[155]

A final example to consider is the Belgian federation. Its Constitution empowers the Community and Regional Governments of Belgium—Governments of the Flemish, French, and German-speaking Communities[156]—to conclude treaties regarding matters that fall within the competence of their respective Parliaments.[157] Thus, Belgium must obtain the consent of its constituent units before it enters into treaties if the treaties relate to matters that fall within their competence. This was shown for example by the recent declaration by Belgium concerning the EU-Canada Comprehensive Economic and Trade Agreement (CETA) to the effect,

---

[148] Article 16(2), Austrian Constitution. Article 16(2) states that the approval is deemed to have been given if the Federal Government has not within eight weeks from the day that the request for approval reaches the Federal Chancellery told the Governor that approval is withheld.
[149] Article 32, the Basic Law of Germany.
[150] *Ibid.*
[151] Wolfrum et al. (2015), p. 9.
[152] Friesen (1994), p. 1416.
[153] *Canada (AG) v. Ontario (AG)* [1937] UKPC 6, [1937] A.C. 326.
[154] *Ibid*, p. 1431.
[155] *Ibid*, pp. 1436–1437.
[156] Article 121, Belgian Constitution.
[157] *Ibid*, Article 167(3).

among others, that unless their respective parliaments decide to the contrary, "the Walloon region, the French Community, the German-speaking Community, the Francophone Community Commission and the Brussels Capital Region do not intend to ratify CETA on the basis of the system of Investor-State dispute settlement provided in chapter 8 of CETA, as it stands at the moment of signature".[158]

Coming to the case of Ethiopia, as earlier noted, the power to conduct foreign affairs in general and treaty-making power in particular falls under the exclusive competence of the federal government.[159] The Constitution explicitly assigns the power to formulate and implement foreign policy and negotiate and ratify international agreements to the federal government. This means that the federal government can enter into treaties with other states or other subjects of international law on potentially any matter, even if the matter in question falls within state's competence in terms of the vertical division of constitutional powers between the two levels of government. While this is what emerges from the explicit wording of the federal Constitution, there are however certain practical developments over the last several years that seem to have loosened the exclusivity of treaty making competence. In reality, the states of the federation are allowed to enter into agreements with foreign states that share international borders with them.[160] This could be based on a prior authorization by the federal government, somewhat along the lines of the Austrian constitutional dispensation[161] noted above. But, there is no official explanation of the practice or the requirements and procedures for the competence of states to conduct foreign affairs.

8 Conclusion

The paper has shown that non-treaty sources of international law are not clearly recognized in the national laws of Ethiopia except in criminal law areas. It has also shown that Ethiopia receives treaties into its legal system through ratification and attaches no further requirements to the domestic application of treaties. The Ethiopian constitutional dispensation also shows that ratified treaties are in principle self-executing capable of direct application in Ethiopia. It is not clear from the Ethiopian Constitution whether the executive can enter into international agreements without the legislature's approval. In view of this, the paper argued that the relevant rules of the Constitution should be given meaning that accepts the executive's competence to make international agreements on matters falling within its

---

[158] <http://worldtradelaw.typepad.com/ielpblog/2016/10/belgian-ceta-declaration-informal-english-translation-from-french-version-opening-procedural-paragra.html> (accessed on 9 December 2016).

[159] Articles 51(8), 55(12), 77 (4), 77(8).

[160] *See*, e.g., Fana Broadcasting Corporate News (2016). Here, it was reported that an agreement was signed between the Amhara Regional State's representative and the Administrator of the adjacent Sudanese Gedaref State.

[161] See above, n 148 and accompanying text.

general or departmental responsibilities. The paper has also argued that, in terms of hierarchical status, treaties rank below the Constitution. In regards to the sub-constitutional laws, although the Constitution is not explicit, the Ethiopian government maintained in the Core Document Forming the Initial Part of the Reports of Ethiopia to the UN treaty bodies that treaties rank higher than ordinary laws of the country. It has also been explained that treaties have the modes of direct or indirect application in Ethiopia. The paper has also shown that Ethiopian constituent units do not have constitutional competence in relation to foreign affairs more broadly and treaty-making specifically.

Acknowledgement I am grateful to the editors of the Yearbook and to the anonymous reviewers for their constructive comments. I am solely responsible for any remaining errors.

References

Abebe AK (2012) Litigating constitutional human rights in Ethiopia. Ethiop Bar Rev 4(2):49–76

Amare G (1998) The Ethiopian Human Rights Regime, Federal Democratic Republic of Ethiopia's Constitution and International Human Rights Conventions Ethiopia has ratified. Unpublished paper: Addis Ababa

Asrat A (2016) Ethiopia, Sudan sign accord to cement people-to-people ties at border areas. Fana Broadcasting Corporate News (4 June 2016). http://www.fanabc.com/english/index.php/component/k2/item/6075?Itemid=674. Accessed 13 Nov 2016

Assefa G (2001) Problems of implementation of [international] human rights laws by Ethiopian courts. In: Fiseha A, Regassa T (eds) Proceedings of the symposium on the role of courts in the enforcement of the constitution. Berhanena Selam Printing Press, Addis Ababa, pp 88–107

Assefa G (2009) Is publication of a ratified treaty a requirement for its enforcement in Ethiopia? A comment based on [Federal] Cassation File No. 23632. J Ethiop Law 23(2):162–170

Bradley CA, Goldsmith JL (2000) Treaties, human rights, and conditional consent. Univ Pa Law Rev 149:399–468

Bulto TS (2009) The Monist-Dualist divide and the supremacy clause: revisiting the status of human rights treaties in Ethiopia. J Ethiop Law 23(1):132–161

Christenson GA (1995/96) Customary international human rights law in domestic court decisions. Gonzaga J Int Comp Law 25:225–254

Constituent Assembly, Ethiopia (December 1994) Minutes, vol 2

Currie I, de Waal J (2005) The bill of rights handbook, 5th edn. Juta and Company

Declaration of the establishment of the Federal Democratic Republic of Ethiopia Proclamation No. 2/1995

De wet E (2015) The reception of international law in the South African legal order: an introduction. In: de Wet Erika E, Wolfrum R, Hestermeyer H (eds) The implementation of international law in Germany and South Africa. Pretoria University Law Press, Pretoria, pp 23–51

Dinokopila BR (2015) The implementation of African Union Law in South Africa. In: de Wet E, Wolfrum R, Hestermeyer H (eds) The implementation of international law in Germany and South Africa. Pretoria University Law Press, Pretoria, pp 468–494

Ethiopian Constitution, 1931

Ethiopian Constitution, 1955

Ethiopian Constitution, 1987

Ethiopian Constitution, 1995

Ethiopian Transitional Period Charter, 1991

Federal Courts Establishment Proclamation No. 25/1995 (Ethiopia) (with Amendments)

Federal Negarit Gazeta Establishment Proclamation, No. 3/1995 (Ethiopia)

Fercot C (2008) Perspectives on federalism-diversity of constitutional rights in federal systems: a comparative analysis of German, American and Swiss Law. Eur Const Law Rev 4:302–324

Friesen JF (1994) The distribution of treaty-implementing powers in constitutional federations: thoughts on the American and Canadian models. Columbia Law Rev 94(4):1415–1450

Garcia MG (2013) "International Law and Agreements: Their Effect upon U.S. Law" (Congressional Research Service Series, January 2013) available at: http://jjustice.org/wordpress/wp-content/uploads/Garcia-M.-J.-2014.pdf. Accessed 21 Aug 2016

Haile M (2005) Comparing human rights in two Ethiopian constitutions: the Emperor's and the "Republic's"—*Cucullus Non Facit Monachum*. Cardozo J Int Comp Law 13(1):1–60

Hestermeyer H (2015) The implementation of European Union Law in Germany. In: de Wet E, Wolfrum R, Hestermeyer H (eds) The implementation of international law in Germany and South Africa. Pretoria University Law Press, Pretoria, pp 444–467

Iadarola A (1975) Ethiopia's admission into the League of Nations: an assessment of motives. Int J Afr Hist Stud VIII(4):601–622

Idris I (2000) The place of international conventions in the 1994 federal democratic republic of Ethiopia constitution. J Ethiop Law 20:113–138

International Human Rights Instruments, Core Document Forming the Initial Part of the Reports of State Parties: Ethiopia, UN Doc HRI/CORE/ETH/2008 (6 February 2009)

Kirby M (2010) Domestic courts and international human rights law: the ongoing judicial conversation. Utrecht Law Rev 6(1):168–181

Marcus H (1975) The life and times of Menelik II Ethiopia 1844–1913. Clarendon Press, Oxford

Marcus H (2002) A history of modern Ethiopia. University of California Press, Oakland

Marcus H (2005) Racist discourse about Ethiopia and Ethiopians before and after the Battle of Adwa. In: The Battle of Adwa: reflections on Ethiopia's historic victory against European colonialism: interpretations and implications for Ethiopia and beyond. Algora Publishing, New York, pp 229–237

Phooko MS (2014) Legal status of international law in South Africa's municipal law: government of the Republic of Zimbabwe v. Fick and others (657/11) [2012] Zasca 122. Afr J Int Comp Law 22:399–419

Sandholtz W (2015) How domestic courts use international law. Fordham Int Law J 38(2):595–638

Shelton D (2011) Introduction. In: Shelton D (ed) International law and domestic legal systems: incorporation, transformation, and persuasion. Oxford University Press, Oxford, pp 1–22

Sloss D (2011) Domestic Application of Treaties (2011). Available at: http://digitalcommons.law.scu.edu/facpubs/635. Accessed 30 Aug 2016

Soriano MC (2008) The reception process in Spain and Italy. In: Keller H, Sweet AS (eds) A Europe of rights: the impact of the ECHR on national legal systems. Oxford University Press, Oxford, pp 392–450

Sweet AS, Keller H (2008) Assessing the impact of the ECHR on national legal systems (2008). Faculty Scholarship Series, Yale Law School. Available at http://digitalcommons.law.yale.edu/fss_papers/88/. Accessed 14 Nov 2016

Treaty Making Procedure Proclamation No. 25/1988 (Ethiopia)

UK Human Rights Act (1998)

Woldemeskel M (1970) ZikreNeger, 2nd edn. (in Amharic). (n.p.), Addis Ababa

Wolfrum R, Hestermeyer H, Vöneky S (2015) Reception of international law in the German legal order: an introduction. In: de Wet E, Wolfrum R, Hestermeyer H (eds) The implementation of international law in Germany and South Africa. Pretoria University Law Press, Pretoria, pp 3–22

Wondimagegnehu T (1989) Tewodros II and the regime of extra-territoriality under the Anglo-Abyssinian treaty of 1849. J Ethiop Law 14(1):91–117

Zewde B (2002) A history of modern Ethiopia, 1855–1991. James Currey/Ohio University Press/Addis Ababa University Press, Oxford/Athens/Addis Ababa

Getachew A. Woldemariam is an Associate Professor in law at Addis Ababa University, and holds LLB, LLM & PhD degrees.

Ethiopia's WTO Accession at the Crossroads

Derk Bienen

Abstract The Government of Ethiopia started the process of accession to the World Trade Organisation (WTO) in 2003. The Memorandum of the Foreign Trade Regime (MFTR) was prepared and submitted to the WTO Secretariat in December 2006. The goods offer as well as the various information documents were submitted to the WTO in 2011 and 2012, and the services offer has been prepared. Nevertheless, since 2012 no tangible progress has been made, although there are now indications that the accession process may resume. Meanwhile, developments in the WTO have been ambiguous. On the one hand, the organisation will soon have 164 members and is thus approaching universal membership. On the other hand, the failure to conclude the Doha Development Round has prompted members to redirect their policy attention to negotiate and conclude trade agreements with trading partners on a bilateral or regional basis. Some observers have indeed suggested that the WTO may have outlived itself. Ethiopia thus faces the decision of whether and to what extent to prioritise multilateral or regional trade integration.

This paper analyses the potential implications of these alternative policy directions. To do so, the anticipated benefits and challenges of acceding to the WTO and of staying outside of the WTO are compared. The paper concludes that Ethiopia should revive the accession process and develop a comprehensive trade policy in which WTO accession should be a core element.

1 Introduction

Most countries in the world are either members of the WTO or in the process of accession: at the end of 2015, the WTO has 162 members, and an additional two, Afghanistan and Liberia, had their accession packages approved in December 2015. WTO members account for more than 97% of world trade. Ethiopia is one of five

D. Bienen (✉)
BKP Development Research & Consulting, München, Germany

Addis Ababa University, Addis Ababa, Ethiopia
e-mail: d.bienen@bkp-development.de

East African countries which are not yet members,[1] although the accession process started more than a decade ago, when the Government of Ethiopia applied for membership in the WTO in January 2003. The Memorandum of the Foreign Trade Regime (MFTR) was prepared and submitted to the WTO Secretariat in December 2006. The goods offer and various information documents were submitted to the WTO in 2011 and 2012, and the services offer has been prepared. Nevertheless, since 2012 no tangible progress has been made, although there are now indications that the accession process may resume.

Meanwhile, developments in the WTO have been ambiguous. The organisation is approaching universal membership. However, the failure to conclude the Doha Development Round has prompted members to redirect their policy attention to negotiate and conclude trade agreements with trading partners on a bilateral or regional basis, and some observers have indeed suggested that the WTO may have outlived itself.

In view of these developments, Ethiopia faces the decision of whether and to what extent to prioritise multilateral or regional trade integration. This requires a careful reassessment of the anticipated benefits and challenges of acceding to, and being a member of, the WTO compared to non-membership. Although such an assessment is ultimately to be undertaken by the Government in collaboration with the private sector and civil society, this paper aims at contributing to the process by analysing the potential implications of the alternative policy directions. To do so, the costs and benefits of acceding to the WTO (Sect. 2), the level of alignment between Ethiopia's economic development strategy as expressed in the Second Growth and Transformation Plan (Sect. 3), and the costs and benefits of staying outside of the WTO are assessed (Sect. 4).

2 An Overview of the Costs and Benefits of WTO Accession

It is sometimes argued that it is odd for countries to remain outside the WTO when the organisation's membership is almost universal. Yet, Ethiopia's WTO accession should not be pursued because most other countries are also members but because it is in Ethiopia's own interest to become a member. This requires an analysis of the benefits and costs of accession and membership for Ethiopia.[2]

---

[1]Of these, Sudan is also an acceding country, having started the accession process in 1994. Following a process of dormancy, Sudan signalled its interest to re-start the process in July 2015. The other East African non-members are Eritrea, Somalia and South Sudan.

[2]The costs and benefits of WTO accession have been discussed extensively in the literature; see for example Martin and Ianchovichina (2001), Evenett and Braga (2005) or, most recently, the contributions in Dadush and Osakwe (2015). This section summarises the main arguments and applies them to Ethiopia.

2.1 Benefits

The extent of the benefits of WTO membership differs from one country to another and hinges on an acceding country's specific situation. In the case of Ethiopia, WTO membership becomes an objective for several reasons.

First, WTO membership guarantees secure market access for Ethiopia's exports on a non-discriminatory basis because WTO member countries must practice and are entitled to the application of the most-favoured-nation (MFN) principle. In other words, they benefit (but also have to grant) non-discriminatory market access from and to all other member countries.[3] In addition, MFN tariffs can only be increased up to the bound tariff levels. This does not apply to non-members. Put differently, a WTO Member cannot only apply different (higher) tariffs on imports from non-members, but also there is no upper boundary for such tariffs. Therefore, securing market access has been one of the main reasons for seeking WTO membership for big economies and large exporters like China.[4] For Least Developed Countries (LDC) like Ethiopia this might not be an immediate concern, given the still relatively limited export capacity and the fact that it currently benefits from several preferential schemes accorded by her trading partners. However, with increasing exports the likelihood of being affected by discriminatory trade measures will increase for Ethiopia, and the risk of facing negative discriminatory treatment may become real. Conversely, WTO membership ensures the predictability, security and transparency of market access conditions and creates a rule-based framework with a secured MFN treatment for each member's exports; it provides basic protection against discriminatory treatment for all members.

This risk assessment also applies to preferential treatment, which Ethiopia as an LDC currently benefits from. Unilateral preferential market access granted to LDCs by major markets like the United States (under the African Growth and Opportunity Act, AGOA) or the European Union (EU, under the Everything But Arms initiative, EBA) can be withdrawn or tied to political concessions from the benefiting country; in the former case, security of preferential market access is at stake, and in the latter case, preferential access is "paid for" by a reduced domestic policy space. In contrast, for LDC members, the WTO's Bali Ministerial Decision on Duty-Free and Quota-Free Market Access for Least Developed Countries[5] or the Decision on Preferential Treatment to Services and Service Suppliers of Least-Developed

---

[3]Exceptions to the MFN principle are free trade agreements and customs unions, which are authorised under GATT Art. XXIV, or the Enabling Clause (Decision on Differential and More Favourable Treatment, Reciprocity and Fuller Participation of Developing Countries, of 28 November 1979), which enables developed members to give differential and more favourable treatment to developing countries, without the need for reciprocity.

[4]Martin and Ianchovichina (2001), p. 6.

[5]WT/MIN(13)/44 – WT/L/919, 11 December 2013.

Countries[6] (the "Services Waiver"), as well as other decisions, have further strengthened trading conditions. These decisions compare favourably with unilateral preferential access schemes because only preferential treatment accorded directly through the WTO decisions carries legal certainty, whereas unilateral preferential treatment provided by WTO Members under the Enabling Clause does not. For example, Kenya—which became a beneficiary of the EU GSP in October 2014 after previously having benefitted from duty-free access to the EU—would face MFN tariffs for its cut flower exports to the EU from January 2017 in case the Economic Partnership Agreement is not signed, as a result of the EU's considering that the industry in Kenya has graduated.[7]

A second expected benefit of WTO accession is constituted by the economic gains which are realised through progressive reforms and the "locking in" of policies. As a multilateral institution, the WTO serves to encourage reform minded and progressive governments to build domestic institutions to guide the market economy, promote welfare enhancing trade policies and ease the acceding country's integration into the global economy. WTO rules help improve the business environment domestically by building market-supporting mechanisms such as secure property rights, administrative transparency in government agencies (commitments made can be easily looked up through the WTO), and regulatory predictability (commitments made are unlikely to be affected by future policy changes). Ethiopia can and does, of course, adopt welfare-increasing economic policies irrespective of WTO membership. However, unlike unilateral policy reforms, policy reforms supported by multilateral commitments and concessions are more credible and provide the Ethiopian government and businesses with defence mechanisms against potential policy reversals. In addition, although it is true that the overall thrust of WTO accession is towards a more open foreign trade regime, greater transparency and predictability is also accorded to those areas and sectors which Ethiopia chooses not to open up.

Third, achieving WTO membership is seen as a credible means of gaining an enhanced international reputation. This in turn helps countries like Ethiopia to attract solid investment by translating concessions into international legal commitments, and thereby providing powerful guarantees of the government's policy directions to foreign and domestic investors.[8] Increased FDI, in turn, contributes

---

[6]WT/L/847, 19 December 2011; implementation of the Services Waiver has however been slow. Until the Nairobi Ministerial Conference in December 2015 only 22 Members had made notifications, prompting another Ministerial Decision on the Implementation of Preferential Treatment in Favour of Services and Service suppliers of Least Developed Countries and Increasing LDC Participation In Services Trade, WT/MIN(15)/48 – WT/L/982, 21 December 2015.

[7]See Commission Implementing Regulation (EU) 2016/330 of 8 March 2016 suspending the tariff preferences for certain GSP beneficiary countries in respect of certain GSP sections in accordance with Regulation (EU) No 978/2012 applying a scheme of generalised tariff preferences for the period of 2017–2019 (OJ L 69, 9.3.2016, p. 9).

[8]For example, in Cambodia foreign direct investment inflows sharply increased from less than USD 200 million per year in the years 1999–2003 (the year of WTO accession) to more than USD 2 billion per year in the years 2006–2009. See Chea (2012).

to improved supply and quality and lower costs to the benefit of Ethiopian consumers.

Fourth, the WTO dispute settlement system serves the shared interest of all WTO members in establishing and enforcing the rule of law in world trade. What makes the WTO attractive is the possibility of resolving disputes in a binding and enforceable manner through the dispute settlement mechanism. This is in particular important for small economies (by global comparison) and LDCs like Ethiopia, as it increases their leverage in trade disputes.

Fifth, membership in the WTO enables countries to influence the rules of the multilateral trading system, by participating in the negotiations where multilateral trade rules and disciplines are set, concessions are negotiated and trade liberalisation and policies are monitored. This gives Ethiopia the chance to contribute to the shaping of future rules and disciplines of the WTO. If Ethiopia, as a member of the WTO, carefully identifies its priorities, prepares its positions and works in partnership with other members, it will be in a position to have an impact on the evolution of the rules of the trading system.[9] Admittedly, considering the present state of the Doha Round, the possibility for a developing country to influence the rules of the WTO might look overly optimistic. Nevertheless, even if the probability is low: without WTO membership, Ethiopia has no options except to comply with rules that it has no part in making.

As a result of the combination of these factors, research has found that WTO accession normally leads to an acceleration in a country's growth rate—both a temporary pick up in the growth rate after the initial application, and a distinct growth spurt after the actual accession.[10] Most studies of individual countries also find that WTO accession leads to increased trade (both imports and exports), investment, employment, and GDP,[11] notwithstanding the possibility of negative transitional or short-term effects which result from adjustments in the economic structure of accession countries between growing exporting sectors and potentially shrinking import-substituting sectors. However, the findings regarding increasing imports and the ensuing adjustments in these studies primarily depend on the assumption that acceding countries reduce their applied import tariffs, which is not necessarily required during and in the short-term after accession to the WTO. For Ethiopia in particular, based on the experience of acceded LDCs,[12] WTO

---

[9]These steps are best (and normally) taken in cooperation with other, like-minded countries with which Ethiopia would act as a member of coalitions. There are already several coalitions in place in Geneva to which the country would be a natural member (African Group, LDC Group, etc.). It is also worth noting that Ethiopia already has a permanent mission in Geneva, which gives it greater capacity to make full use of its membership than is the case for the many WTO members that still remain non-resident.

[10]This is the result of an econometric analysis based on data from 42 countries that acceded to the WTO between 1990 and 2001. See Tang and Wei (2006).

[11]The estimated impact of WTO accession on the GDP of selected countries ranges from 0.5% in Laos (Kyophilavong et al. 2010) to 4.4% in Ethiopia (Chala et al. 2010).

[12]See Bienen (2014).

accession is unlikely to lead to reduced applied import tariffs, except possibly in selected sectors, e.g. if Ethiopia would agree to participate in sectoral initiatives such as the Information Technology Agreement.

In sum, as outlined above the main expected benefits of WTO accession for Ethiopia would not primarily come from changes in tariffs but changes in the regulatory system, increased FDI and the way markets operate.

2.2 Costs

On the other hand, accession to and membership in the WTO also entail costs. First, one potential cost factor, already mentioned, is that local businesses in some sectors may face increased competition caused by the liberalisation in specific sectors, both goods and services. Concerns over this—in particular in relation to financial and telecommunication services—are indeed one of the reasons for the current dormant state of the accession negotiations process. Nevertheless, although often a defensive view is taken regarding the opening up of markets, and this is considered as a cost, a more nuanced assessment of the wider costs and benefits of such market opening, and its implications on economic development, needs to be undertaken in addition to the effect of increased competition on affected domestic businesses.

Second, in addition to the costs of actual market opening acceding countries are required to bind tariffs and commit to minimum levels of services sector openness vis-à-vis WTO members, which results in a loss of policy space. Although this can be considered as a benefit of WTO accession (as mentioned above, it reduces uncertainty about future policy reversal and hence creates a more enabling environment for trade and investment), it can also be seen as an opportunity cost for the acceding country, as policy measures which the government may potentially consider as useful or necessary for economic development may no longer be possible (or at least be very difficult to implement) as a WTO member. Examples of such policy measures are certain types of subsidies (in particular export subsidies), tariff increases above the bound rates, conditions to be imposed on foreign investment, and protection of intellectual property rights (IPR). The economic development literature provides many arguments why policy space in these areas may be important for developing countries. For example, with regard to IPR the prevailing view is that the WTO Agreement on Trade Related Aspects of Intellectual Property Rights (TRIPS) establishes minimum standards of protection which go beyond the interest and capacities of (many) developing countries and therefore primarily reflect the interests of developed country members.[13] These costs need to be carefully considered by the acceding country. Fortunately, however, many of the acceding country's commitments are negotiated and can be tailored to minimise the cost, through transition periods or flexibilities. In addition, as has been mentioned

---

[13] See, e.g., Deere (2008).

above, staying outside of the WTO and benefitting from preferential market access in exchange for certain political conditionalities also constitutes a loss of policy space.

Finally, WTO accession and membership also raise costs for the government. Many of these are related to the requirements of the accession process, which entails lengthy negotiations between the acceding country and WTO members, which consume substantial human and financial resources of the acceding country, as well as typically multiple changes in laws and regulations. However, such resource constraints are comparatively—when compared to other acceding countries—limited in Ethiopia: the country has already accumulated relevant technical knowledge and negotiation experience during the WTO accession process, has established a relatively well staffed department in charge of WTO accession at the Ministry of Trade, has undertaken numerous technical studies, and has a well-developed institutional set-up, which includes private sector representatives, for discussing technical and political matters related to accession.

Once Ethiopia becomes a member, regular costs for government, apart from membership duties, will arise from membership obligations, such as the need to maintain bodies providing information about trade issues,[14] prepare and submit notifications about trade measures[15] and explanatory documents.[16] In addition, participation in negotiations and in WTO disputes, regardless in which role, also requires (sometimes substantial) resources, e.g. for economic or legal advice, although these costs are sometimes reduced, in particular for LDCs, by donor support or pro bono work offered by experts.

2.3 Conclusion

In general terms, the benefits of WTO accession for Ethiopia clearly outweigh the costs. Moreover, costs can be reduced by careful formulation of accession commitments. However, two questions remain to be addressed. The first one is whether the positive cost-benefit analysis still applies in the current situation, where the Doha negotiations have all but failed, regionalism has been on the rise, as have been protectionist measures, and some observers have in fact suggested that the WTO may have outlived itself as a negotiating forum.[17] However, even if this was true it does not distract from other advantages that the WTO offers to its members, and notably the economically less powerful ones.

---

[14]Examples are notification authorities and enquiry points, such as for technical barriers to trade or sanitary and phytosanitary measures.

[15]Notification requirements can be substantial. Under the Agreement on Agriculture alone, 12 different notifications are distinguished; see World Trade Organisation (2015).

[16]E.g. government reports under the trade policy review mechanism.

[17]See e.g. Altman (2011).

The second question to be addressed is whether, leaving the general cost-benefit assessment aside, WTO accession is compatible with Ethiopia's current economic development strategy. This is addressed in the next section.

3 WTO Accession and Ethiopia's Economic Development Objectives and Strategy

WTO accession is not an end in itself; it is a means to an end. Its overarching objective is the economic development and transformation of Ethiopia, as expressed in the Second Growth and Transformation Plan (GTP II), and the achievement of middle income status by 2025. Specifically, the "GTP II aims to achieve an annual average real GDP growth rate of 11 percent within [a] stable macroeconomic environment while at the same time pursuing aggressive measures towards rapid industrialization and structural transformation."[18] Objectives for exports are ambitious: the share of goods exports is planned to increase from 6.4% of GDP in 2014/15 to 11.8% in 2019/20.[19] These objectives are to be achieved through a range of measures grouped into nine pillars: (1) Maintaining rapid, sustainable and equitable economic growth and development; (2) Improve the quality, productivity and competitiveness; and increase the production capacity of productive sectors to reach the potential production capacity of the economy; (3) Enhancing the transformation of domestic private sector; (4) Expand the accessibility and ensure the quality of infrastructure development through strengthening the implementation capacity of the construction sector; (5) Fostering the governance and management of rapid urbanisation to accelerate economic growth; (6) Accelerating and ensuring the sustainability of Human Development and Technological Capability; (7) Promote democratic and developmental good governance through enhanced implementation capacity and public engagement; (8) Promote women and youth empowerment, participation and equity; and (9) Building a climate resilient green economy.

Ethiopia's accession to, and membership in, the WTO might directly impact on most of the pillars, except the management of urbanisation, and the promotion of women and youth empowerment, both of which would only be linked indirectly. The question to be addressed therefore is to what extent Ethiopia's WTO accession is supportive of or conflicting with the GTP II objectives and pillars. Specifically, the implications of WTO membership on the stability of the macroeconomic environment and on industrialisation and structural transformation need to be considered.

---

[18] National Planning Commission (2015), p. 16.
[19] National Planning Commission (2015), p. 22.

3.1 Macroeconomic Environment

To ensure the continuity of a stable macroeconomic environment, the GTP II specifically includes the pillar of promoting democratic and developmental good governance through enhanced implementation capacity and public engagement. It also aims at maintaining the fiscal deficit at a sustainable level and keeping inflation at single digit levels.[20] WTO membership clearly contributes to these objectives, although only indirectly—the WTO itself does not regulate macroeconomic policies. However, it requires countries to adopt a transparent framework for economic policy making, strengthen judicial oversight over the implementation of economic policies, and engage in non-discriminatory, inclusive and non-preferential economic policies. Also, WTO rules require that foreign exchange regulations allow the country to engage in international trade and limit restrictions to certain exceptional situations (e.g. in cases of balance of payments problems).

3.2 Industrialisation and Structural Transformation

The strong focus of the GTP II on the related objectives of industrial development and structural transformation is evident throughout the strategy. The most relevant specific objective of the GTP II in this context is "to bring significant growth of the manufacturing industry so that it plays leading role in job creation, technology learning structural shift in Ethiopia's export and address trade imbalance."[21] No less than six of the nine GTP II pillars address these issues[22]: The pillar "Maintaining rapid, sustainable and equitable economic growth and development" foresees the strengthening of forward and backward linkages between sectors to create value chains. In a similar vein, the pillar "Improve the quality, productivity and competitiveness; and increase the production capacity of productive sectors to reach the potential production capacity of the economy" will address challenges related to technology imitation, designing development, fabrication and adaptation of technology, inter alia by enhancing the competitiveness of exporters applying the Kaizen approach and building industrial parks. Under the third pillar, "Enhancing the transformation of domestic private sector", a concerted effort will be made to increase both domestic and foreign private sector investment, and to facilitate the transition of micro and small enterprises into larger, more competitive ones. Measures foreseen under the pillar "Expand the accessibility and ensure the quality of infrastructure development through strengthening the implementation capacity of the construction sector" include the establishment of incentives for increased domestic investment aimed at the substitution of imports

---

[20]National Planning Commission (2015), p. 22.
[21]National Planning Commission (2015), p. 29.
[22]See National Planning Commission (2015), pp. 17–20.

in construction materials and services. The pillar "Accelerating and ensuring the sustainability of Human Development and Technological Capability" is expected to expand the accessibility and ensure the quality of education and health services, as well as support for research and development (both by public and private entities), and the development of networking between research institutions and companies for innovation. Finally, under the pillar "Building climate resilient green economy" the government proposes measures to enhance the productivity of crop and livestock sub-sectors, expand renewable energy generation, and promote modern and energy efficient technologies in transport, industry and construction.

Table 1 provides an overview of how WTO accession and membership would impact on these pillars. Ultimately, most of the pillars rely on three types of instruments: investment, technology transfer, and incentives. While the impact of WTO accession on the first two is positive, it is ambiguous on the third one.

With regard to investment, WTO rules are aimed at creating a non-distorting and liberal trade and investment environment which facilitates the attraction of foreign direct investment and transfer of technology. This is enshrined not only in the specific WTO agreements addressing investment issues—notably the General Agreement on Trade in Services (GATS) and the Agreement on Trade Related Investment Measures (TRIMs)—but also a result of the general promotion of a stable economic environment which is conducive to investment, both by domestic and foreign investors.

The most direct linkage between WTO membership and investment is in the services sectors, addressed by the GATS, where Ethiopia will need to make commitments for market access and national treatment including in services trade mode 3, commercial presence (i.e., investment).[23] Substantive commitments will be expected by WTO members.[24] Thus, making no market access commitment at all in the construction sector, which constitutes the focus of GTP II pillar 3,[25] might be inacceptable. The same applies to two other important services sectors which provide inputs to the productive sector, but which are not specifically addressed in the GTP II, i.e. financial and telecommunication services, as well as transport

---

[23]Investment rules in goods sectors are not the subject of WTO accession negotiations.

[24]For overviews of the commitments made by acceding countries in services sectors, see Bienen (2014), p. 22ff and Carzaniga et al. (2015).

[25]With regard to the construction services sector, the GTP II aims at "Enhancing investment in the sector and pursuing import substitution strategy that reduce the pressure on foreign exchange demand, as well as offer opportunity for technology learning and job creation. Private sector investment in infrastructure development will be promoted through providing the necessary incentives and support to enhance the private sector participation in allowed investment areas" (National Planning Commission 2015, p. 18). Investment in construction services is currently open for foreign investors only for grade 1 construction. See item 6 of the Schedule to the Investment Incentives and Investment Areas Reserved for Domestic Investors Council of Ministers Regulations No. 270/2012, Federal Negarit Gazeta No. 4 of 29 November 2012, p. 6663.

Table 1 Links between GTP II and Ethiopia's WTO accession and membership

GTP II pillars	Measures foreseen	Potential effect of WTO accession/membership
(1) Maintaining rapid, sustainable and equitable economic growth and development	Strengthen forward and backward linkages between sectors	**Positive.** Creation of and insertion into global value chains requires investment, enhancing technologies, and trade facilitation, all three of which are supported by WTO membership. Conditions for potential protection of infant industries to be negotiated (e.g. higher bound tariffs)
(2) Improve the quality, productivity and competitiveness; and increase the production capacity of productive sectors to reach the potential production capacity of the economy	Enhance competitiveness of exporters (kaizen approach); build industrial parks	**Positive.** Investment, enhancing technologies, and trade facilitation supported by WTO membership. Better support services for industry. Incentive schemes (e.g. industrial parks) may **potentially conflict** with WTO rules (e.g. if contingent on use of domestically produced inputs) but are possible under certain conditions (including some to be negotiated during accessions, such as export subsidies)
(3) Enhancing the transformation of domestic private sector	Increase domestic and foreign private sector investment; facilitate transition of micro and small enterprises into larger, more competitive ones	**Positive.** WTO membership contributing to investment. Conditions for potential protection of infant industries to be negotiated (e.g. higher bound tariffs). Incentive schemes foreseen may **potentially conflict** with WTO rules but are possible under certain conditions
(4) Expand the accessibility and ensure the quality of infrastructure development through strengthening the implementation capacity of the construction sector	Substitute imports in construction materials and services through increased domestic investment, facilitated by incentives	**Potential conflict** if purely focused on support for domestic businesses; commitments in construction services to be negotiated during accession (opening based on conditions). Same argument applies to financial and telecommunication services
(5) Fostering the governance and management of rapid urbanisation to accelerate economic growth	Improve urban planning and management; develop urban infrastructure	No direct linkage

(continued)

Table 1 (continued)

GTP II pillars	Measures foreseen	Potential effect of WTO accession/membership
(6) Accelerating and ensuring the sustainability of Human Development and Technological Capability	Expand accessibility/ensure quality of education and health services; support research and development (both by public and private entities); develop networks between research institutions and companies for innovation	**Positive**, depending on commitments made by Ethiopia: foreign investment in health and education can expand accessibility and increase quality; international STI networks are facilitated by more secure investment environment
(7) Promote democratic and developmental good governance through enhanced implementation capacity and public engagement	Prudent fiscal and monetary policies; improve tax and urban administration (including of land rights); implement efficient customs system	**Positive**. WTO rules aim at ensuring transparency and predictability of the general policy environment for trade and investment, in addition to ensuring that rules for imports and exports, customs issues, and trade related policies are not disruptive for trade
(8) Promote women and youth empowerment, participation and equity	Women and youth initiatives to enhance access to credit and ownership of productive assets; promote gender equality	No direct linkage
(9) Building a climate resilient green economy	Enhance productivity of crop and livestock sub-sectors; expand renewable energy generation; promote modern and energy efficient technologies in transport, industry and construction	**Positive**. Investment in such technologies and technology transfer facilitated by WTO membership by strengthening the framework under which technology transfer takes place

services, all of which are currently at least partially reserved for domestic investors or subjected to restrictions in Ethiopia.[26]

However, the extent of market opening is to be negotiated between WTO members and Ethiopia. For example, services sectors can be fully or partially reserved for domestic investors, or market entry can be subjected to conditions in terms of technology transfer, limitations of foreign ownership or employment. The experience of other acceded countries provides useful guidance on the flexibility available for acceding countries. For LDCs like Ethiopia, the degree of flexibility has been further reinforced by the LDC Accession Guidelines of July 2012.[27]

---

[26]See Proclamation No. 769/2012. A Proclamation on Investment, Federal Negarit Gazeta No. 63 of 17 September 2012, p. 6572, and Investment Incentives and Investment Areas Reserved for Domestic Investors Council of Ministers Regulation No. 270/2012.

[27]WTO 2012: Accession of Least-Developed Countries. Decision of 25 July 2012, WT/L/508/Add. 1, 30 July 2012.

As a result of this, WTO accession could actually help clarify the status of sectors which are currently reserved for domestic investors or are subjected to other conditions such as minimum capital requirements; in addition to the GTP II (specifically pillar 3) the provisions contained in the 2012 Investment Proclamation and its Regulations thus provide a natural starting point for negotiations. During the accession negotiations, Ethiopia would then explicitly limit the degree of openness it is willing to grant in the selected sectors by registering such limitations in the services schedule, thereby stating the "rules" or commitments transparently. Appropriately phrased commitments in these sectors can contribute to the achievement of infrastructure development objectives formulated in the GTP II.

Technology transfer is a function of both the level of investment by experienced companies (often foreign ones) and the import of equipment and other inputs for domestic industry. While the positive relation between WTO accession and investment has already been discussed, WTO accession also contributes to the latter, not only by offering an opportunity to bind low tariffs for key inputs but also by applying the rules established under the WTO for facilitating trade[28] and for the protection of IPR.[29]

Finally, the provision of incentives or subsidies[30] by WTO members is limited and subjected to certain conditions under the WTO Agreement on Subsidies and Countervailing Measures. In particular, incentives which are contingent on export performance or import substitution are prohibited by the Agreement.[31] These limitations set by the WTO are potentially in conflict with incentives envisaged by the GTP II under various pillars,[32] depending how they would be constructed. A review of the incentives foreseen in the 2012 Investment Incentives Regulation indeed shows that some of them would require some negotiation to be continued as they are conditional upon export performance.[33] Export subsidies are normally not allowed under WTO rules. While LDC members of the WTO may nevertheless maintain export subsidies under the special and differential treatment accorded under Article 27.2 of the Agreement on Subsidies and Countervailing Measures, Ethiopia, as an acceding country would not automatically be granted the same

---

[28]This would include, among others, the agreements on Sanitary and Phytosanitary Measures, Technical Barriers to Trade, Customs Valuation, Preshipment Inspection, Rules of Origin, and Import Licensing, as well as, once it has entered into force, the Trade Facilitation Agreement.

[29]Indeed, recent research has shown a clear positive relationship between protection of IPR (as facilitated by the TRIPS agreement) and the inflow of FDI. See Zhang and Yang (2016) and Klein (2016).

[30]The use of the term "incentives" in Ethiopia largely equates to "subsidies" in WTO terminology.

[31]Article 3.1.

[32]For example, pillar 3 foresees incentive packages for domestic private sector transformation, and pillar 4 for the construction sector and infrastructure development.

[33]See e.g. Article 7 of the Investment Incentives and Investment Areas Reserved for Domestic Investors Council of Ministers Regulations No. 270/2012, as amended by Article 2(3) of the Investment Incentives and Investment Areas Reserved for Domestic Investors Council of Ministers (Amendment) Regulation No. 312/2014.

treatment, but this would have to be negotiated; for example, Cambodia and Lao PDR have reserved the right to continue using export subsidies.[34] To the extent that incentives for export promotion are currently an important policy issues in Ethiopia, its negotiation position on the maintenance of export subsidies would likely be firm.

3.3 The Missing Element: GTP II and Trade

Although export growth is the fundamental strategic direction of the GTP II, the pillars and measures foreseen under it are predominantly oriented at increasing the productive capacity, rather like an industrial policy. Trade and export policies and measures, such as market access issues and trade facilitation, play no important role, apart from individual measures being scattered across the nine pillars (e.g. customs modernisation), and one short section on trade, which is primarily aimed at domestic trade. The strategic direction is described as follows:

> improving the transparency and competitiveness of the sector, promote competitive and fair trade practice that satisfy producers, consumers and traders, strengthening capacity, combat rent seeking attitudes and practices, develop reliable and modern trade information system. In addition, strengthening international and regional trade integration will be given due emphasis during the plan period.[35]

The measures foreseen to support the development of Ethiopia's international trade—some other measures are primarily targeting domestic commerce—include:

> Inspect quality of Imported and Exported goods. Transparent, fair competitive, efficient and economical modern marketing system will be practiced by introducing modern trade information system; Integrating the country into multilateral trading system, create conducive environment and promote export market opportunity, increase annual commodity exchange capacity and introduce new agricultural items in the commodity exchange system[36]

As can be seen, international and regional trade integration are mentioned but not prioritised, nor are they ranked. Some of the proposed measures again aim at strengthening the supply side, while trade facilitation and demand side/market access issues play no prominent role.

In any case, WTO accession would be an important contributor to this pillar of the GTP II. Not only is it the key institutional expression of Ethiopia's "integrating into the multilateral trading system", but WTO rules also facilitate the specific actions foreseen to improve transparency, enhance trade information, and improve the quality infrastructure. The respective WTO Agreements[37] provide guidance on

---

[34]See the final accession Working Party Reports for Cambodia (WT/ACC/KHM/21, 15 August 2003, paras. 116–120) and Lao PDR (WT/ACC/LAO/45, 01 October 2012, paras. 106–108).

[35]National Planning Commission (2015), p. 39.

[36]National Planning Commission (2015), p. 39f.

[37]Notably, the SPS, TBT and Trade Facilitation Agreements.

how to implement these actions in a non-distorting manner and avoiding trade disruptions. Of course, WTO membership is not a necessary condition for the implementation of the GTP II measures related to developing trade, but it would set a regulatory floor for Ethiopia by making compliance with the WTO rules mandatory, thereby leveraging the implementation of reform measures already planned under the GTP II.

3.4 Conclusion

In sum, there is vast alignment of WTO accession with Ethiopia's economic transformation strategy, both as included explicitly in the GTP II and as required implicitly. The few areas of potential conflict can be turned into synergies by a careful formulation of WTO accession commitments.

Nevertheless, the fact that WTO accession and Ethiopia's economic transformation strategy are aligned does not necessarily mean that WTO accession should also be the preferred option. To compare it to alternative policy options—i.e. trade policies that would not include WTO accession—the implications of these policy alternatives have to be considered. This is done in the next section.

4 The Costs and Benefits of Trade Policy Outside the WTO: Regionalism, Bilateralism, Unilateralism

For Ethiopia, three alternative approaches to a multilaterally oriented trade policy can be distinguished. First, regionalism would mean that Ethiopia prioritises economic and trade integration within the Eastern African region. Bilateralism would involve the promotion of trade, through agreements and otherwise, with selected key trading partners, in particular, Ethiopia's largest and fastest growing export markets. Finally, unilateralism would mean staying outside of trade agreements, and trade under MFN and preferential access.

4.1 Regionalism

Regional economic integration has, at least until recently, not been a strategy pursued by Ethiopia. Although the country is a member in several regional integration arrangements, such as the Common Market for Eastern and Southern Africa (COMESA), the Intergovernmental Authority on Development (IGAD) and the

Sana'a Forum for Cooperation (SFC), this regional integration has only marginally comprised preferential trade. Ethiopia so far only participates in the COMESA Free Trade Area (FTA) in a limited way by granting (and profiting from, in partner countries) a 10% duty discount on imports from other COMESA members. Regionalism is also, as mentioned, largely absent in the GTP—none of the regional clubs is even mentioned in the document. Nevertheless, at the 2015 Summit of COMESA, Ethiopia committed to joining the COMESA FTA in a phased approach.[38] Ethiopia has also signed, in June 2015, the *Sharm El Sheikh Declaration Launching the COMESA-EAC-SADC Tripartite Free Trade Area* (TFTA),[39] although not the TFTA Agreement itself.

Exports to regional markets account for approximately 10% of Ethiopia's total exports (Table 2), but have been growing less in recent years than total exports—over the period 2011–2015 at an annual average of 9.8%, compared to a total annual export growth of 17.8%. Improving access to regional markets through participation in FTAs with the intention of increasing regional exports is thus a rational strategy.

The potential benefits from regional integration are access to a larger market, economies of scale, and learning effects, not least resulting from increased competition with imports on the domestic market—indeed, such concerns over Ethiopia's limited competitiveness with other regional producers were the main reason why the country chose not to join the COMESA FTA when it was established in 2000.

The example of Kenya however also shows the limits of a regional integration approach. For Kenya, regional integration has indeed provided a larger market—mostly stemming from the relatively deep integration in the East African Community (EAC)—thereby possibly supporting the realisation of scale economies, but also possibly reducing external competitiveness, given the relatively high rate of protection. Regional sourcing has remained limited to raw materials in light manufacturing, while more complex regional value chains are absent, not least because of the lack of large firms in Kenya that could organise such value chains. Also, regional integration has not offered Kenyan firms an opportunity to benefit from knowledge spillovers—as Kenyan firms are already comparatively more developed than their partners in the other EAC countries, learning effects have been limited—these occur primarily when exporting to more advanced countries and in direct interaction with demanding foreign clients. Hence, regional integration has not supported a rapid move up the technology ladder.

These lessons would also seem to apply to Ethiopia, all the more so as the COMESA FTA and the TFTA constitute comparatively shallow forms of regional economic integration. Regional trade integration, although undoubtedly providing

---

[38] See Final Communiqué of the Eighteenth Summit of the COMESA Authority of Heads of State and Government, Addis Ababa, Ethiopia, 31 March 2015.

[39] http://repository.eac.int/bitstream/handle/123456789/591/FINAL%20SHARM%20EL%20SHEIKH%20DECLARATION%20ON%20THE%20%20LAUNCH%209%20JUNE%202015%201750HRS.pdf?sequence=1&isAllowed=y. Accessed 16 April 2016.

Table 2 Ethiopia's main export markets, 2011–15 (USD million)

Export market	2011	2012	2013	2014	2015	Total 2011–15	% of total	CAGR 2011–15
EU	881.4	821.9	1047.7	1237.1	1216.9	5205.2	25.7%	8.4%
Somalia	243.3	259.8	651.1	707.2	671.7	2533.2	12.5%	28.9%
TFTA	327.8	356.2	425.4	457.7	476.9	2044.1	10.1%	9.8%
China	283.4	320.9	329.1	533.2	378.5	1845.1	9.1%	7.5%
Saudi Arabia	167.4	191.4	395.5	571.9	357.1	1683.3	8.3%	20.9%
Kuwait	3.1	1.8	94.2	800.7	643.1	1543.0	7.6%	279.1%
USA	98.0	116.1	147.4	185.3	277.8	824.6	4.1%	29.8%
Switzerland	129.4	177.0	158.8	158.8	160.3	784.3	3.9%	5.5%
UAE	82.5	79.9	95.5	143.7	124.5	526.2	2.6%	10.8%
Israel	67.2	70.9	117.8	134.4	94.7	485.0	2.4%	8.9%
Japan	35.9	75.4	111.7	144.4	96.8	464.2	2.3%	28.1%
Turkey	45.2	50.6	81.7	77.2	50.5	305.2	1.5%	2.8%
India	33.8	44.5	39.7	59.8	75.8	253.5	1.3%	22.4%
Pakistan	13.4	45.9	52.4	41.7	47.8	201.2	1.0%	37.5%
Others	203.0	279.0	329.0	413.8	354.9	1579.6	7.8%	15.0%
Total	2614.9	2891.3	4076.9	5666.9	5027.5	20,277.6	100.0%	17.8%

Source: Calculations by the author based on UN COMTRADE

benefits, does not contribute significantly to the GTP II objective of structural transformation, mostly because it fails to promote investment and technology transfer in the same way as WTO membership, i.e. by ensuring the predictability of a sound environment for trade and investment.

4.2 Bilateralism

Ethiopia's largest non-regional export markets are the EU, China, various Arab countries, and the United States (Table 2 above). Enhancing and ensuring market access to these markets could be pursued through bilateral agreements. However, no such agreements are currently in place and only one, the Economic Partnership Agreement (EPA) with the EU, is under negotiation, but not formal talks have been held since 2011.

Indeed, the attractiveness of bilateral agreements for Ethiopia appears to be limited. With regard to the EU, as an LDC Ethiopia currently already benefits from preferential treatment under the EBA. The EPA would only marginally improve market access, e.g. because of enhanced rules of origin, but these would come at the cost of the requirement for Ethiopia to open up its market for imports from the EU.

A similar argument applies to trade with the United States, where Ethiopia is eligible to export duty-free under AGOA and the US Generalised System of Preferences (GSP). In addition, in negotiations for a bilateral trade agreement, the

US offensive interests would hardly differ from their offensive interests in the WTO negotiations, and include financial and telecommunications sector opening, therefore providing no advantage, in defensive terms, over Ethiopia's accession to the WTO.

Even for China, the existence of a preference scheme, from which a substantial part of Ethiopia's exports to China benefits, reduces the attractiveness of negotiating a bilateral agreement.[40]

As a result, a trade policy focusing on bilateral agreements e.g. with Arab countries, could play only a residual role for Ethiopia; it does not constitute a substitute for WTO Membership.

4.3 Unilateralism

The GTP II considers that market access provided for Ethiopian exports under

> the African Growth and Opportunity Act (AGOA) as well as access to European markets through the EU's Everything But Arms (EBA) initiative are appropriate to be exploited in the course of implementing GTP II. Utilizing these market opportunities are important avenues for the realization of the envisaged huge expansion of agro-processing based manufactured exports and export diversification. Effective utilization of these market opportunities is key for the realization of the objectives of Ethiopia's export-led manufacturing expansion.[41]

However, it would appear that this strategy is not without risks, as it is based on preferential market access provisions with limited predictability. As they have been provided unilaterally by trading partners they can also be withdrawn unilaterally. For example, eligibility for AGOA is contingent upon meeting certain economic and political requirements,[42] and indeed eligibility for AGOA has been withdrawn, and in some cases re-instated for a number of African countries with different justifications.[43] Furthermore, if Ethiopia succeeds in achieving middle income status, it will by default no longer be eligible for AGOA and EBA access, resulting in a high risk of falling into the middle income trap.

---

[40]In 2005, China provided duty-free access for 190 products; the list was extended in 2008 to 454 products; see Co and Dimova (2014), p. 3.

[41]National Planning Commission (2015), p. 49.

[42]Section 104 of the African Growth and Opportunity Act.

[43]For example, Madagascar's eligibility for AGOA was removed on 01 January 2010 following a 2009 coup d'état, and reinstated in June 2014. Swaziland lost its eligibility on 01 January 2015 over US concerns about worker rights; see Office of the United States Trade Representative (2014).

Ethiopia's WTO Accession at the Crossroads   113

4.4 Conclusion

As the quick discussion in this section has shown, none of the alternatives to WTO membership provide a comprehensive and compelling strategy for Ethiopia's trade policy. A bilateral approach could only open selected markets but would require substantial domestic market opening—substantially higher than that required as part of WTO accession. Regionalism offers some benefits but fails to provide the environment for technology transfer and investment which are needed to achieve the structural transformation Ethiopia needs, and aspires to achieve with the help of the GTP II, to become a middle income country on a sustainable basis. Finally, the unilateral approach which Ethiopia has taken until recently, but which is gradually beginning to change, fails to provide the secure market access that is needed for sustained investment and technological change. It may constitute a sensible medium-term strategy but will face increasing issues as Ethiopia develops and comes to be seen as a competitor on international markets.

In the same context, the free-riding aspect of staying outside the WTO—many benefits of the WTO also generally apply to non-members: rules hardly differentiate between trading partners, and MFN duties are also typically applied to both other WTO members and non-members—will also weigh heavier and negatively impact on the perception of Ethiopia by her trading partners. In sum therefore, regionalism, bilateralism and unilateralism do not constitute viable alternative long-term strategies for Ethiopia when compared with WTO membership.[44]

5 WTO Accession, Regionalism, and the Need for a Trade Policy

Accession to the WTO is not currently high on the policy agenda in Ethiopia—the GTP II does not even mention it, and refers to integration into the multilateral trading system in passing. In general, the GTP II addresses trade in a very limited way. It primarily and overwhelmingly addresses supply side and productive capacity issues without giving due attention to issues at or beyond the border. Neither does it specify clear measures or even a coherent strategy for the country's trade policy. This is an important gap as the Plan is framed as an export oriented strategy. Ethiopia's economic and trade relations with the world are too important to be left to a collection of uncoordinated measures.

---

[44]Another aspect to be considered in this regard is the potential cost of delayed membership. Although over time, the cost of accession, in terms of commitments to be made and concession to be given, has remained largely stable (Bienen 2014), there is always the risk of increasing demands by WTO Members to be met. Note also that middle-income acceding countries are the ones that tend to pay a higher cost of entry than LDCs; see Pelc (2011).

A coherent trade policy to support structural transformation and the industrial policy on which it is based should rest on two pillars. The first one is Ethiopia's accession to the WTO: as has been shown in this paper, it is a necessary (although by no means sufficient) ingredient for achieving structural transformation, because it guarantees—unlike the alternative trade policy approaches—a predictable and conducive regulatory framework for trade and investment. In this sense, it is considered superior to alternative trade policy approaches. Arguably, Ethiopia's best guarantee of realising coherent and consistent international trade policies is to be found inside the rules-based multilateral system, rather than in a network of bilateral and regional agreements. In addition, joining the WTO sends a clear message to the international community about Ethiopia's commitment to openness of foreign trade, rule of law and good governance. Conversely, the consequences of further delays in the accession process could include the loss of Ethiopia's credibility among key trading partners, as well as the loss of confidence among (potential) investors.

The chances for reviving the accession process exist. Movements have been registered in at least one main contentious area, financial services, where the government has recently taken steps towards the opening of the sector.[45] On the other hand, for the time being the government continues to reject liberalisation of the telecommunication sector.[46]

As mentioned before, although WTO accession can be considered as a necessary condition for Ethiopia's structural transformation, it is by no means a sufficient one, but needs to be complemented by other policies, including in relation to trade. In this context, regionalism, bilateralism and unilateralism can indeed be considered as complements, rather than alternatives, to Ethiopia's multilateral integration—while priority should be accorded to the multilateral dimension. Such a combination of trade policies has for example been applied by Kenya[47] and could be emulated by Ethiopia.

---

[45] See Mwanza (2015) and Yewondwesson (2016).

[46] "No room for foreign telecom operators, Ethiopia declares", The Citizen, 31 October 2015. http://www.thecitizen.co.tz/News/No-room-for-foreign-telecom-operators–Ethiopia-declares/-/1840340/2937572/-/xn9a3uz/-/index.html (accessed 17 April 2016).

[47] Kenya has been following an export-led strategy since the 1990s which recently has been manifested in a three-pronged trade policy: First, regional integration behind relatively high tariffs against third parties has been the main approach to ensure access to regional markets for manufactured products. Kenya is a member of various regional clubs. Of these, COMESA and the EAC are particularly important as they constitute the major markets for Kenya's manufacturing exports and thereby allow Kenyan firms to attain economies of scale. Second, Kenya has also signed the EPA with the EU, an important step to ensure continued duty free and quota free access to that important market for Kenya's agricultural products (including tea, coffee, fruits and vegetables, and cut flowers). This strategy should not necessarily be emulated by Ethiopia which, being an LDC, benefits from duty free access to the EU under EBA, unlike Kenya. Finally, Kenya has been an active supporter of multilateral trade liberalisation under the WTO, evidenced by the hosting of the 10th Ministerial Meeting of the WTO Doha Round in December 2015.

What Ethiopia needs in any case is a coherent and comprehensive trade strategy. WTO accession should be a central part of it.

References

Altman D (2011) Why the WTO is obsolete. http://bigthink.com/experts-corner/why-the-wto-is-obsolete. Accessed 17 Apr 2016

Bienen D (2014) What can LDCs acceding to the WTO learn from other acceded countries?, Trade and development discussion paper no. 01/2014. BKP Development, Munich, 05 February 2014

Carzaniga A, Lim AH, Lee J (2015) Services market opening: salience, results and meaning. In: Dadush U, Osakwe C (eds) WTO accessions and trade multilateralism. Case studies and lessons from the WTO at twenty. World Trade Organisation/Cambridge University Press, Geneva/Cambridge etc.

Chala AT, Reda HT, Measho DA (2010) Impact of WTO accession on growth, poverty and inequality: lessons from integrated dynamic CGE model for Ethiopian economy, Draft, February 2010

Chea S (2012) Lessons learnt from WTO accession of Cambodia, WTO-ITC workshop on trade capacity for WTO accession of Liberia, 11–14 December 2012, Monrovia

Co CY, Dimova R (2014) Preferential market access into the Chinese market: how good is it for Africa? IZA Discussion Paper No. 7908. Institute for the Study of Labor, Bonn, January 2014

Dadush U, Osakwe C (eds) (2015) WTO accessions and trade multilateralism. Case studies and lessons from the WTO at twenty. World Trade Organisation/Cambridge University Press, Geneva/Cambridge etc.

Deere C (2008) The implementation game: the TRIPS agreement and the global politics of intellectual property reform in developing countries. Oxford University Press, Oxford

Evenett SJ, Braga CAP (2005) WTO accession: lessons from experience. World Bank Trade Note 22, 06 June 2005

Klein MA (2016) Foreign direct investment and intellectual property protection in developing countries. https://economics.indiana.edu/home/conferences/2016-jordan-river-economics-conference/files/2016-04-29-12.pdf. Accessed 04 July 2016

Kyophilavong P, Takamatsu S, Ko J-H (2010) Laos' world trade organization accession and poverty reduction. In: Thirteenth annual conference on global economic analysis, 15 April 2010

Martin W, Ianchovichina E (2001) Implications of China's accession to the world trade organization for China and the WTO. World Bank Working Paper, 24 September 2001

Mwanza K (2015) Ethiopia cautiously opens up financial sector to regional banks. AFK Insider, 29 October 2015. http://afkinsider.com/105691/ethiopia-cautiously-opens-up-financial-sector-to-regional-banks/. Accessed 17 Apr 2016

National Planning Commission (2015) The Second Growth and Transformation Plan (GTP II) (2015/16-2019/20) (Draft), September 2015

Office of the United States Trade Representative (2014) President Obama removes Swaziland, reinstates Madagascar for AGOA Benefits. https://ustr.gov/about-us/policy-offices/press-office/press-releases/2014/June/President-Obama-removes-Swaziland-reinstates-Madagascar-for-AGOA-Benefits. Accessed 10 Apr 2016

Pelc KJ (2011) Why do some countries get better WTO accession terms than others? Int Organ 65 (04):639–672

Tang M-K, Wei S-J (2006) Does WTO accession raise income? When external commitments create value, June 2006. http://www.nber.org/~wei/data/tang%26wei2006/WTO-Accession_journal_version_060706.pdf. Accessed 10 Apr 2016

World Trade Organisation (2015) Handbook on notification requirements under the agreement on agriculture, June 2015. https://www.wto.org/english/tratop_e/agric_e/ag_notif_e.pdf. Accessed 10 Apr 2016

Yewondwesson M (2016) Ethiopia's financial sector starts to open, Capital, 03 February 2016. http://www.capitalethiopia.com/index.php?option=com_content&view=article&id=5718:ethiopias-financial-sector-starts-to-open&catid=54:news&Itemid=27. Accessed 17 Apr 2016

Zhang H, Yang X (2016) Trade-related aspects of intellectual property rights agreements and the upsurge in foreign direct investment in developing countries. Econ Anal Policy 50:91–99

Derk Bienen is a trade law consultant at BKP Development Research & Consulting, and Adjunct Honorary Professor at the School of Economics at Addis Ababa University.

Competition for Natural Resources and International Investment Law: Analysis from the Perspective of Africa

Melaku Geboye Desta

Abstract Africa is abundantly endowed with natural resources, such as minerals, oil and gas. To exploit those resources and bring them to the market, it has been necessary to involve foreign multinational extractive companies that have the required technical and managerial expertise. While the terms on which these companies undertook such projects were determined for long by brute force, the instrument of choice today is the web of treaties, contracts, and institutions that may be collectively termed international investment law. This article examines the complex relationship between this body of international law, on the one hand, and the sovereignty of states over their natural resources, on the other, from the perspective of African countries. Adopting historical, theoretical and jurisprudential analyses, this contribution argues that the competition between developed countries and developing countries for control of extractive resources defined both the content and the evolution of international investment law. This article further finds that contemporary international investment law significantly erodes the state's sovereignty over its natural resources by, at the minimum, (1) limiting its legislative jurisdiction through the doctrine of internationalisation of the investment contract and stabilisation clauses, and (2) virtually eliminating its judicial jurisdiction through the almost uniform adoption of international arbitration as the means to settle investment disputes. The article concludes by calling on African countries to work together through their regional and continental institutions, develop common positions, conduct a comprehensive review of their respective bilateral and other investment treaties and related national legislation and natural resources contracts, terminate those that undermine their national interests or renegotiate them based on regionally- and/or continentally-harmonised policy frameworks.

M.G. Desta (✉)
Faculty of Business, De Montfort University, Leicester, UK
e-mail: melaku.desta@dmu.ac.uk

1 Introduction

Africa is endowed with abundant natural resources, including minerals, oil and gas.[1] While Africa is still known as the least-explored continent[2] for its sub-surface resources, in 2012 the African Development Bank put the Continent's share of the world's total mineral reserves at about 30%[3]; in 2015 *The Economist* observed that Africa is home to "a third of the planet's mineral reserves, a tenth of the oil and it produces two-thirds of the diamonds."[4]

However, this resource wealth has not benefited the bulk of African citizens. On the contrary, for generations of Africans in far too many countries, resource endowments have brought them only colonial and neo-colonial occupation and exploitation, displacement and environmental devastation, poverty and civil conflict. The question of whether a natural resources-rich country succeeds or fails appears to depend primarily on how that country is governed rather than how well or how poorly it is endowed with such resources.[5]

To exploit those resources and bring them to the market, it is typically necessary to involve foreign multinational extractive companies that have the technical and managerial expertise. Historically, the terms on which these companies undertook such projects were determined by brute force, but the weapon of choice today is the web of treaties, contracts, and institutions that may be collectively termed international investment law. The purpose of this article is to examine the complex relationship between this body of international law, and the sovereignty of states over their natural resources, from the perspective of African countries.

Natural resources,[6] such as oil and gas reserves or mineral deposits, are often in such high demand that resource companies are mostly willing to put their capital and reputation at serious risk to acquire a stake in their development. Likewise, as soon as the presence of a reasonable deposit of some valuable resource in the territory of a particular country becomes public, governments come under intense 'economic and political pressure' to develop them.[7] The comparative lack of complete geological information in most developing countries means that the

---

[1]The 2012 US Geological Survey reported that Africa "ranks first or second among the continents in share of world reserves of bauxite, chromite, cobalt, ilmenite, industrial diamond, manganese, phosphate rock, platinum-group metals (PGM), rutile, soda ash, vermiculite, and zirconium." See Yager et al. (2012).

[2]As the Africa Progress Panel (APP) observed, on a per square kilometer basis, Africa spends less than a tenth of what major producers such as Australia and Canada spend on exploration. See Africa Progress Panel (2013), p. 41.

[3]See African Development Bank (2012).

[4]*The Economist* (10 January 2015).

[5]As the Africa Progress Panel put it, "there is no automatic relationship between resource wealth and progress in human development. What counts is well-designed public policy, backed up by government commitment." *APP Report* (2013), 19.

[6]Throughout this paper, I use the term 'natural resources' to mean hydrocarbons and minerals.

[7]See Stevens et al. (2013), p. x.

majority of new and worthwhile resource discoveries today and in the future are likely to be in these countries, while only firms from mainly developed countries have the necessary financial, technical and managerial capability to unlock the resource and transform it into actual wealth.[8]

Almost inevitably, the involvement of foreign firms, especially if they are successful in their primary task of producing and exporting the resource, tends to provoke nationalist sentiment and accusations about loss of host country sovereignty, or worse. As a result, the story of investment in natural resources is mostly a story of foreign private firms operating in developing countries, on terms usually negotiated on project-specific bases and kept hidden from public view, while their exploration, production and exportation activities are all too visible to the local communities in the form of adverse environmental and social externalities and, in far too many cases, a 'resource curse' situation where resource revenues are used to maintain unaccountable ruling elites in power, often leading to violent competition for control of resources and civil conflict.[9] From this perspective, the natural resources sectors particularly in developing countries have been the laboratory within which the legal experiment to find the optimal point between host state sovereignty, and attraction and protection of foreign investment, has been taking place for a long time. That optimal point has, however, been elusive, fluctuating with the investment cycle itself, commodity prices on world markets, and the dominant ideology of the day.

This article starts with a highlight of the literature on the relationship between foreign investors and host states in the extractive sectors. Focusing on Raymond Vernon's obsolescing bargains model,[10] Sect. 2 introduces this highly insightful theoretical perspective. Section 3 provides a brief introduction to the principle of sovereignty over natural resources and how it interacts with the evolving regime of international investment law. There is ample literature on this subject already[11] and this contribution is a narrowly focused examination of how the fast-evolving body of international investment law affects the host state's exercise of permanent sovereignty over its natural resources. To this end, I start the section with an outline of the major principles of international investment law, which I describe simply as principles of international law designed to protect foreign investment from the host

---

[8]This picture is changing with the arrival of major resource companies from emerging countries, such as Brazil, China and Malaysia, but by far the dominant players in the sector still come from the OECD.

[9]For more on this, see World Bank (2009). UNCTAD also reported 'a strong link between dependence on natural resources and the risk of civil war and other conflicts and their prolongation', as well as 'detrimental impacts of natural resource dependence on governance and human rights, ... particularly in sub-Saharan Africa. Oil and diamonds in Angola, diamonds in Sierra Leone and Liberia, cobalt and other minerals in the Democratic Republic of the Congo and oil in Sudan have fuelled lengthy civil wars.' See UNCTAD (2008), p. 95.

[10]See Vernon (1971).

[11]See Schrijver (1997) and Pahuja (2011).

state.[12] I then look at the principle of sovereignty in very broad terms, as a bundle of powers and prerogatives that are available only to a state with internal and external dimensions. Internally, sovereignty manifests itself in the inherent qualities of the state as being endowed with supreme authority to do as it pleases within its territory subject only to constraints it has wilfully undertaken, while the external dimension implies the right to be left alone (non-intervention from abroad) and the right to be recognised and treated as an equal in international affairs.[13] Section 4 then considers the broad question of whether, or to what extent, international investment law hampers the exercise of sovereignty by the state over its natural resources. Section 5 concludes with thoughts about the current trends, threats and opportunities. Using historical and doctrinal approaches, this contribution attempts to examine the issues from the perspective of poor developing countries like those in Sub-Saharan Africa.

2 Theoretical Insights: The Obsolescing Bargains Model

Too many countries with abundant natural resources, such as potentially valuable fossil fuel and mineral deposits, suffer from extreme poverty and political instability while, at the same time, there is often a world market out there that offers attractive prices for their resources. Although governments in these countries are desperate to develop their resources, there is little they can do by themselves. In the absence of home-grown capital, technology and knowhow, attracting foreign investment becomes the only option.[14] Depending on the quality and quantity of resource endowment and the situation on the market for the relevant commodities, countries may have to compete amongst themselves to stand out in the eyes of foreign firms, such as by way of enacting new laws, reducing royalties and other taxes, promising exemptions from import and export duties and the like.[15]

---

[12]There is a large and growing body of literature in this area. For an authoritative and critical analysis of the investment regime, see Sornarajah (2004).

[13]See, e.g. Domingo (2009), noting at 1557 that sovereignty is 'a property inherent to any state, which gives it supreme power in its territory, control of its legal system, and the right to recognize external bodies or entities that establish contact with it.'

[14]International financial institutions, such as the World Bank and regional development banks, could also provide some limited financing for natural resources projects, but they often put the involvement of foreign mining or oil and gas companies as a condition for financing such projects. As Professor Wälde noted three decades ago, 'financial institutions are unwilling to contribute capital if they are not assured that an experienced mining company will be in charge of operations and will assume strict completion guarantees.' Wälde (1983), p. 245.

[15]To attract foreign investment, World Bank advice to resource-rich countries would emphasise the need to put in place a guarantee of mining rights before starting exploration, to institute a well-established mining code and a system of contractual stability, a stable fiscal regime, accelerated depreciation and amortisation, opportunities for profit repatriation, and access to foreign exchange at realistic rates. See World Bank (1992), p. 17.

Once investor-companies have set their eyes on a particularly attractive-looking country, the chances of winning additional concessions are often highest at the outset. Unlike in most developed countries where the major terms of investment are provided in general legislation, investment terms in many developing countries are decided by negotiations, a game that typically brings overly keen but inexperienced host government officials face to face with a foreign investor that is likely to be a repeat player in the negotiations game, with a wealth of professional experience and expertise to draw on. The resulting investment contract is often so comprehensive, and its terms so specific, that it can effectively replace national law for most purposes of the investment.[16] In case that might not be enough, and recognising that such good days never last forever, investment contracts in the extractive industries in particular often contain a 'stabilization' clause that aims to freeze, as of the date of the contract, the legal regime governing their operations for up to several decades into the future.[17] Finally, they also typically provide for the use of international arbitration to settle any future disputes, further insulating the investment not just from the application of local law but also from the jurisdiction of local courts. While investment contracts are generally intended to protect foreign firms from non-commercial risks that are inherent in such long-term and vulnerable projects,[18] in practice they are also used to lock in terms and conditions extracted from the host state at a time when its bargaining power is at its weakest.[19] It is also this far-reaching nature of investment contracts and the lack of balance they embody that usually raises sovereignty concerns not long after they are signed and puts their continued validity under question mark.

In his prize-winning book about ExxonMobil, Steve Coll recounts the widely-reported story of the contract signed between Exxon (along with Chevron and Petronas as project partners) and the government of Chad, for the exploration, exploitation and transportation of Chad's hydrocarbon resources.[20] Coll observes that the terms of the contract were highly favourable to Exxon, which were insulated from subsequent unilateral government action by a stringent stabilisation and supremacy clause under which the terms of the contract were to prevail over any existing or future law of Chad. Coll then quotes Christ Goldthwait, then US

---

[16] The World Bank also observed that "[a]n investment agreement is often an indispensable condition for foreign investors for major projects in developing countries where the risk of unilateral changes by the government to the investment rules is considered unduly high by investors because of political circumstances, lack of track record and economic difficulties." See World Bank (1992), p. 25.

[17] For a recent survey of stabilisation clauses, see Shemberg (2009).

[18] The World Bank noted that average return on equity required or targeted on investment in developing countries was 25–30%, with a payback of 2–4 years as opposed to 20% and a payback of 5–6 years in industrialised countries. See World Bank (1992), p. 17.

[19] Through these contracts, firms win "special privileges or exemptions regarding taxes and foreign exchange regulations". See World Bank (1992), p. 30.

[20] According to Coll, 'Chad's take of less than two thirds of revenue after expenses compared to rates closer to 90 percent in Nigeria'. Coll (2012), p. 160.

Ambassador to Chad, as marvelling: 'just how much control the government [of Chad] has ceded to Esso [Exxon's local subsidiary] over what happens in the south, almost a loss of sovereignty!'[21] It is here that Vernon's theory comes in as a helpful device to explain, and perhaps even predict, the behaviours and expectations of the main protagonists in the natural resources contractual relationship.

The obsolescing bargains theory predicts that once an agreement has been reached between the foreign investor and the host government, and a certain amount of foreign capital invested in projects, the bargaining power starts to shift from companies to host states. In his pioneering analysis, Raymond Vernon showed that investment contracts in the natural resources sector are 'generally assumed' to come unstuck through a process that 'leads governments repeatedly—almost predictably—to reopen the issues involved in the exploitation of raw materials.'[22] This, according to Vernon, is inter alia because the initial contractual obligations on the government side 'consist of a series of self-denying commitments', which make them obsolete in the eyes of the government almost immediately after signature of the contract.[23]

Vernon's insights are not limited to the political economy of the natural resource investment contract; he also understood the legal innovations that were taking place to deal with the perceived extra political and regulatory risks involved for multinational corporations operating in the developing world. 'If the raw material operation is located in an advanced country', wrote Vernon, 'as a rule, the enterprises have been brought into the country under the provisions of general law, without extraordinary concessions of an extensive sort, and they are expected to continue on that basis' while in the less-developed countries, 'special provisions generally surround the foreign operations'.[24]

The enduring validity of Vernon's perception on this particular issue has been confirmed and reconfirmed by subsequent research and analysis.[25] Writing in the mid-1990s, Wälde and Ndi observed that 'Developed Western nations rarely contract with foreign investors under a specific, individual investment regime derogating from the generally applicable law'[26] while Cameron wrote, in 2012, that 'stabilization clauses in state contracts remain near-standard practice around

---

[21] Id., 170. Coll does not say when the *Convention for Exploration, Exploitation and Transportation of Hydrocarbons* was signed but we can find an indication of the time from the fact that Goldthwait served as US Ambassador to Chad between October 1999 and January 2004.

[22] Vernon (1971), p. 46. Wälde and Ndi call this the "unavoidable, natural tendency of governments to seek adjustments to long-term investment relations in response to both political pressure and the evolution of circumstances." Wälde and Ndi (1996), p. 220.

[23] Vernon (1971), p. 47.

[24] Vernon (1971), p. 48.

[25] See also Lehavi and Licht (2011), pp. 115–166 (highlighting the political economy context within which Vernon coined the theory, the empirical evidence from the 1970s that proved the predictive power of the theory, and the debt crisis of the 1980s, along with the triumph of market liberalism starting from the late 1980s, which led to a marginalisation of the theory).

[26] See Wälde and Ndi (1996), p. 221.

the world but are rarely ever conceded by governments in OECD countries in their attempts to attract investment in their natural resources.'[27] Finally, Vernon also showed how natural resources operators particularly in the poorest developing countries are likely to undermine the sovereignty of their hosts by dominating the national economy, and sometimes dictating national policy as governments depend on tax or other revenues from such companies for their daily operations.[28]

Vernon's powerful insights have been further refined by subsequent analyses, the work of Hogan and Sturzenegger being perhaps the most recent and comprehensive.[29] Using the notion of the 'natural resources trap' as their analytical tool, Hogan and Sturzenegger make a compelling case as follows:

> Because MNCs anticipate expropriation, they will offer a contract that compensates them for the risk. But this forces the [host country] to expropriate; if they do not firms will be rewarded with windfall gain that may be politically intolerable. It is a double trap, because lack of credibility not only creates a contract that in itself is more vulnerable, but also because it forces even those governments that would prefer to operate in a stable and law-abiding context to fall in the vicious cycle with the rest.[30]

The logical conclusion of Vernon's obsolescence bargaining model or Hogan and Sturzenegger's natural resources trap model appears clear: that whatever states give at the beginning of the investment relationship they will try to take back afterwards, making a dispute with the foreign investor all but inevitable. The natural assumption that investment contracts are designed to maximise the investor's share of the pie at the expense of the host state's, and the 'self-denying' nature of the initial commitments, are likely to lead the state to overreaction later. It is also worth noting that this unfortunate cycle is by no means unique to developing countries; it is only more frequent there. Dieter Helm described the UK's own processes of nationalisation and privatisation in the second half of the twentieth century as a classic time-inconsistency problem in which governments have 'an incentive to promise ex ante that investors will be able to earn at least normal profits but then ex post to intervene to force down prices, claw back profits, and change outputs.'[31]

When states take regulatory action or infringe on the contractual or property rights of the investor, they often justify it through one ill-defined and often least-understood notion—sovereignty. Their argument can take many different forms:

---

[27]Cameron (2013), p. 313.

[28]Vernon wrote: 'As foreign raw material operations become more and more integrated in the economic life of host countries – through increasing payments to government and the increasing use of local labor, materials, and resources – the vulnerability of the economy to changes in these operations inevitably seems to increase. The psychic sense of dependence on foreign interests generated by this situation has produced occasional eruptions. ... the sense of dependence that host governments experienced was at times beyond bearing.' Vernon (1971), p. 52.

[29]See Hogan and Sturzenegger (2010, eds.).

[30]Id., p. 3.

[31]See Helm (2010), p. 294. Frankel defines the time-inconsistency problem to mean the situation where "the incentive you have to promise ahead of time is different from the incentive you have after the investment has been made". Frankel (2010), p. 326.

the terms of the original investment contract were unduly skewed in favour of the foreign investor and therefore contrary to the host country's national interest; those terms undermine the sovereign rights of the host state over its natural resources, making the agreements null and void; the political-economy circumstances within which the contract was negotiated have undergone significant transformation, making continued validity of the contract anomalous; etc. The sad fact that poor countries that are rich in natural resources are prone to suffer from the resource curse[32]—also known as the 'paradox of plenty'—makes it all the more likely that their governments will also try to find a scapegoat in foreign investors. Today's international investment law regime[33] is the direct or indirect product of competing claims and counterclaims as they evolved over time. The story of this evolution can be told as a process of fine-tuning the point of equilibrium between the claim for the fullest possible measure of sovereignty in traditionally capital-importing (host) states and the desire for the fullest possible protection of foreign investment by capital-exporting (home) states.

3 Sovereignty v Investment Protection: Historical Overview

Under traditional international law, the right of diplomatic protection through the home state was essentially the only peaceful remedy available to an alien that has suffered damage at the hands of a host state.[34] Diplomatic protection itself was available only on restricted grounds, and normally only after exhaustion of local remedies.[35] That has changed now, and today's international investment law is probably unrecognisable to international lawyers of just a generation ago. It is my thesis that the decolonisation of a large part of the world after the Second World War, which promised thitherto-inconceivable luxuries of sovereignty to the former colonies, exposed the inadequacies of diplomatic protection to safeguard continuing foreign economic interests inside the territories of those newly-born states. Two types of interests were in need of special protection from the threats of sovereignty in these new states: access to their natural resources through foreign direct

---

[32] Professor Paul Collier describes the resource curse phenomenon as 'the tendency for many low-income commodity exporters to experience slower economic growth than countries that are less well-endowed with resources.' Collier (2008), p. 11. See also Duruigbo (2006), noting that the problem in this area can better be described as a "leadership curse" whereby "kleptocratic rulers cause a wake of thieving frenzy, a cascade of catastrophes." Id. 34.

[33] For a treatment of present-day international investment law as a *regime*, see Salacuse (2010).

[34] Under the principle of diplomatic protection, if a foreign investor company suffers from an unlawful act, 'the general rule of international law authorizes the national State of the company alone to make a claim.' See *ICJ, Barcelona Traction* (Belgium v. Spain) Judgment of 5 February 1970, ICJ Rep 3.

[35] See, e.g. Dodge (2000).

investment, and access to their markets through trade—the same twin motives that drove the colonial project in a previous era.[36]

The special protection agenda was set right in the middle of World War II in the *Atlantic Charter*, a short but highly influential joint 'communiqué' between US President Franklin D. Roosevelt and British Prime Minister Winston Churchill on August 14, 1941.[37] By this document, the two superpowers of the day 'deem[ed] it right to make known certain common principles in the national policies of their respective countries on which they base their hopes for a better future for the world'.[38] The fourth principle in a list of eight commits the two powers to 'endeavor, with due respect for their existing obligations, to further the enjoyment by all States, great or small, victor or vanquished, of *access, on equal terms, to the trade and to the raw materials of the world which are needed for their economic prosperity.*'[39] The International Trade Organisation (ITO) project that was launched right after the War was designed to give effect to this principle of the Atlantic Charter.[40]

Fifty-three countries signed the ITO Charter but only Liberia ratified it; all others were waiting for the US to move first but when, in 1950, the US government decided not to seek ratification from Congress, the ITO Charter was effectively dead.[41] There are several reasons for this failure, including dissatisfaction in capital-exporting nations with overly sovereignty-protective provisions of the Charter's investment chapter.[42] At this point, the supposedly provisional General Agreement on Tariffs and Trade (GATT) was put in charge of the trade concerns—which was essentially a market-opening tool for industrial goods, the type produced only in the advanced countries, while leaving national governments free with respect to goods in which the poorest countries have a comparative advantage, such as agricultural products and other primary commodities. No GATT-type multilateral alternative existed for the issue of access to natural resources, which took a different direction altogether. With the decolonisation movement about to enter its 'most active phase',[43] international law needed an innovative solution for the problem.

---

[36]The dominant economic view of the era of economic imperialism demanded possession of African territory, which was deemed 'necessary in order to serve as a market for the products, and a source of the raw materials of the industry, of the citizens of European States.' Woolf (2012), p. 324.

[37]The Atlantic Charter was just that, a communiqué; it was not even signed by the two leaders 'in order to avoid having to have it ratified as a treaty by the U.S. Senate. For an insightful account of the drafting history of the Atlantic Charter, see Steil (2013), pp. 118–121.

[38]See US Department of State (1941).

[39]Id., emphasis added. Steil describes the negotiation process on the fourth principle as 'the hornet's nest'. Steil (2013), p. 119.

[40]On the history of the ITO project, see Irwin et al. (2008).

[41]See GATT (1995), p. 6.

[42]See Salacuse (2010), p. 88.

[43]See Craven (2007), p. 90. Ghana became the first country in Sub-Saharan Africa to gain its independence in 1957.

3.1 Independence: The Promises and Challenges of Sovereignty

When the newly-independent countries looked inside the sovereignty box, they sensed that it was different from the one their former colonial masters had enjoyed for a long time; they realised that independence did not necessarily mean full sovereignty over their natural resources; the political independence they proudly proclaimed appeared to lack sufficient economic content. They realised that, even after independence, companies from metropolitan territories were to continue with large, generous and long-term concessions granted prior to independence; international commitments undertaken on their behalf by former colonial rulers would remain valid potentially for ever; their inheritance was not just the great assets they had expected, but also enormous constraints and potential liabilities.[44] It was clear that recognition of the sovereignty of these countries was, at least in economic terms, mere 'courteous pretence.'[45] Frustrated by this perceived injustice, but also encouraged by their growing numerical strength in global bodies such as the UN General Assembly, developing countries launched their quest for an unequivocal affirmation of their rights over their natural resources as early as 1952. The delegate of Burma to the UN at the time is quoted to have said: 'The principle of the sovereign rights of nations over their own resources would seem so obvious as not to require elucidation.'[46] As subsequent developments demonstrated, he was clearly right and clearly wrong at the same time.

Indeed, no one in their right minds would have questioned the sovereignty of, say, the United Kingdom over the natural resources within its territory; that was merely an aspect of British territorial sovereignty. The very concept of sovereignty would lose its core meaning if it did not imply at least this much. British sovereignty was indivisible. The only question was whether the newly-independent countries of the Third World were fit enough to assert that same principle on the same basis as Britain. Again, there was nothing new here; historians have shown that Grotius himself 'insisted that "[s]overeignty beyond Europe, unlike sovereignty within Europe, was... very much a divisible notion and was to remain so within all subsequent conceptions" of relationship with the non-Western world.'[47] It took 10 years for these new states to get a declaration of their sovereignty over their natural resources, in the form of the famous UN General Assembly Resolution

---

[44] For early views of the debate whether newly independent states were to start with a clean slate or be subjected to restrictions and commitments undertaken during colonial days, see Bedjaoui (1968), arguing that 'a concessionary contract must end with the extinction of the personality of the ceding State and could survive the change of sovereignty only at the express wish of the new authority'. Id., 115. For a modern analysis of the doctrines of clean slate v succession, see Craven (2007), pp. 29–52.

[45] Strange (1996), p. 13.

[46] See Schwebel (1963), p. 463.

[47] Pagden (2006) as quoted in Chimni (2007), p. 202.

1803.[48] However, far from a simple acknowledgment of their sovereignty over their natural resources, Resolution 1803 was drafted as a compromise between the state's sovereign rights, on the one hand, and its obligations towards the foreign investor, on the other.

If we look at some of the provisions of Resolution 1803 just on the surface, the first paragraph declares: 'The right of peoples and nations to permanent sovereignty over their natural wealth and resources must be exercised in the interest of their national development and of the well-being of the people of the state concerned.' This was immediately followed, in paragraphs 2 and 3, by a recognition that decisions on the exploration of resources, and whether or not to allow foreign investment for the purpose, shall be left to the free choice of the state, but then adds: 'In cases where authorization is granted, the capital imported and the earnings on that capital shall be governed by the terms thereof, by the national legislation in force, and by international law. The profits derived must be shared in the proportions freely agreed upon in each case, between the investors and the recipient state, due care being taken to ensure that there is no impairment, for any reason, of that state's sovereignty over its natural wealth and resources.' (Para 3). Likewise, paragraph 7 affirms that 'Violation of the rights of peoples and nations to sovereignty over their natural wealth and resources is contrary to the spirit and principles of the Charter of the United Nations and hinders the development of international co-operation and the maintenance of peace.' Paragraph 8 then brings the investor's side back, this time with a sense of elevation of the investment contract to a quasi-treaty: 'Foreign investment agreements freely entered into by, or between, sovereign states shall be observed in good faith; states and international organizations shall strictly and conscientiously respect the sovereignty of peoples and nations over their natural wealth and resources in accordance with the Charter and the principles set forth in the present resolution.' As will be explained further down, this requirement to respect foreign investment agreements in particular was later used to support the emerging concept of internationalisation of state contracts. Finally, paragraph 4, which recognises the state's right to nationalise foreign investments under certain circumstances, makes the right conditional on the payment of 'appropriate compensation, in accordance with the rules in force in the state taking such measures in the exercise of its sovereignty and in accordance with international law'; and in the event of a dispute, it reaffirms the doctrine of exhaustion of local remedies, but also introduces consensual international arbitration as an option.

Needless to say, the title of Resolution 1803—'permanent sovereignty over natural resources'—does not adequately represent its content; in fact, it is a resolution as much about sovereignty over natural resources as it is about protection of foreign investment. A better title would probably have been something like 'the state's sovereignty over its natural resources and its obligations towards the foreign

---

[48]UNGA Resolution 1803 (XVII), 1962 was passed by 87 votes in favour, two against, and 12 abstentions. See Schwebel (1963).

investor.' By keeping the investment protection aspect of Resolution 1803 out of the title, the drafters left us with a false sense that this is the beginning of the Permanent Sovereignty over Natural Resources (PSNR) principle; in fact this same resolution also represented the start of the post-War experiment to develop a new species of international law for the protection of foreign investment from the risks posed by these newly-independent states. That this happened within the natural resources sector is just as it had to be; virtually all foreign investment at the time was concentrated in the natural resources sector, a fact that remains largely the case in Sub-Saharan Africa even today.[49] Furthermore, continuing access to natural resources was a matter of national security and strategic priority for the major powers at the time.[50] Only with these economic realities and strategic imperatives in mind can one appreciate the conjoined nature of the birth of PSNR and investment protection principles as we know them today. In no other sector do these two sets of principles clash so directly, and in no other multilateral instrument before the 1962 resolution can one find the substantive and procedural principles of investment protection articulated in so much detail, and with so much similarity to their modern form.

Resolution 1803 was broadly considered a success, but not unanimously, nor indefinitely. On further reflection, some developing countries began to feel that Resolution 1803 may have 'harmed rather than furthered' their interests.[51] This perception, coupled with the continuing rapid increase in the ranks of new members of the UN General Assembly in the 1960s and early 1970s, led to many more resolutions reasserting sovereignty over natural resources in ever more strident language, culminating in Resolution 3201 (S-VI: 1974) on the establishment of the New International Economic Order (NIEO)[52] and Resolution 3281 (XXIX: 1974) on the Charter of Economic Rights and Duties of States.[53] The PSNR principle was recognised as one of several principles on the full respect of which 'the new international economic order should be founded'.[54] By rejecting the earlier concept of internationalisation of state contracts, this Resolution explicitly put investment and PSNR on a direct collision course, stating: 'In order to safeguard these resources, each State is entitled to exercise effective control over them and their exploitation with means suitable to its own situation, including the right to

---

[49]See, e.g., UNCTAD (2011), p. 33 and UNCTAD (2005), pp. 9 and 69.

[50]Daniel Yergin, in his authoritative account of the oil industry in the twentieth century, recounts the story of oil contract renegotiations that started with the fifty-fifty formula in Venezuela in 1943 and spread to Saudi Arabia and others around 1950 and the nationalisation of the Anglo-Iranian oil company by the Mossadegh government in 1951, the nationalisation of the Suez Canal company by the Nasser government in Egypt in 1956, etc., all of which would naturally have shaped the position of the capital exporting countries during the PSNR negotiations. See Yergin (1991), pp. 431–498. The formation of OPEC in 1960 could only exacerbate their concerns.

[51]See Anghie (2005), p. 221.

[52]See UNGA Resolution 3201 (S-VI), 1974, para. e.

[53]See UNGA Resolution 3281 (XXIX), 1974.

[54]See UNGA Resolution 3201 (S-VI), 1974, para. e.

nationalisation or transfer of ownership to its nationals, this right being an expression of the full permanent sovereignty of the State. No State may be subjected to economic, political or any other type of coercion to prevent the free and full exercise of this inalienable right'.[55] Mainly because of its aversion to the foreign investor's rights, the Texaco tribunal that recognised Resolution 1803 (1962) as a codification of existing international customary law specifically rejected Resolution 3201 (S-VI: 1974) on the establishment of the NIEO and Resolution 3281 (XXIX: 1974) on the Charter of Economic Rights and Duties of States.[56] Stephen Schwebel later called the 1974 Charter 'the high water mark of disregard, if not denigration, of the international law relating to foreign investment'.[57] The 1974 Charter also represented the highpoint of the NIEO movement.[58]

3.2 Investment Protection: Deflating Sovereignty

Richard Gardner, by then already an influential figure inside the US government, wrote in *Foreign Affairs* in 1974 that 'in three decades of negotiations since [the Atlantic Charter], our focus has been almost exclusively on access to markets. In the next decades, we will need to place new emphasis on arrangements to assure reasonable access to scarce resources.'[59] This agenda was pursued systematically, consistently and, with the benefit of hindsight, successfully. While developing countries were arguing passionately over the PSNR text and its successors in New York and elsewhere, the blueprint of the future investment protection project was being developed, quietly, at the World Bank in Washington.[60] The Washington Convention of 1965, which established ICSID, is the product of that sketch.[61] Professor Andreas Lowenfeld, who participated in the process representing the US, recalls that the World Bank prepared the Washington Convention text using only legal experts, and not national diplomats or politicians, because '[t]hey did not want this effort to replicate the experience of the United Nations'.[62] As Puig noted in his recent historical study of ICSID, 'one of the reasons ICSID was established under the auspices of the WB was to insulate the discussion from the UN General

---

[55]Ibid.
[56]See *Texaco* award, 17 I.L.M. (1978), paras. 88–91.
[57]See Schwebel (2004), p. 28.
[58]See Alvarez (2011a), p. 124.
[59]Gardner (1974), p. 564.
[60]Thomas Wälde later observed that some global institutions like the World Bank 'act as successors to the former colonial administrations, with a social-engineering mandate for economic development that seems to succeed rarely if ever.' See Wälde (2004), p. 14.
[61]For a fascinating story of how the negotiations for this Convention took place, see Lowenfeld (2009).
[62]See Lowenfeld (2009), p. 52.

Assembly.'[63] Instead of calling a diplomatic conference as is usual in such matters, the Bank got the Convention approved by a resolution of its Board of Governors—a body whose decision-making procedures more accurately reflect the prevailing balance of power than the size of its membership. The resolution was passed despite 21 developing countries voting against it. According to Lowenfeld, 'this was the first time that a major resolution of the World Bank had been pressed forward with so much opposition'.[64] Just as it was born without any diplomatic fanfare, ICSID lived its early days quietly and unthreateningly; only after the arrival of bilateral investment treaties (BITs) of the highly investor-protective variety since the late 1980s did it start to bite properly.[65]

The claim of sovereignty over natural resources that was asserted with so much passion and emotion has since faded, while the investment protection agenda has never been stronger. The lesson for developing countries is clear: numerical superiority alone is not enough to bring changes to international law. They now realise that, in the words of Professor Michael Reisman, '[i]nternational law's arithmetic may be one state-one vote, but international political arithmetic ... still holds that ninety-nine minus one ofttimes equals zero, and that one plus one ofttimes equals one hundred. Getting your numbers wrong in world politics is as perilous as getting your physics wrong on a superhighway'.[66]

Developing countries got their arithmetic wrong, and found themselves driving the BIT superhighway, one at a time. Several initiatives for a multilateral investment agreement failed, leaving the bilateral route almost as the only option, and many took it—in some cases probably without much serious thought.[67] Those who led the development of ICSID through the World Bank Board of Governors prepared their own model BITs to further their interests as capital exporters, took them to the capitals of developing countries, and got them signed with little modification; they became the treaty-equivalent of the contracts of adhesion.[68] They might be typical of 'agreements between a lion and a rabbit',[69] but they

---

[63] Puig (2013), pp. 542–543.

[64] See Lowenfeld (2009), p. 54.

[65] As Lowenfeld noted, 'only eleven disputes were brought to the Centre in its first fifteen years, and only six resulted in a final award.' Lowenfeld (2009), p. 55. As Alvarez reminds us, although the first BITs date back to the late 1950s, they were mostly weak; it was in the 1980s that truly investor-protective BITs emerged, and the US played a leading role in their birth. See Alvarez (2011a), p. 126.

[66] Reisman (1987), p. 137.

[67] For an insightful summary of the competing explanations as to why so many developing countries advocated the NIEO principles so passionately and signed BITs that completely undermine the letter and spirit of the NIEO movement, see Alvarez (2011a), pp. 123–143.

[68] Carlos Calvo's home state Argentina signed a BIT with the US 'whose text is, except for its Protocol, identical to that of the 1987 U.S. Model BIT Text.' Alvarez and Khamsi (2009), p. 408.

[69] According to Nico Schrijver, Nigeria used this expression during UN General Assembly debates on Resolution 1803, apparently referring to the phrase 'freely entered into', presumably in paragraph 8 of the Resolution, which provides: 'Foreign investment agreements freely entered into by, or between, sovereign states shall be observed in good faith'. See Schrijver (1997), p. 263.

meet the formalistic requirements of consent under international law. In the circumstances, it will certainly be difficult to disagree with Jan Paulsson when he says: 'those who challenge the legitimacy of international adjudication ... criticize the principle of the supremacy of international law when their real complaint has to do with the political choices of their own government in making the bargains reflected in international treaties.'[70]

But, of course, whether those "political choices" truly existed can be legitimately challenged.[71] Indeed, the first BIT involving an African country was signed on 11 August 1960 between Chad and France,[72] ironically the day on which Chad attained its independence from France.[73] A "treaty" signed between a former colony and its former colonial power on the day of the independence of the former from the latter cannot be the product of "political choice", nor reflect any bargaining process between them. Prof. Joseph Weiler said it well when he wrote of "the shameful exploitations and arbitral biases that are now part of the thousands (!) of bilateral investment treaties (BITs) which are for the most part offered on a take-it-or-leave-it basis between bilateral unequal partners."[74] The next question then is this: to what extent, if at all, has this development undermined the PSNR principle?

---

[70]Paulsson (2010), p. 349.

[71]A recent survey by UNECA shows that of the roughly 2750 BITs in the world today, over 850 involve an African country; 157 of them are intra-African while the remaining 696 are with the rest of the world. See UNECA (2016), p. 16.

[72]See UNCTAD (2000), p. 53. It is notable that no reference to this treaty appears in UNCTAD's otherwise most resourceful Investment Policy Hub available at http://investmentpolicyhub.unctad.org/IIA/CountryBits/39 (accessed 03 December 2016).

[73]The first BIT between two African countries was signed on 25 September 1982 by Egypt and Somalia. See http://investmentpolicyhub.unctad.org/IIA/CountryBits/194#iiaInnerMenu (accessed 03 December 2016). Ethiopia signed its first BIT (with Germany) only on 21 April 1964 while its second came 30 years later when it signed one with Italy on 23 December 1994. See UNCTAD Investment Policy Hub at http://investmentpolicyhub.unctad.org/IIA/CountryBits/67#iiaInnerMenu (accessed 03 December 2016). The number of BITs involving African countries has continued to grow since, but the amount of FDI flowing to Africa in general, and sub-Saharan Africa in particular, has remained miniscule. Africa's share of global FDI in 2014 was just under 4.4%. See UNCTAD (2016), p. 34. Even more importantly, if we exclude FDI in services in Africa, which is highly concentrated in just a few countries, the little FDI that traditionally goes to sub-Saharan Africa is heavily concentrated in the extractive sector—minerals, oil and gas resources. See UNCTAD (2008), p. 82. Finally, there is generally little direct relationship between the national economic policy of a country and its ability to attract this type of FDI; what seems to decide here is the geology rather than the political-economy of these countries. See UNCTAD (2016), p. 8 (noting: "the geography of natural resources determines FDI in extractive industries to a high degree").

[74]See Weiler (2015).

4 Sovereignty Over Natural Resources: The Retreating Host State

Before we attempt to answer the above question, a brief discussion of the general concept of sovereignty itself is in order. The concept of sovereignty is complex, dynamic and controversial; it is often condemned and dismissed as out of date,[75] as it is defended and upheld as our salvation from chaos.[76] Professor John Jackson wonders whether the concept of sovereignty is 'perhaps purposefully, misleading'[77]; for Professor Louis Henkin, state sovereignty is 'essentially a mistake, an illegitimate offspring'[78] that we must get rid of if we can. It is notable, however, that most—though not all—of the criticisms of sovereignty mainly derive from the history of abuse of the doctrine by repressive regimes that have used it as a shield against foreign intervention while perpetuating some of the most heinous human rights violations within their territories.[79] This aspect of sovereignty is out of date and must be rejected.[80] In this paper, I am looking at sovereignty as it relates to the management of national natural resources, where I believe sovereignty remains positively relevant. For my purposes, I find Richard Haas's characterisation of sovereignty a good starting point:

> First, a sovereign state is one that enjoys supreme political authority and a monopoly over the legitimate use of force within its territory. Second, it is capable of regulating movements across its borders. Third, it can make its foreign policy choices freely. Finally, it is recognized by other governments as an independent entity entitled to freedom from external intervention.[81]

Sovereignty described in these forms is far from absolute. After all, mere assertion of the abstract principle of sovereignty by a resource-rich developing country cannot make a meaningful difference until that resource is properly explored and exploited, which requires capital, technology and management knowhow. Sovereignty over natural resources is 'a mere abstract potentiality

---

[75]No less an authority than Louis Henkin has argued that 'for legal purposes at least, we might do well to relegate the term sovereignty to the shelf of history as a relic from an earlier era.' Henkin (1995) quoted in Jackson (2006), p. 69.

[76]See Alvarez (2011b, Return of the State), p. 263 (referring to Michael Walzer as saying that 'only those lucky enough to live in a functioning state can afford to suggest that [sovereignty] is "withering away."')

[77]See Jackson (2006), p. 69.

[78]In simpler days, wrote Henkin, sovereignty 'implied several key elements. Primarily, it meant political independence. It also meant territorial integrity and virtually exclusive control and jurisdiction within that territory.' Henkin (1999), p. 2 (footnotes omitted).

[79]Henkin (1999), pp. 1–14, at 2 (footnotes omitted). For a recent analysis of the use of sovereignty to challenge the jurisdiction of regional courts in Africa, see Alter et al. (2016).

[80]For an eye-opening discussion of the type of atrocities, genocide and crimes against humanity that have been committed under the watch of the UN, and the struggles to stop them, see Annan (2012).

[81]See Haass (2003).

when the means for developing these resources are lacking. The freedom to exploit natural resources implies, therefore, at least some cooperation between developed and developing states, since it is only the former that can provide to the latter the means for developing their resources. Precisely for that reason, states regularly use their sovereignty as currency in bilateral and multilateral negotiations with one another to maximize mutual gains, and in the process to voluntarily concede pieces of their sovereign space in exchange for concessions of a similar nature from others.'[82] Or, to use Richard Haas's language, governments 'trade freedom of action for the benefits of multilateral cooperation.'[83] The question, then, is on what terms that cooperation will take place. The international investment regime represents a significant part of the answer to this question at any particular point in time.

To analyse the relationship between sovereignty over natural resources and investment protection law, I build on Haas's characterisation and consider sovereignty as a bundle of powers and prerogatives, available only to a state. Translated into the natural resources sector and contextualised within the domain of international investment law, governments have supreme political authority internally to make and enforce laws for the management, development and utilisation of their natural resources ('internal authority' or 'exclusive jurisdiction within their own territory'); they have supreme authority to determine whether or not foreign capital can be employed to develop those resources and, once developed, whether or not the final product stays within their borders or is exported to the world market (border control); they have complete authority to determine their foreign policy and international relations with respect to natural resources and do so on an equal basis with every other state in the world and free of unwanted intervention (non-intervention).[84]

Understood in this way, the three traditional functions of the state—to make laws through its chosen legislator (also known as legislative jurisdiction), to administer those laws through its own executive (also known as executive jurisdiction), and to interpret those laws and administer justice through its courts (also known as judicial jurisdiction)—are all derived from, and manifestations of, national sovereignty. The key question, then, is whether, or to what extent, international investment law hampers the exercise of these three components of sovereignty in the natural resources sector. I argue that modern investment law significantly erodes the state's sovereignty over its natural resources by, at the minimum, (1) limiting its legislative jurisdiction through the doctrine of internationalisation of the investment contract and stabilisation clauses, and (2) virtually eliminating its judicial jurisdiction through the almost uniform adoption of international arbitration as the means to settle investment disputes.

---

[82]Fatouros (1964), p. 804.

[83]Haass (2003).

[84]This paraphrasing is based on Haas's description of the four main characteristics of sovereignty, Id.

4.1 Legislative Sovereignty and Internationalisation of Contracts

Internationalisation of contracts refers to a process by which the parties to an international investment contract, i.e. the foreign investor and the host state, could 'remove their agreement from the scope of the contracting State's legislative sovereignty'[85] and put them directly under international law.[86] The roots of this innovation date back to the 1930 *Lena Goldfields* award,[87] where the tribunal split the question of applicable law in two and ruled that, for all domestic matters, such as those relating to performance of the contract by both parties inside the USSR, Soviet law applied, while for all other purposes 'the *general principles of law* such as those recognised by Article 38 of the Statute of the Permanent Court of International Justice ... should be regarded as "the proper law of the contract"'.[88] It was from this curious and unwarranted split[89] of the applicable law concept that one of the most successful legal innovations of international investment law originated. That was the first time Article 38 of the Statute of the PCIJ was used as a source of law governing the relations between a state and a private investor. Although there was little enthusiasm or recognition of the significance of this innovation when it first came out, the decolonisation process of the 1950s and 1960s, and the accompanying sovereignty risks to foreign property in the newly-independent states, gave new meaning and relevance to the doctrine of internationalisation. Already in 1957 Arnold McNair, a leading authority in international law who had just retired from his position as President of the ICJ, was thus able to assert an emerging 'general consensus of opinion' that general principles of law recognised in civilised nations provided 'the system of law governing these contractual relationships'.[90] And, as noted earlier, in 1962 Resolution 1803 effectively elevated the investment contract to a quasi-treaty by prescribing the state's obligation to observe its contractual commitments in good faith.[91] Greenwood thus observed that 1962 was 'the high point of acceptance' of the theory of internationalisation of state contracts, which was soon followed by 'growing

---

[85] See Greenwood (1982), p. 41.

[86] For a useful summary of the extensive debate surrounding the concept of internationalisation of state contracts, see Maniruzzaman (2001), pp. 309–328.

[87] Nussbaum (1950), pp. 31–53. The award of the tribunal in *Lena Goldfields* was published in *The Times* of London on 3 September 1930 and reproduced in Nussbaum. For a modern and comprehensive account of this case, see Veeder (1998), pp. 747–792.

[88] *Lena Goldfields* award, para. 22, extracts reproduced in Nussbaum (1950), p. 50 (emphasis added).

[89] Arthur Nussbaum rightly commented that 'such a splitting of applicable legal systems was not warranted; the "proper law" of the entire contract was Soviet.' Nussbaum (1950), p. 36.

[90] See McNair (1957a, b), pp. 1–19.

[91] For early reflections on this practice, see Greenwood (1982).

opposition from the developing States' who considered it an insult to sovereignty of a contracting State.[92]

Be that as it may, if an investment contract were to be removed from the legislative sovereignty of the host state, one would think that the parties must include an unambiguous choice of law clause to that effect.[93] But this has not always been the case.[94] In the *Abu Dhabi* arbitration, the closest to a choice of law clause was limited to a declaration by the parties to 'base their work in this Agreement on goodwill and sincerity of belief' and to interpret the Agreement 'in a fashion consistent with reason.'[95] The sole arbitrator in the case started with a rhetorical question of what the proper law of the contract was and wrote: 'This is a contract made in Abu Dhabi and wholly to be performed in that country. If any municipal system of law were applicable, it would prima facie be that of Abu Dhabi.'[96] The arbitrator continued: 'But no such law can reasonably be said to exist. The Sheikh administers a purely discretionary justice with the assistance of the Koran; and it would be fanciful to suggest that in this very primitive region there is any settled body of legal principles applicable to the construction of modern commercial instruments.'[97] Thus the arbitrator conferred on himself an unlimited discretion to determine the law applicable to the construction of the contract. At first, he rejected the municipal law of England as inapplicable because, 'Clause 17 of the agreement ... repels the notion that the municipal law of any country, as such, could be appropriate.'[98] Interestingly, however, the arbitrator ended up applying English law on the grounds that 'some of its rules are ... so firmly grounded in reason, as to form part of this broad body of jurisprudence—this "modern law of nature"', a body of 'principles rooted in the good sense and common practice of the generality of civilised nations.'[99]

The *Abu Dhabi* award might stand out for its candour today, but it was by no means unique in its dismissal of host state laws as totally inadequate. As Lalive has observed, many tribunals have ruled that 'the State party to the contract and to the litigation had no law of contracts, no commercial law capable of meeting the

---

[92] Id., 43.

[93] As Judge Higgins put it, 'the best way to avoid sole reliance on domestic law is, one has to say, by having a governing law clause that introduces international law. If, in the bargaining process, the private party has been unable to accomplish this, it seems doubtful that international arbitrators should remedy that which one of the negotiating parties was unable to achieve.' Higgins (1994), p. 141.

[94] According to Maniruzzaman, the theory of internationalisation suggests that, 'no matter what law the parties to [a state] contract choose as the proper law of the contract, international law superimposes their choice and applies automatically as the overriding governing rule.' See Maniruzzaman (2001), p. 309.

[95] *Abu Dhabi* arbitration (1952), p. 250.

[96] *Abu Dhabi* arbitration (1952), p. 252.

[97] Id., 252–253.

[98] Id., 253.

[99] Id., 253. The arbitrator understood this 'modern law of nature' to mean Ibid.

intricacies of modern international trade relations.'[100] Lalive then opined that this argument 'is not very convincing and should as a rule be disregarded.'[101] In this spirit, the *Aminoil* tribunal showed its sensitivity by emphasising that 'Kuwait law is a highly evolved system ... established public international law is necessarily a part of the law of Kuwait. In their turn the general principles of law are part of public international law ... and that this specifically applies to Kuwait oil concessions, duly results from the clauses included in these.'[102]

In *Abu Dhabi*, English law was brought in as applicable law because it represented some form of 'modern law of nature'; in *Aminoil*, those same English law principles would apply because they would represent general principles of law recognised in a civilised nation, forming part of established public international law that is 'necessarily part of the law of Kuwait'. The routes could be straightforward as in Abu Dhabi, or meandering as in Aminoil, but the destination remained the same in all cases. The 'general principles of law recognised in civilised nations' that were used as the tool to make new law applying to new states are still on the ICJ Statute as a legitimate source of international law.

Professor Alvarez suggests that today's international lawyers 'no longer distinguish the rules applicable to the "civilized" versus "uncivilized" worlds in order to use the former to dispossess the latter.'[103] The evolution of the applicable law concept in international investment law and its practical application in the hands of international arbitrators might leave a question of whether Alvarez's statement here is a result of hope rather than experience. The *Abu Dhabi* award may be dismissed as a case of the bad old days, but national law was never given the last word in investment arbitration; at the very least, it has always been subject to the international minimum standard. To the extent its substantive rules and principles are taken from the general principles of law in those 'civilized states', the international minimum standard is reminiscent of Lord Asquith's rejection of English law as inapplicable, only to bring it back through the back door with a different name—as a 'modern law of nature'.[104] As Mohammed Bedjaoui put it, the general principles of law are 'in fact merely the transposition into international law of the principles of the Western countries' own domestic law.'[105] Article 42(1) of the ICSID Convention puts host state law and international law as applicable law by default in the absence of a choice of law clause in the contract. But, in practice, and regardless of whether or not the parties have included a choice of law clause, arbitrators apply

---

[100] See Lalive (1964), p. 1009.

[101] See Lalive, Id.

[102] See *Aminoil* arbitration (1982), p. 1000.

[103] Alvarez (2009) Empire of Law, pp. 943–975.

[104] But, the application of the international minimum standard to a country as a minimum threshold that it must make available to foreign investors in its territory is not the same as making international law the only applicable law. For a discussion of the distinction between these two, see Maniruzzaman (2001).

[105] Bedjaoui (1979), p. 101.

host state law subject to international law—i.e. in the event of a conflict between the two, international law is given precedence over host state law.[106] As Dame Higgins noted two decades ago, 'whether there is only a domestic-law-proper law clause; or whether there is a mixed "international-law and domestic-law" clause (as in the Libyan arbitrations or in Article 42 of the [ICSID]), international arbitrators are very likely to find international law relevant.'[107] Many BITs that are pervasive today take this a significant step further—through the so-called umbrella clause, which purports to lift all and any investment contracts to the realm of international law.[108]

4.2 Legislative Sovereignty and Stabilisation Clauses

Stabilisation clauses are provisions in investment contracts that aim 'to freeze the law of the host state at the time of contracting or to insulate the contract against the impact of future legislative changes'.[109] Traditionally, stabilisation clauses are designed to freeze the law of the host state as of the day of the investment contract.[110] This is reflected in the definition adopted by the arbitral tribunal in *Total v Argentina*, which understood stabilisation clauses as clauses in state contracts 'with the intended effect of freezing a specific host State's legal framework at a certain date, such that the adoption of any changes in the legal regulatory framework of the investment concerned (even by law of general application and without any discriminatory intent by the host State) would be illegal.'[111]

Generally intended as tools for the management of political risk, stabilisation clauses were first introduced to fill whatever room was left for national legislative sovereignty from the application of the doctrine of internationalisation. But, unlike the doctrine of internationalisation, which first came into existence through an arbitration award and later moved to contract drafting, stabilisation clauses were

---

[106]See, e.g. Dolzer and Schreuer (2008), p. 271.

[107]Higgins (1994), p. 141.

[108]The umbrella clause expressly requires the host state 'to observe any obligation it may have entered into with regard to foreign investments, that is converting (or purporting to convert) contracts subject to domestic law into international obligations.' See Lowenfeld (2009), p. 58.

[109]Delaume (1997), p. 23. For a recent and thorough analysis of stabilisation clauses, see Shemberg (2009).

[110]However, stabilisation obligations today may come from international treaties, as well as unilateral undertakings contained in municipal law. This article deals with traditional stabilisation clauses as contained in international investment contracts, for the simple reason that to the extent they are contained in municipal law or international treaties, stabilisation clauses impose constraints on sovereignty just like every other law does and in every country. Stabilisation clauses contained in investment contracts, on the other hand, are as a matter of empirical fact limited to developing countries. For more, see Shemberg (2009).

[111]*Total v Argentina,* (2010), para. 100 (emphasis added).

the creation of contracts from the 1950s, receiving recognition by arbitral tribunals afterwards. When they started in the 1950s and 1960s, they were introduced as part of the post-colonial regime to manage the impending 'sovereignty risk' in the newly sovereign states of the South.[112] Starting in the 1980s, however, stabilisation clauses were more or less wilfully accepted by capital-starved developing countries that looked at them as 'an important tool of foreign investment promotion policy.'[113] Today, stabilisation clauses are a common feature of investment contracts, particularly those in the extractive industries between foreign companies and African governments,[114] though rare or non-existent in advanced countries.[115] In this sense, stabilisation clauses are a premium developing countries pay to attract private foreign capital and technology; indeed, considering administrative and institutional problems that are often associated with these countries, this might be termed a rule-of-law premium. As a result, a state party to an international investment contract that contains a stabilisation clause might commit breach of contract by the mere act of passing a new law, or as we have seen in recent jurisprudence and contract practice,[116] even a new interpretation of a pre-existing law.[117]

Given that the state has consented to such a clause in the first place, it is hardly surprising that today's international law affirms that this contractual breach entails state responsibility.[118] As an ICSID tribunal emphasised recently, a stability undertaking in an investment agreement is of 'undoubted importance for investors' because it 'freezes the laws, rules and regulations applicable to it, as they were in existence at the time the Agreement was concluded'.[119] The investor expectations created by such a clause are also likely to be considered 'legitimate', thereby triggering claims of breach of the fair and equitable treatment clause in a BIT.[120] In a recent award, the *Mobil v Canada* tribunal observed that a state may be held responsible if it is established that it made 'clear and explicit representations ... in

---

[112] As Cameron rightly pointed out, the debate on stabilisation clauses first began when "the post-colonial investment regime [was] in place". Cameron (2013), p. 312.

[113] Wälde and Ndi (1996), p. 218.

[114] See Shemberg (2009), pp. 17, 21–22 and 32.

[115] Id. p. v. In fact, many OECD countries do not just exclude stabilisation clauses; they often explicitly reserve the power to unilaterally modify contracts with private operators. For a discussion of such clauses in France, the UK and the US, see Norton (1991), pp. 492–493.

[116] For a useful analysis, see (2010).

[117] See *Duke Energy v. Peru* (ICSID Case No. ARB/03/28, 18 August 2008b), para. 227. For analysis of this case, see Cotula (2010).

[118] This might look obvious in the face of today's virtual consensus in the arbitration jurisprudence, but as recently as 1960, Dr Mann argued otherwise. See Mann (1960), pp. 587–588.

[119] See *Aguaytia Energy, LLC v Republic of Peru* (ICSID Case No ARB/06/13, award of 11 December 2008a), para. 95.

[120] See, e.g., *Total v Argentina*, ICSID Case No. ARB/04/1, Decision on Liability (27 December 2010), para. 117.

order to induce the investment', that such representations were 'reasonably relied upon by the Claimants', and it subsequently repudiated those representations.[121]

Unlike in earlier days,[122] however, the obligation of the state under a stabilisation clause is generally limited to the payment of compensation to affected foreign investors rather than repeal of legislation.[123] As a result, the limitations to legislative sovereignty resulting from modern stabilisation clauses have diminished over time. However, the mere fact that stabilisation clauses are common in international investment contracts for the exploitation of natural resources in developing countries, with consequent constraints on the powers of the state to change its laws—albeit remediable through financial compensation—provides further evidence that international investment law unduly and discriminatorily restricts the sovereign legislative space available to these states to manage their natural resources sectors.

In a further sign of hope, the Israeli Supreme Court recently upheld a petition brought before it by the Movement for Quality Government in Israel, a citizen watchdog organisation, challenging the legality of a stability undertaking given by the Government of Israel in an investment contract to develop the offshore Leviathan gasfield.[124] In that undertaking, the Government of Israel had committed "to a decade during which it not only will not legislate but will also object to any legislation that is against the provisions of the Outline [contract]".[125] The Court ruled, by majority, that the Government's stabilisation undertaking "was prescribed ultra-vires and is void. . . . the Government does not have the power and authority to decide not to decide or not to take action. It was emphasised that this is all the more relevant when at hand is a matter that is subject to real political dispute, and when the authority wishes to restrict the discretion of its successors, the composition of which and the ideology it may hold may be different than that of the present government."[126] This is an example that governments and the national judiciary particularly in Africa must consider in their efforts to rebalance their regulatory frameworks in the field. However, it must also be clear that there can be

---

[121] See *Mobil v Canada*, ICSID Case No. ARB(AF)/07/4, Award, 22 May 2012, para. 154.

[122] See the Texaco Award, where the arbitrator ordered specific performance as a remedy, but this aspect of the award became irrelevant as Libya and the companies reached a settlement soon after the award was issued. See Elder (1997).

[123] A good example of this came from the mid-1970s when the ICSID tribunal in *Alcoa Minerals of Jamaica v. Jamaica*, ruled that Jamaica was in breach of the stabilisation clause contained in the long-term contract it had signed with Alcoa for bauxite mining. For more on this, see Igbokwe (1997), p. 120.

[124] See the Supreme Court of Israel, *High Court of Justice 4374/15, 7588/15, 8747/15, 262/16, The Movement for Quality Government v. The Prime Minister of Israel, Regarding the Gas Outline that was Prescribed in Government Decision 476 Summary of Judgment*, dated 27 March 2016, available at http://elyon1.court.gov.il/files_eng/15/740/043/t63/15043740.t63.pdf.

[125] Id. p. 2.

[126] See Id., opinion of Deputy President E. Rubinstein, p. 2. See also Joel Greenberg, "Israel's supreme court blocks Leviathan gasfield deal", *Financial Times*, 28 March 2016. The Court gave the government a year to revise the deal, failing which the entire deal would be cancelled.

circumstances where stabilisation commitments may have a place in African natural resources contracts; the main argument here is against the power-based process by which they are "imposed" and the absolute sense in which they are implemented in practice.[127]

4.3 Judicial Sovereignty and International Arbitration

As noted earlier, one key manifestation of sovereignty involves the inherent power of the state as the supreme authority to administer justice within its territory. Translated into the natural resources industry, this would inevitably mean the power to subject all natural and legal persons operating within its territory to the jurisdiction of its courts. In practice, however, this is where the investment law experiment in the natural resources sector has succeeded in almost completely obliterating prior international law. In perhaps the most successful innovation designed to insulate Western corporations operating in the poorest developing countries from the jurisdiction of the local courts, access to international arbitration has since become an almost unconditional right for the foreign investor.[128]

The reputation of many of these countries as lacking independent and competent courts with the capacity to administer justice impartially explains, at least in part, investors' and home states' insistence on access to international arbitration as a condition for commitment to operate in those countries. Today, BITs have effectively guaranteed them this privilege. If the doctrine of internationalisation of state contracts was intended to ensure foreign investors to remain subject only to the laws of their home countries (through the reference to general principle of law recognised in civilised nations or some other less crude language), the provision

---

[127] As the African Peer Review Mechanism (APRM) Country Review Report for Zambia found, "Enforcement of effective environmental and social ethical standards in the mining sector has been gravely complicated by the Development Agreements executed between the Government and the mining giants, which ... provided for periods of stability of up to 20 years during which mining companies would be exempted from any changes in legal framework. This immunity coupled with the weak legal framework for this sector has led to grave unethical practices." APRM Country Review Report No. 16 (2013), p. 214. In discussions held with several government officials particularly from resource-rich west African countries, the author has learnt that in some cases the duration of stabilisation commitments can be as long as 75 years during which beneficiary companies resist or frustrate government attempts to make regulatory changes in a variety of ways, including by refusing to comply with new laws when issued.

[128] What is interesting is that even some of the leading authorities of the day did not see this coming. Writing in 1963, Professor Brierley described the doctrine of diplomatic protection, identified some of its defects, such as the fact that the home state of the foreign investor might not be willing to take up his case, possible delays, and the like, and noted: 'It has been suggested that a solution might be found by allowing individuals access in their own right to some form of international tribunal for the purpose.' Brierley then added: 'For the time being, however, the prospect of states accepting such a change is not very great.' J L Brierley (1963) at 277, quoted in Blackaby and Partasides (2011), p. 467.

of direct access to international arbitration is the modern day replacement of the consular courts that had exclusive jurisdiction during the colonial days.[129] Traditional international law of course had an older, fairer, and well-established mechanism of dealing with such issues by allowing foreign investors access to diplomatic protection, or even international arbitration if there was a specific agreement to that effect, once they have exhausted available remedies within the host state. General Assembly Resolution 1803 recognised this possibility when it provided: 'In any case where the question of compensation gives rise to a controversy, the national jurisdiction of the state taking such measure shall be exhausted. However, upon agreement by sovereign states and other parties concerned, settlement of the dispute should be made through arbitration or international adjudication.'[130] As Professor Lowenfeld pointed out, the language of this provision was the result of serious negotiations and compromises.[131] If the use of the stronger language of 'shall' indicated that the doctrine of exhaustion of local remedies was left intact, subsequent developments under the auspices of the World Bank, sowed the seed for its lasting reversal in the shape of the 1965 Washington Convention that established ICSID.[132] The doctrine of exhaustion of local remedies remains the default rule to this day,[133] except when it comes to the relations between foreign investors and developing countries, for which BITs mostly provide access to international arbitration without any such requirement.[134]

---

[129] For a discussion of capitulation agreements and how they were applied through consular courts, see Salacuse (2010), p. 82; and more generally Anghie (2005).

[130] UNGA Resolution 1803 (1962), para. 4. The rest of this paragraph contains the following: 'Nationalization, expropriation or requisitioning shall be based on grounds or reasons of public utility, security or the national interest which are recognized as overriding purely individual or private interests, both domestic and foreign. In such cases the owner shall be paid appropriate compensation, in accordance with the rules in force in the state taking such measures in the exercise of its sovereignty and in accordance with international law.'

[131] See Lowenfeld (2009), pp. 48–49 (pointing out that 'in comparison with the draft proposed by the Special Commission to the General Assembly, the first sentence was changed from "should" to "shall"—i.e. stronger for the host country, while the second sentence was changed from "may" to "should,"—i.e. stronger for the investors.')

[132] For more on the history of ICSID, see Lowenfeld (2009), p. 51.

[133] The exhaustion of local remedies rule is 'an established procedural rule of customary international law that a State may not espouse the claim of one of its nationals against another State unless the national has exhausted local remedies.' Foster (2011), p. 204.

[134] As Professor Schrueur put it, 'international investment arbitration dispenses with the requirement to exhaust local remedies, at least in principle. Article 26 of the ICSID Convention specifically does away with this traditional requirement "unless otherwise stated"'. Schreuer (2005), p. 1. Schreuer adds that while countries can insist on exhaustion of local remedies in their BITs, 'clauses of this kind seem to be rare and are found mostly in BITs of older vintage.' Id., 2.

5 Conclusion

A state's sovereignty over its natural resources is now one of the most prominent principles of international law that has been already recognised as a principle of customary international law. Indeed, when Resolution 1803 was issued by the General Assembly in 1962, it was 'generally considered at the time to be evidence of customary international law'.[135] Whatever doubt may have remained about its status has been cleared since. The ICJ has also, for the first time, ruled that the PSNR principle 'is a principle of customary international law'.[136] At the level of relevant treaties, too, this principle has been articulated in various instruments and in varying degrees of detail; the Energy Charter Treaty may be mentioned as just one example.[137] Finally, Professor Vaughan Lowe refers to the PSNR principle as one of the possible examples for *jus cogens* norms of international law on the same level as the principle for the prohibition of apartheid-type racial discrimination.[138] This, however, is only the easy part. As I noted earlier; I do not believe the sovereignty of states over their natural resources, per se, was ever seriously questioned; only the sovereignty of the newly independent states was—and by extension their sovereignty over their natural resources.

The real question is one of balance between this principle and the principles of international law for the protection of foreign investment. This balance has been shifting increasingly towards the latter especially over the last two decades. The changes brought about by BITs in these two decades are so revolutionary that, according to Judge Schwebel, they represent what until recently he would have considered the 'ideal' law of international investment: 'BITs specify in terms more explicit, detailed, and far-reaching than was ever advanced under what was customary international law in the time of Cordell Hull what may be described as an ideal law of international investment.'[139] Many of the capital-importing developing countries that fought hard in the corridors of the United Nations until the mid-1970s have come to realise that all their fears had materialised, shattering their hopes for a more balanced future under the law. The dawn of hope and independence in the 1960s, which was further invigorated by the commodity price boom and accompanying confidence and assertiveness of the 1970s, was quickly replaced by the debt crisis and the pro-market ideological shift of the 1980s, the BITs of the 1990s, and the dreaded arbitrations of the 2000s.

---

[135] See Greenwood (1982), pp. 27–81, at 42. Former ICJ Judge Stephen Schwebel also noted that the resolution 'is the capstone of more than ten years of consideration of the subject by the General Assembly, the Human Rights Commission, the Economic and Social Council and a special Commission on Permanent Sovereignty over Natural Resources.' See Schwebel (1963), p. 463.

[136] ICJ, Armed Activities on the Territory of the Congo (Dem. Rep. Congo v Uganda), Judgment 19 December 2005, P 77, para. 244. For analysis of the significance of this ruling, see Dufresn (2008).

[137] See Energy Charter Treaty, Art. 18:1.

[138] See Lowe (2007), p. 59.

[139] See Schwebel (2004), p. 28.

Competition for Natural Resources and International Investment Law: Analysis... 143

However, I conclude not with despair, but with hope. There are presently some promising signs of change in the right direction, dictated mainly by such underlying economic factors as the role reversal of traditionally home states of FDI in the Global North increasingly finding themselves in the unusual position of having to answer for their own practices at the behest of investors coming from the traditional host states of the Global South.[140] As a result, these countries are reconsidering their traditional positions, and in the process coming slightly closer to the position long advocated by the Global South. As Professor Alvarez observed in 2011, 'many recent investment protection treaties accord FDI host states greater room to maneuver, while simultaneously granting foreign investors fewer rights'.[141] Alvarez added that the US 'led the charge in favor of investor protections' in the 1980s, but 'it now appears to be leading the drive in the opposite direction.'[142] The recent negotiations on the Transatlantic Trade and Investment Partnership (TTIP) between the EU and the US have taken the resistance to the ever-expanding protection afforded to foreign investors to a higher level. Indeed, it is ironic, indeed hypocritical, to observe that countries like France and Germany—historically major sponsors and active users of the BIT system with investor-state dispute settlement (ISDS) as the norm—are leading the rejection of ISDS in TTIP.[143] Again, to quote Joseph Weiler:

> The European hue and cry at the ISDS of TTIP is ugly and self-serving when one considers that they themselves have imposed the very same provisions they find so otiose when applied to Europe (in the context of North American investment) in their bilateral investment relations with developing and other countries (where the fear of reciprocal action is negligible) and happily use them, extensively, when the boot is on their foot. These horrible provisions are, it appears, altogether Kosher when applied to others, but oh, so unacceptable when threatening us. It's the NIMBY [not in my backyard] of international economic law: fine so long as it is not in my back yard.[144]

---

[140] See, e.g., Melnitzer (2016) describing the case of the first BIT claim brought against Canada by a developing-country investor (by Egypt). As Melnitzer observed, "the irony here is palpable. After all, investor-state dispute-resolution mechanisms were originally intended to protect investors from developed countries against unfair treatment from developing countries, where democracy and the rule of law were not necessarily priorities. As far back as 1994, NAFTA's Chapter 11 was included in the treaty to protect US and Canadian investors against corruption in Mexico."

[141] Alvarez (2011b Return of the State), p. 235.

[142] Alvarez (2011b Return of the State), p. 235. Alvarez also shows that several other countries, including Canada and China, are following this US lead in terms of their model BITs, while several countries are also making revising their national investment laws in more sovereignty-enhancing ways; interestingly, Alvarez also suggests that even some arbitral tribunals are turning in this direction: 'The efforts to re-balance the rights of sovereigns vis-à-vis foreign investors [are] increasingly evident in the text of BITs, national laws, and even some arbitral awards....' Id., 251–252.

[143] See Barbière (2016), noting: "Paris and Berlin want ... ISDS removed from the transatlantic trade treaty currently being negotiated with Washington", quoting French Secretary of State for Foreign Trade Matthias Fekl as saying he would "never allow private tribunals in the pay of multinational companies to dictate the policies of sovereign states, particularly in certain domains like health and the environment."

[144] See Weiler (2015), p. 76.

Other major players, including India,[145] Indonesia and South Africa,[146] are also reviewing, and in some cases terminating, their existing BITs with a view to negotiating new ones based on model BITs they themselves prepare.[147] More generally, African countries are beginning to actively engage in this field in different forms. For example (1) a number of Regional Economic Communities, such as the East African Community (EAC), the Economic Community of West African States (ECOWAS) and the Southern Africa Development Community (SADC) have developed regionally-harmonised model BITs for use in future negotiations; (2) an initiative by the African Union (AU) to develop a Pan-African Investment Code (PAIC) is at advanced stages; and (3) the ongoing negotiations for the Continental Free Trade Area (CFTA) envisage an investment chapter in the second phase of these negotiations.[148] All this is encouraging, but it needs to be taken to its logical conclusion so that each African country conducts a comprehensive review of its network of bilateral and other investment treaties and related national legislation and natural resources contracts, terminate those that do not serve its national interests or renegotiate them based on regionally- and/or continentally-harmonised policy frameworks.[149] This way lies the opportunity for African countries to exercise their sovereignty over their natural resources in a manner that best serves their national interests.[150]

---

[145] See, e.g. Singh and Ilge (2016).

[146] See Nolan (2016), noting South Africa and Indonesia "have terminated existing BITs that include ISDS provisions. ... South Africa began terminating treaties in 2012 after a two-year review of its investment treaty obligations" which "followed ISCID arbitration by investors from Luxembourg and Italy in response to South Africa's 2002 Mineral and Petroleum Resources Development Act." Id., 434.

[147] For example, India's 2015 Model BIT makes access to ISDS conditional on exhaustion of local remedies (see Art. 14.3 of Model BIT, available at https://www.mygov.in/sites/default/files/master_image/Model%20Text%20for%20the%20Indian%20Bilateral%20Investment%20Treaty.pdf) (accessed 03 December 2016).

[148] See Mbengue (2016).

[149] Otherwise, as Alvarez warned, many African countries "will likely remain parties to older much more pro-investor BITs based on models comparable to those of the U.S. Model BIT of 1984." Alvarez (2011b Return of the State), p. 260.

[150] For an excellent analysis, see Carim (2015), "International Investment Agreements and Africa's Structural Transformation: A Perspective from South Africa", *South Centre Investment Policy Brief* (No. 4 August 2015), https://www.southcentre.int/wp-content/uploads/2015/08/IPB4_IIAs-and-Africa's-Structural-Transformation-Perspective-from-South-Africa_EN.pdf (making some well-thought recommendations to African policy-makers and experts, including to use the AU platform to conduct a comprehensive review of all their international investment agreements (IIAs), to pause signing new IIAs, and to consider developing an Africa-wide investment protection framework that serves their particular needs and interests.)

References

Abu Dhabi Arbitration (1952) In the matter of an arbitration between Petroleum Development (Trucial Coast) Ltd. and the Sheikh of Abu Dhabi, Award of 1952. Int Comp Law Q 1:247–261

Africa Progress Panel (2013) Equity in extractives: stewarding Africa's natural resources for all

African Development Bank (2012) Mining industry prospects in Africa. http://www.afdb.org/en/blogs/afdb-championing-inclusive-growth-across-africa/post/mining-industry-prospects-in-africa-10177/. Accessed 03 Dec 2016

Alter J, Gathii J, Helfer R (2016) Backlash against international courts in west, east and southern Africa: causes and consequences. Eur J Int Law 293–328

Alvarez J (2009) Contemporary foreign investment law: an 'Empire of Law' or the 'Law of Empire'. Ala Law Rev 60:943–975

Alvarez J (2011a) The public international law regime governing international investment. Pocketbooks of The Hague Academy of International Law

Alvarez J (2011b) The return of the state. Minnesota J Int Law 20(2):223–264

Alvarez J, Khamsi K (2009) The argentine crisis and foreign investors: a glimpse into the heart of the investment regime. In: Sauvant K (ed) Yearbook on international investment law & policy, 2008–2009. Oxford University Press, Oxford

Aminoil Arbitration (1982) Award in the matter of an arbitration between Kuwait and the American Independent Oil Company (Aminoil), award 24 March 1982. ILM 21:976

Anghie A (2005) Imperialism, sovereignty and the making of international law. Cambridge University Press

Annan K with Mousavizadeh N (2012) Interventions: a life in war and peace. Allen Lane, 2012

Barbière C (2016) France and Germany to form united front against ISDS. http://www.euractiv.com/section/trade-society/news/france-and-germany-to-form-united-front-against-isds/. Accessed 03 Dec 2016

Bedjaoui M (1968) First report on succession of States in respect of rights and duties resulting from sources other than treaties, ILC A/CN.4/204

Bedjaoui M (1979) Towards a new international economic order. Holmes and Meier, New York, London

Blackaby N, Partasides C with Redfern A and Hunter M (2011) Redfern and Hunter on international arbitration. Oxford University Press, Oxford

Brierley J (1963) The law of nations. Oxford University Press, Oxford

Cameron (2013) Reflections on sovereignty over natural resources and the enforcement of stabilization clauses. In: Sauvant K (ed) Yearbook on international investment law & policy 2011–2012. Oxford University Press, Oxford

Carim X (2015) International investment agreements and Africa's structural transformation: a perspective from South Africa. South Centre Investment Policy Brief. https://www.southcentre.int/wp-content/uploads/2015/08/IPB4_IIAs-and-Africa's-Structural-Transformation-Perspective-from-South-Africa_EN.pdf. Accessed 03 Dec 2016

Chimni B (2007) Just world under law: a view from the south. Am Univ Int Law Rev 22:199–220

Coll S (2012) Private Empire: ExxonMobil and American Power. Allen Lane

Collier P (2008) Essay: laws and codes for the resource curse. Yale Hum Rights Dev Law J 11:9–28

Cotula L (2010) Pushing the boundaries vs striking a balance: some reflections on stabilization issues in light of Duke Energy International Investments v. Republic of Peru. Transnational Dispute Management. https://www.transnational-dispute-management.com/article.asp?key=1571. Accessed 03 Dec 2016

Craven M (2007) The decolonization of international law: state succession and the law of treaties. Oxford University Press, Oxford

Delaume G (1997) The proper law of state contracts revisited. ICSID Rev – Foreign Invest Law J 12:1–28

Desta MG (2015) Sovereignty over natural resources and international investment law: the elusive search for equilibrium. In: Hofmann R, Schill SW, Tams CJ (eds) International investment law and development: friends or foes? Edward Elgar, pp 223–255

Dodge W (2000) National courts and international arbitration: exhaustion of remedies and Res Judicata under Chapter Eleven of NAFTA. Hastings Int Comp Law Rev 23:357–383

Dolzer R, Schreuer C (2008) Principles of international investment law. Oxford University Press, Oxford

Domingo R (2009) The crisis of international law. Vanderbilt J Transnatl Law 42:1543–1593

Dufresn R (2008) Reflections and extrapolation on the ICJ's approach to illegal resource exploitation in the armed activities case. N Y Univ J Int Law Polit 40:171–217

Duruigbo E (2006) Permanent sovereignty and peoples' ownership of natural resources in international law. George Wash Int Law Rev 38:33–100

Elder E (1997) The case against arbitral awards of specific performance in transnational commercial disputes. Arbitr Int 38:1–32

Fatouros A (1964) International law and the third world. Va Law Rev 50:783–823

Foster G (2011) Striking a balance between investor protections and national sovereignty: the relevance of local remedies in investment treaty arbitration. Columbia J Transnatl Law 50:201–267

Frankel J (2010) Comment on Helm. In Hogan and Sturzenegger (2010)

Gardner R (1974) The hard road to world order. Foreign Aff 52:556–576

GATT Secretariat (1995) Analytical index: guide to GATT law and practice. Geneva

Greenwood C (1982) State contracts in international law – the Libyan oil arbitrations. Br Yearb Int Law 53:27–81

Haass R (2003) Sovereignty: existing rights, evolving responsibilities: remarks to the School of Foreign Service and the Mortara Center for International Studies, Georgetown University (Washington, DC). http://2001-2009.state.gov/s/p/rem/2003/16648.htm. Accessed 03 Dec 2016

Helm D (2010) Credibility, commitment, and regulation: ex ante price caps and ex post intervention. In Hogan and Sturzenegger (2010)

Henkin L (1995) International law: politics and values. Kluwer

Henkin L (1999) Lecture: that 'S' word: sovereignty, and globalization, and human rights, et cetera. Fordham Law Rev 68:1–14

Higgins R (1994) Problems and process: international law and how we use it. Oxford University Press, Oxford

Hogan W, Sturzenegger F (eds) (2010) The natural resources trap – private investment without public commitment. The MIT Press, Cambridge

ICJ, Barcelona Traction (Belgium v. Spain) Judgment of 5 February 1970, ICJ Rep 3

ICJ, Armed Activities on the Territory of the Congo (Dem. Rep. Congo v Uganda) Judgment 19 December 2005

ICSID, Aguaytia Energy, LLC v Republic of Peru (ICSID Case No ARB/06/13) award 11 December 2008a

ICSID, Duke Energy v. Peru, Award on the Merits (ICSID Case No. ARB/03/28) award 18 August 2008b

ICSID, Total v Argentina (ICSID Case No. ARB/04/1) Decision on Liability, 27 December 2010

ICSID, Mobil v Canada (ICSID Case No. ARB(AF)/07/4) Award, 22 May 2012

Igbokwe V (1997) Developing countries and the law applicable to international arbitration of oil investment disputes - has the last word been said? J Int Arbitr 14:99–124

Irwin D, Mavroidis C, Sykes A (2008) The genesis of the GATT. Cambridge University Press

Jackson J (2006) Sovereignty, the WTO, and changing fundamentals of international law. Cambridge University Press

Lalive J (1964) Contracts between a state or a state agency and a foreign company: theory and practice: choice of law in a new arbitration case. Int Comp Law Q 13:987–1021

Lehavi A, Licht A (2011) BITs and pieces of property. Yale J Int Law 36:115–166

Lowe V (2007) International law. Oxford University Press, Oxford

Lowenfeld A (2009) The ICSID convention: origins and transformation. Ga J Int Comp Law 38:47–61

Maniruzzaman M (2001) State contracts in contemporary international law: Monist versus Dualist controversies. Eur J Int Law 12:309–328

Mann FA (1960) State contracts and state responsibility. AJIL 54:572–591

Mbengue M (2016) The quest for a Pan-African Investment Code to promote sustainable development. http://www.ictsd.org/bridges-news/bridges-africa/news/the-quest-for-a-pan-african-investment-code-to-promote-sustainable. Accessed 03 Dec 2016

McNair A (1957a) The applicability of "General Principles of Law" to contracts between a state and a foreign national. American Bar Association: Section of Mineral & Natural Resources Law Proceedings 168–176

McNair A (1957b) The general principles of law recognized by civilized nations. Br Yearb Int Law 33:1–19

Melnitzer J (2016) Protectionism in reverse. Lexpert Magazine, 28 November 2016. http://www.lexpert.ca/article/protectionism-in-reverse/?p=&sitecode=lex. Accessed 14 May 2017

Nolan M (2016) Challenges to the credibility of the investor-state arbitration system. Am Univ Bus Law Rev 5:429–446

Norton P (1991) A law of the future or a law of the past? Modern tribunals and the international law of expropriation. Am J Int Law 85:474–505

Nussbaum A (1950) The arbitration between the Lena Goldfields, Ltd. and the Soviet government. Cornell Law Q 36:31–53

Pagden A (2006) The empire's new clothes: from empire to federation, yesterday and today. Common Knowl 12:36–46

Pahuja S (2011) Decolonising international law: development, economic growth and the politics of universality. Cambridge University Press

Paulsson J (2010) The power of states to make meaningful promises to foreigners. J Int Dispute Settlement 1:341–352

Puig S (2013) Emergence & dynamism in international organizations: ICSID, investor-state arbitration & international investment law. Georgetown J Int Law 44:531–608

Reisman M (1987) The cult of custom in the late 20th century. Calif West Int Law J 17:133–145

Salacuse J (2010) The emerging global regime for investment. Harv Int Law J 51:427–473

Sauvant KP (ed) (2009) Yearbook on international investment law & policy 2008–2009. Oxford University Press, New York

Sauvant KP (ed) (2013) Yearbook on international investment law & policy 2011–2012. Oxford University Press, New York

Schill S et al (eds) (2015) International investment law and development bridging the gap. Edward Elgar

Schreuer C (2005) Calvo's grandchildren: the return of local remedies in investment arbitration. Law Pract Int Courts Tribunals 4:1–17

Schrijver N (1997) Sovereignty over natural resources: balancing rights and duties. Cambridge University Press

Schwebel S (1963) The story of the U.N.'s declaration on permanent sovereignty over natural resources. Am Bar Assoc J 49:463–469

Schwebel S (2004) Investor-state disputes and the development of international law: the influence of bilateral investment treaties on customary international law. AJIL 98:27–30

Shemberg A (2009) Stabilization clauses and human rights. http://www.ifc.org/wps/wcm/connect/9feb5b00488555eab8c4fa6a6515bb18/Stabilization%2BPaper.pdf?MOD=AJPERES. Accessed 03 Dec 2016

Singh K, Ilge B (2016) Remodeling India's Investment Treaty Regime. The Wire, 16 July 2016. http://thewire.in/52022/remodeling-indias-investment-treaty-regime/. Accessed 03 Dec 2016

Sornarajah M (2004) The international law on foreign investment. Cambridge University Press

Steil B (2013) The Battle of Bretton Woods: John Maynard Keynes, Harry Dexter White, and the making of a new world order. Princeton University Press

Stevens P et al (2013) Conflict and coexistence in the extractive industries: a Chatham House report. https://www.chathamhouse.org/sites/files/chathamhouse/public/Research/Energy,%20Environment%20and%20Development/chr_coc1113.pdf. Accessed 03 Dec 2016

Strange S (1996) The retreat of the state: the diffusion of power in the world economy. Cambridge University Press

Supreme Court of Israel, High Court of Justice 4374/15, 7588/15, 8747/15, 262/16, The Movement for Quality Government v. The Prime Minister of Israel, Regarding the Gas Outline that was Prescribed in Government Decision 476 Summary of Judgment, dated 27 March 2016. http://elyon1.court.gov.il/files_eng/15/740/043/t63/15043740.t63.pdf. Accessed 03 Dec 2016

Texaco Overseas Petroleum Company v. The Government of the Libyan Arab Republic, award 19 January 1977. in ILM, 1978, at 1 et seq

The Economist, African economic growth: the twilight of the resource curse? (10 January 2015). http://www.economist.com/news/middle-east-and-africa/21638141-africas-growth-being-powered-things-other-commodities-twilight. Accessed 03 Dec 2016

UNCTAD (2000) Bilateral investment treaties 1959–1999

UNCTAD (2005) Economic development in Africa: rethinking the role of foreign direct investment. United Nations

UNCTAD (2008) World Investment Report 2007: transnational corporations, extractive industries and development

UNCTAD (2011) World Investment Report 2010: investing in a low-carbon economy. United Nations

UNCTAD (2016) World Investment Report 2015

UNECA (2016) Investment policies and bilateral investment treaties in Africa: implications for regional integration

UNGA Resolution 1803 (XVII) on the Permanent Sovereignty over Natural Resources, 14 December 1962

UNGA Resolution 3201 (S-VI), Declaration on the Establishment of a New International Economic Order (A/RES/S-6/3201, 1 May 1974)

UNGA Resolution 3281 (XXIX) on the Charter of Economic Rights and Duties of States (A/RES/29/3281, 12 December 1974

US Department of State (1941) The Atlantic Charter. http://avalon.law.yale.edu/wwii/atlantic.asp. Accessed 03 Dec 2016

Veeder V (1998) The Lena Goldfields arbitration: the historical roots of three ideas. Int Comp Law Q 47:747–792

Vernon R (1971) Sovereignty at bay: the multinational spread of US enterprises. Basic Books, New York

Wälde T (1983) Permanent sovereignty over natural resources: recent developments in the mineral sector. Nat Res Forum 7:239–251

Wälde T (2004) International standards in transnational investment & commercial disputes: the role of international standards, soft law, guidelines, voluntary and self-regulation in international arbitration, negotiation and other forms of dispute management: preliminary study, Transnational Dispute Management. https://www.transnational-dispute-management.com/article.asp?key=272. Accessed 03 Dec 2016

Wälde T, Ndi G (1996) Stabilizing international investment commitments: international law versus contract interpretation. Texas Int Law J 31:215–267

Weiler J (2015) European Hypocrisy: TTIP and ISDS, EJIL Talk (21 January 2015). http://www.ejiltalk.org/european-hypocrisy-ttip-and-isds/. Accessed 03 Dec 2016

Woolf L (2012) Empire and commerce in Africa: a study in economic imperialism. Forgotten Books, London

World Bank (1992) Strategy for African Mining (World Bank Technical Paper Number 181). http://documents.worldbank.org/curated/en/722101468204567891/Strategy-for-African-mining. Accessed 03 Dec 2016

World Bank (2009) The World Bank Group Program of Support for the Chad-Cameroon Petroleum Development and Pipeline Construction Program Performance Assessment Report (Report No 50315). http://www-wds.worldbank.org/external/default/WDSContentServer/WDSP/IB/2009/09/29/000333037_20090929000309/Rendered/PDF/503150PPAR0P05101Official0use0only1.pdf. Accessed 03 Dec 2016

Yager T et al (2012) The mineral industries of Africa: 2012 minerals yearbook. http://minerals.usgs.gov/minerals/pubs/country/2012/myb3-sum-2012-africa.pdf. Accessed 03 Dec 2016

Yergin D (1991) The prize: the epic quest for oil, money and power. Pocket Books

Melaku Geboye Desta is professor of International Economic Law, Leicester De Montfort University School of Law, De Montfort University, England, UK (currently on sabbatical), and Principal Adviser, Capacity Development Division, UNECA. Dr Desta has published widely in the fields of international economic law and policy in general and agriculture and natural resources in particular. Dr Desta has consulted for a number of international organisations and national governments and served as arbitrator in international disputes. All views expressed in this article are exclusively personal to the author and do not in any way reflect or represent the views of any institution with which he is associated at any time. This article builds on Melaku Geboye Desta, "Sovereignty over natural resources and international investment law: The elusive search for equilibrium", in Stephan W. Schill, Christian J. Tams and Rainer Hofmann (eds.), International Investment Law and Development Bridging the Gap (Edward Elgar, 2015), pp. 223–255. I am grateful to two anonymous peer reviewers for helpful comments.

The Global Goals: Formalism Foregone, Contested Legality and "Re-imaginings" of International Law

Duncan French

Abstract The Global Goals adopted in 2015 are the next phase in the UN's plans to tackle poverty and the systemic causes of under-development and other global problems. As with the previous Millennium Development Goals, the Global Goals are expressly political in nature. This paper considers the function, status and role of international law in global development and, in particular, how the Global Goals might be perceived in legal terms. The paper rejects the argument that they represent customary international law due to weaknesses in State practice and *opinio juris*, and is unpersuaded that it is helpful to categorise them as soft law as their purpose is aspirational and not regulatory. Thus, the Goals exist in an arena of contested legality. Two "re-imaginings" of international law are proposed; first, by connecting them to the non-binding Maastricht Principles on the Extraterritorial Obligations of States in the Area of Economic, Social and Cultural Rights and secondly, by linking them to ideas of international solidarity. The paper concludes that neither provides easy solutions. Nevertheless, what both do—in their own way—is to force us to question why international law is not viewed as an acceptable conduit for the advancement of global development?

> ...development is a mutually beneficial concept. The objective is to raise the tides and lift all boats. International law, with its unique structure and binding language, represents the levies, docks and canal works, channelling the waters and ensuring access and fair play for all involved.[1]

---

[1] de Serpa Soares (2015), p. 3.

D. French (✉)
University of Lincoln, Lincoln, UK
e-mail: dfrench@lincoln.ac.uk

1 Introduction

The United Nations General Assembly adopted the Sustainable Development Goals (SDGs)—more commonly known as the "Global Goals"—in September 2015[2] to run from 2016 to 2030, as the successor to the Millennium Development Goals (MDGs), which were to expire at the end of that year. The MDGs had, to some extent, and in some quarters, been a surprising success, certainly when contrasted against the low expectations many had placed in previous attempts by the UN to promote and support global development programmes and opportunities. The hope is that despite their differences—discussed in more detail below—the Global Goals will again resonate with (and within) the international community towards proactive and progressive implementation.

From the perspective of international law, however, the Global Goals—as with the MDGs—remain conceptually and programmatically indeterminate. Eschewing formal legal conceptualisation, the Global Goals remain outside the framework of normative rules and international legal processes. Though embedded and finding expression within the work-plans and strategies of the UN and other global and regional bodies (as well as non-governmental organisations), the Global Goals are not only explicitly political they are, more specifically and overtly, non-legal. While one might make a case to argue international organisations (especially those within the UN system) are required to act to support the Goals, the commitment of States towards them is much more difficult to categorise.

Whether the Goals might separately be construed as "soft law" is invariably part of the discourse, but that only takes us so far, as soft law often—and I would argue invariably—presupposes some movement of travel towards a level of bindingness, and it is unclear whether that it is even relevant in this context. What this paper therefore seeks to consider are certain broader normative questions; should the Global Goals be re-imagined as international law, what that might look like and how might that be distinct from what exists now? Two putative routes are considered; namely the recently proposed (non-binding) Maastricht Principles on the Extraterritorial Obligations of States in the Area of Economic, Social and Cultural Rights and the ongoing work of the Independent Expert on Human Rights and International Solidarity. Though there are genuine questions as to whether clearer normativity would make objectives such as the Global Goals more, or less, effective—many suspect the latter—there is perhaps a broader, more overarching, question of why should not they be binding? Why is not international law viewed as an acceptable conduit and process for advancement of global development priorities? Placing the quotation at the beginning into a question, is international law part of the international toolkit to 'raise the tides and lift all boats'?

---

[2]For information on the Global Goals, see http://www.globalgoals.org/.

2 Development, the MDGs and the Global Goals: False Starts and Winning Formulas?

The United Nations has international development as one of its core purposes, building on Article 1(3) of the Charter, which recognises the Organisation's pivotal role 'in solving international problems of an economic, social, cultural, or humanitarian character'. The Economic and Social Council, in particular, was established within the United Nations to promote and coordinate institutional action and intergovernmental discussion on, *inter alia*, development. Amongst the bodies and programmes established by States, or through the UN, over the years to consider these issues include the UN Development Programme (UNDP), the World Health Organization (WHO), the Food and Agriculture Organization (FAO), UNICEF (UN Children's Fund), and UNESCO (UN Educational, Scientific and Cultural Organization). Overseeing all of this is the General Assembly. In addition, the Bretton Woods institutions of the World Bank and the International Monetary Fund (IMF) and, somewhat later in development, the World Trade Organization (WTO)—connected to but outside the UN family of institutions—play key, if invariably controversial, roles in both the operational and strategic approach of the global effort towards tackling poverty and underdevelopment. Thus, despite or because of best efforts, institutional fragmentation and strategic in-fighting between institutions has always been a well-recognised feature of global development policy.[3]

It would prove moot to seek to elaborate on the variety of understandings and definitions of development provided over the years and the extent to which these interpretations say more about the internal politics of the authoring institution than the issue itself. Indeed, such definitions determine the parameters of the debate; perhaps no more evident than when development shifted in the middle 1980s onto new ground to incorporate an environmental dimension within the concept of sustainable development[4] to then shift further into more holistic understandings of social and human development, and human security.[5] And though much work has been done on bringing different interpretations together—largely down to the collaborative work around the MDGs—differences in focus and tone remain. So, for instance, whereas the present mission of the World Bank is to 'end extreme poverty within a generation and boost shared prosperity'[6] and that of the UNDP is not dissimilar ('Helping countries to achieve the simultaneous eradication of poverty and significant reduction of inequalities and exclusion'[7]), this is not to

---

[3]See various contributions in Boas and McNeill (eds) (2003).
[4]World Commission on Environment and Development (1987).
[5]UNDP (1994).
[6]http://www.worldbank.org/en/news/feature/2013/04/17/ending_extreme_poverty_and_promoting_shared_prosperity.
[7]http://www.undp.org/content/undp/en/home/librarypage/corporate/Changing_with_the_World_UNDP_Strategic_Plan_2014_17/.

ignore the much broader perspective of development endorsed by the General Assembly itself:

> Sustainable development recognizes that eradicating poverty in all its forms and dimensions, combating inequality within and among countries, preserving the planet, creating sustained, inclusive and sustainable economic growth and fostering social inclusion are linked to each other and are interdependent.[8]

Such understandings are, of course, far from being irreconcilable or mutually exclusive (and both the World Bank and the UNDP also endorse broader approaches to development to include environmental sustainability and social inclusion), but such differences in wording do nevertheless reveal a broader, and deeper, complexity; how to connect (and embed synergies between) the overarching objectives of poverty reduction and development promotion within particular institutional mandates and actions.

It is thus unsurprising that over the decades, the UN (both as an institution *per se* and as a forum for its members) has sought various means by which to tackle development, often in quite disparate ways. They have ranged from the adoption of so-called "decades of development"[9] (the term itself suggesting both the long-term endeavour of the mission and the frustration as one decade of development slipped into the next), the concerted (if acrimonious) attempt by the Global South to establish a New International Economic Order (NIEO),[10] through to now a seeming consensus around headline targets and measurable indicators. Simultaneously, the Bretton Woods institutions have evolved[11]; moving away from the dogmatic Washington Consensus of the 1980s, which represented a strategy and practice often at odds with the vision of the majority of its own developing country membership of the UN. This is a long, and often-repeated, story of global international development, of the imposition of neo-liberalism, tied aid and interference with host States. It has often been a story of international rhetoric *yet* substantive inactivity (or worse, ineffective activity) on development policy and praxis; of the paradox of emotive words combined with the absence of long-term strategy and consequently positive outcomes. The success that was achieved was often low-level, and the results of macro-projects funded through organisations such as the World Bank seemed hopelessly random, with huge social negative externalities often being as prominent as the benefits of such programmes.[12]

Also absent, from the perspective of the international lawyer, was any form of serious international legal engagement in such matters; the Bretton Woods institutions, for instance, have always sought to place their own activities within tightly-woven (and, as importantly, internal) systems of rules and processes, with as little scrutiny from external review—or general international law—as possible. The *quid*

---

[8]UNGA (2015), para. 13.
[9]Various (2011).
[10]Meagher (1979).
[11]Darrow (2003).
[12]Wendt (1999), pp. 149–162.

pro quo offered was that such institutions did not seek to intervene in the internal political affairs of the States in which they operated; the economic rationale of their mandate being a purely technocratic one. Change has come, but it often seems grudging and determined by—and at the pace of—the institutions themselves.

The governance of international trade has equally struggled with balancing the reciprocity of trade commitments with ensuring special and differential treatment for developing countries. The most recent WTO Ministerial Conference in Nairobi in December 2015 revealed a stark realism as to how far long-held hopes for the Doha "development" trade round were no longer driving its agenda,[13] in contrast to the fine words of previous meetings, and even as recently as September of the same year.[14] Regional and pan-regional trading blocs and preferential trade and investment agreements are becoming the increasingly dominant form of intergovernmental agreement,[15] raising not only the question as to the *raison d'être* of the WTO but fundamentally risking the objective of balanced development in trade negotiations.

Similarly, despite decades since the adoption of the Universal Declaration on Human Rights and the 1966 International Covenants on Civil and Political Rights, and Economic, Social and Cultural Rights, human rights law remains stubbornly outside the mainstream of development policy and operational activity.[16] As the Special Rapporteur on Extreme Poverty and Human Rights, Professor Philip Alston, noted in a damning 2015 report:

> For most purposes, the World Bank is a human rights-free zone. In its operational policies, in particular, it treats human rights more like an infectious disease than universal values and obligations. The biggest single obstacle to moving towards an appropriate approach is the anachronistic and inconsistent interpretation of the "political prohibition" contained in its Articles of Agreement. As a result, the Bank is unable to engage meaningfully with the international human rights framework, or to assist its member countries in complying with their own human rights obligations.[17]

This might, of course, be as much the fault of those with responsibility for the advancement of human rights as it is with those with a similar responsibility for development (a point Alston has also had the opportunity to make[18]), but nonetheless normative and institutional barriers as to *who* is responsible for *what* have proved incredibly difficult to breakdown. The 1986 UN Declaration on the Right to

---

[13]WTO (2015), para. 30: 'We recognize that many Members reaffirm the Doha Development Agenda, and the Declarations and Decisions adopted at Doha and at the Ministerial Conferences held since then, and reaffirm their full commitment to conclude the DDA on that basis. Other Members do not reaffirm the Doha mandates, as they believe new approaches are necessary to achieve meaningful outcomes in multilateral negotiations...'.

[14]UNGA (2015), para. 68: 'We call upon all members of the World Trade Organization to redouble their efforts to promptly conclude the negotiations on the Doha Development Agenda'.

[15]See, for instance, the adopted Trans-Pacific Partnership (TPP) and the ongoing negotiations between the US and the EU for a Transatlantic Trade and Investment Partnership (TTIP).

[16]Nevertheless, see Salomon (2007).

[17]Alston (2015), para. 68.

[18]Alston (2005), p. 827.

Development[19]—imperfect as it was—is thus perhaps not so much as anomaly in this area, as a missed opportunity for the General Assembly to take overall strategic responsibility for this issue.

Moreover, international aid ('official development assistance' (ODA)) and the "obligation" to bestow it remains outside the purview of international law. Political commitment to ODA has never found legal expression, though certain States have committed themselves to it within domestic law.[20] The extent to which solidarity and positive cooperation in the field of development have consistently failed to be the subject of normative explanation is mirrored only by the reality that globalising pressures and private resource often makes such public provision, however essential, of secondary importance.

For the international lawyer, overarching this is a realisation that the role of international law in development has traditionally been limited and nuanced. Not just that, but there is little sense of progression; of the gradual evolution of State practice and *opinio juris* that constitutes customary international rules on international development. As noted above, the NIEO was unduly partisan in nature and rejected with suspicion by developed States as one-sided, regardless of the existence or otherwise of any specific merits. Ultimately, it failed under the weight of its own expectations and the lack of political engagement by the United States and the European north. Various attempts have been made to identify and progressively develop legal rules that might frame a broader normative understanding of development—devised often at a non-governmental level[21]—but such arguments remain at best aspirational and perhaps, more notably, marginalised. The traditional response is that developed States will not provide assistance through compulsion; voluntarism is the best form of self-interest.

It was in this context that the General Assembly adopted the 2000 Millennium Declaration, including what subsequently became the Millennium Development Goals.[22] The eight MDGs were headline targets that it was hoped the international community of States, multilateral agencies and NGOs would coalesce around. Perhaps most prominently were the targets reducing extreme poverty by half, reducing child mortality of the under-fives by two-thirds and ensuring universal primary education for all. Though not without criticism,[23] sometimes strident, the MDGs have surpassed the relatively low expectations many had for them. In part, this was because the MDGs were both strategic yet not unduly prescriptive, two faults previously seen in global development policy. As the UN Secretary General

---

[19]UNGA (1986).

[20]See, for instance, as regards the UK: International Development (Official Development Assistance Target) Act 2015, section 1(1): 'It is the duty of the Secretary of State to ensure that the target for official development assistance (referred to in this Act as "ODA") to amount to 0.7% of gross national income (in this Act referred to as "the 0.7% target") is met by the United Kingdom in the year 2015 and each subsequent calendar year'.

[21]ILA (1986), pp. 1–11.

[22]UNGA (2000).

[23]Amin (2006); see also Alston (2005), pp. 762–768.

notes in his foreword to the 2015 Millennium Development Goals Report, worth quoting at length:

> The global mobilization behind the Millennium Development Goals has produced the most successful anti-poverty movement in history. The landmark commitment entered into by world leaders in the year 2000—to "spare no effort to free our fellow men, women and children from the abject and dehumanizing conditions of extreme poverty"—was translated into an inspiring framework of eight goals and, then, into wide-ranging practical steps that have enabled people across the world to improve their lives and their future prospects. The MDGs helped to lift more than one billion people out of extreme poverty, to make inroads against hunger, to enable more girls to attend school than ever before and to protect our planet. They generated new and innovative partnerships, galvanized public opinion and showed the immense value of setting ambitious goals. By putting people and their immediate needs at the forefront, the MDGs reshaped decision-making in developed and developing countries alike.[24]

A high degree of rhetoric, and in danger of transcending into hubris, but there is also a not insignificant element of truth. The MDGs have achieved results. As Bill Gates famously said, they were a 'report card that helps us judge our performance'.[25] It was in this spirit that the international community endorsed in 2012 at the Conference on Sustainable Development (the so-called Rio +20 summit) the beginnings of the work on the next stage. Noticeably, whereas the MDGs had been crafted privately by "experts" within the United Nations, the Sustainable Development Goals (as the Global Goals were initially (and still formally) called) were to be the subject of a 2 year consultative process, involving both States and non-governmental organisations.[26] This process—which, at times, risked becoming subject to the usual global problem of high expectations, and low achievement—emerged into the glare of media and political attention in late summer 2015, just prior to, and then during, the UN summit of world leaders.

Of particular concern had been that the Global Goals would become an unmanageable list of such wide-ranging, yet worthy, objectives that they would be incapable of either sensible implementation or of meaningful cross-cutting connectivity. To take one example, returned to later, there was a significant push by a broad group of organisations and agencies to include culture within the Global Goals, it being noted that the MDGs were noticeably absent in this regard. In and of itself, how could this be objected to? As the Declaration for the Inclusion of Culture states, 'We believe that culture is both a driver and enabler of sustainable development and that the explicit inclusion of targets and indicators for culture in the Sustainable Development Goals will enable transformative change'.[27] Surely it

---

[24] http://www.un.org/millenniumgoals/2015_MDG_Report/pdf/MDG%202015%20rev%20%28July%201%29.pdf.

[25] http://www.gatesfoundation.org/media-center/speeches/2008/09/bill-gates-speaks-at-the-united-nations.

[26] This paper develops on some earlier thoughts on the adoption of the Global Goals, contained in French (2015), pp. 77–79.

[27] http://www.culture2015goal.net/.

would not be wrong to recognise both the generic role of culture in this regard or, indeed, the contributions that different cultures make, thus ensuring critical engagement with different societies, groups and the under-represented in the Goals? Others worried that the simplicity and effectiveness of referencing only headline targets would be lost by seeking to be all-inclusive, of incorporating all interests and many agendas. Such examples of what to include (and to omit) were myriad and cross-cutting, but they often had one thing in common; a fear (real or imaginary) of what exclusion would mean. To return to the above declaration: 'If culture is not mentioned, it will be extremely difficult for countries to elaborate policies and provide funds for projects that rely on culture's role as a driver and an enabler of sustainable development'.

3 Global Goals: What Is Lost in All That Is Included?

Ultimately what transpired in *Transforming our World: the 2030 Agenda for Sustainable Development*,[28] the 'outcome document' of the summit—interesting language itself for an organisation that often likes to see things in terms of declarations—is a balance between what was wanted and what many feared. The Global Goals comprise 17 goals, 169 associated targets and more than 300 indicators of progress. Whether it was the scale of the global ambition required to achieve such various objectives or the spread that such objectives cover that justified the change in name from Sustainable Development Goals to Global Goals is not clear, though their remit is invariably more expansive than the MDGs. As the Outcome Document reflects:

> [t]his is an Agenda of unprecedented scope and significance. It is accepted by all countries and is applicable to all, taking into account different national realities, capacities and levels of development and respecting national policies and priorities. These are universal goals and targets which involve the entire world, developed and developing countries alike.[29]

Moreover, the Global Goals selected range significantly beyond the development priorities of the past—reducing poverty, mortality, hunger etc.—but expressly sought to tackle a broader panoply of issues; arguably to include much more systematically the underlying and systemic causes of unsustainable development, as broadly conceived. Perhaps more noticeably still—and as indicated by the above quotation—is the reach of the Global Goals. Whereas the MDGs were primarily objectives *of* the international community *for* the global South, the Global Goals are objectives both of, and for, the international community more generally. As has been noted, if with some over-generalisation: 'Poorer countries need to make the

---

[28]UNGA (2015).
[29]UNGA (2015), para. 5.

delivery of basic services such as health and education to all their citizens the priorities; emerging economies need to ensure safety and protect human rights; richer countries need to face up to the problems of affluence, such as obesity, and work on building tolerant societies; everyone has a long way to go on environmental sustainability'.[30]

It might be useful at this point to list the 17 Global Goals:

> (1) to end poverty in all its forms everywhere; (2) to end hunger, achieve food security and improved nutrition and promote sustainable agriculture; (3) to ensure healthy lives and promote well-being for all at all ages; (4) to ensure inclusive and equitable quality education and promote lifelong learning opportunities for all; (5) to achieve gender equality and empower all women and girls; (6) to ensure availability and sustainable management of water and sanitation for all; (7) to ensure access to affordable, reliable, sustainable and modern energy for all; (8) to promote sustained, inclusive and sustainable economic growth, full and productive employment and decent work for all; (9) to build resilient infrastructure, promote inclusive and sustainable industrialisation and foster innovation; (10) to reduce inequality within and among countries; (11) to make cities and human settlements inclusive, safe, resilient and sustainable; (12) to ensure sustainable consumption and production patterns; (13) to take urgent action to combat climate change and Its impacts; (14) to conserve and sustainably use the oceans, seas and marine resources for sustainable development; (15) to protect, restore and promote sustainable use of terrestrial ecosystems, sustainably manage forests, combat desertification, and halt and reverse land degradation and halt biodiversity loss; (16) to promote peaceful and inclusive societies for sustainable development, provide access to justice for all and build effective, accountable and inclusive institutions at all levels; and (17) to strengthen the means of implementation and revitalise the global partnership for sustainable development.

By anyone's reckoning, this is a significant list of goals. Whether they are sufficiently coherent and memorable to capture—and retain—global attention only time will tell. For critics, it is a shopping-list of idealism that reveals a chasm of political realism in the workings of the United Nations; a utopian view of what international bureaucracy can achieve.[31] For others, their principal fault will lie with not being ambitious enough. There are fault-lines everywhere; too much or too little State intervention required; too much or too little focus on private investment; and too much or too little attempt to connect the various thematic issues. And so one might go on.

Unlike the MDGs, there are some notable additions, recognising not only the clearer environmental foci of some of the goals (e.g. Goals 13–15) but also the more societally-transformative nature of some of the others (e.g. Goals 4, 5, 10 and 11). Moreover, unlike the MDGs, which were largely macro-targets achievable as much through national economic growth as national policy-making, many of the Global Goals will not be so easily reconciled with, or achieved through, a growth-alone

---

[30]Green (2015).

[31]Hickel (2015): 'The SDGs fail us on this. They offer to tinker with the global economic system in a well-meaning bid to make it all seem a bit less violent. But this is not a time for tinkering'.

approach to development. Targets around gender equality, biodiversity loss and access to justice (to name but three) will require clear, principled and overt strategic intervention and coordinated policies and partnerships. Growth alone with not solve these social issues; in fact, growth without well-considered public policies might make them more difficult to progress.

Nevertheless, a significant issue around all of the Goals is the scale of financial commitment required to ensure their effective implementation. Most assessments have indicated a commitment of several trillion US dollars per annum across domestic, international and private resources to turn the Goals into reality. The 2015 Addis Ababa Action Agenda for Financing for Development,[32] adopted before the Goals themselves, set out a plan (of sorts) to begin mobilising such resource though compromises and disagreements abounded on international tax reform, the clamping down on illicit financial flows and ensuring more equitable distribution of official (never mind private) investment within the global South. This document, like many before it, is replete with many of the right words but, in truth, resource (and action) rarely follows to the same extent.

It is perhaps pertinent here to pause and note the role (and absence) of law in not only achieving the Goals *per se* (something which is returned to) but also around the achievement of financing to support it. The Addis Ababa Action Agenda envisages law, to the extent that it is mentioned at all, as something akin to background fact, as an immovable framework that future programmes and initiatives must work within, as providing "rules of the game" but where the game itself remains unquestioned. Often it seems that there is little recognition that international law is created by the very States that are also negotiating how to resolve contemporary global challenges. Rarely are global rules considered enabling or sufficiently capable of transformative action to prompt or cause fundamental reform.[33] Law is thus both supremely important, yet contemporaneously viewed as marginal in relevance to global development.[34]

Two examples perhaps suffice. On the taxation of multinationals, for instance, the ability to change (or even strengthen) the law is hardly acknowledged; instead, law is seen as a restraint on the regulatory behaviour of any one State, so that it conducts its affairs 'in accordance with national and international laws and policies'.[35] No reference here to the weaknesses in, or limitations of, the present state of

---

[32] UN (2015).

[33] Moreover, as the former on UN Special Representative on Human Rights and Business Enterprises notes, traditional international legal norms are inapplicable directly to private enterprises (Ruggie 2006, para. 64: 'None of these changes, however, support the claim on which the Norms rest: that international law has transformed to the point where it can be said that the broad array of international human rights attach direct legal obligations to corporations, a claim that has generated the most doubt and contestation'). Of course, the Norms referred to were the controversial Draft Norms on the Responsibilities of Transnational Corporations and Other Business Enterprises with Regard to Human Rights (2003).

[34] This should not however ignore the role of private law in development (see, for instance, Rühmkorf 2015).

[35] UN (2015), para. 23.

the law. The contested and evolving nature of international agreements gives way to a fixed sense of normativity, in which the fundamental precepts are removed from, and not part of, the discourse.

Secondly, as regards sovereign debt—a hugely controversial issue—the wording of the document is even more instructive.

> ...We encourage countries, particularly those issuing bonds under foreign law, to take further actions to include [collective action] clauses in all their bond issuance. We also welcome provision of financial support for legal assistance to least developed countries and commit to boosting international support for advisory legal services. We will explore enhanced international monitoring of litigation by creditors after debt restructuring.
>
> We note the increased issuance of sovereign bonds in domestic currency under national laws, and the possibility of countries voluntarily strengthening domestic legislation to reflect guiding principles for effective, timely, orderly and fair resolution of sovereign debt crises.[36]

It is beyond the scope of this paper to consider these issues in anything like the detail they require and deserve.[37] Merely to note at this stage the passive role given to (domestic public) law (as well as the non-existence of international law); certainly in contrast to the primacy given to the assurance of contractual undertakings. To the extent that predatory behaviour of creditors is perceived as a problem, the extent of action is an exploration of future monitoring of litigation practices and patterns. The protection bestowed upon least developed countries is singularly apparent; it is restricted to legal assistance and advice. This is, of course, not to suggest that such initiatives are not constructive and helpful but rather the point is more generic; law as a tool of change is rarely part of the equation. Law is a given, a constraint or, where change is mooted, voluntary and soft. To change the structure, the law—the "rules of the game" themselves—is often viewed as a return to the partisan, and divisive, days of the New International Economic Order. Nevertheless, as Salomon pertinently notes,

> It would seem we need to turn our attention from the poor to the rich, from the victims to the beneficiaries, because it is only by addressing the apparatuses that sustain world privilege that we can understand and hope to confront the mechanisms that maintain world poverty. The adoption and enforcement of legal regimes have, and will continue to play, a critical role in this process.[38]

To thus return to the Global Goals themselves; the absence of law (broadly conceived) is not accidental, but is a clear and explicit attempt to de-legalise the targets.

The next part of this paper will consider some of the consequences that flow from this, and seek to re-imagine alternative scenarios. But it is important to note the chasm between the rhetoric and some very obvious omissions, most notably

---

[36] UN (2015), paras. 100–101.
[37] IMF (2014).
[38] Salomon (2008), pp. 72–73.

around human rights. As has been widely remarked upon, despite the increasing attempt to couple business, development and human rights in recent years,[39] the Global Goals are reflective of the MDGs in overtly failing to utilise human rights, and human rights language, in the text of their wording. Notwithstanding the universalism of human rights, the Global Goals are singularly shorn of their human rights implications, beyond the barest of references.[40] Putting to one side for the moment the myriad of interconnections between the Goals and economic, social and cultural rights (and indeed certain civil and political rights[41]), even as regards those Goals where it would seem almost impossible not to place the relevant Goal within its associated human rights framework, there is nothing.

Take, for instance, gender equality; much was made of how the Global Goals were a fundamental jump-forward in development policy (vis-à-vis the MDGs) on gender issues.[42] Despite this, there are no express references to human rights generally or, more specifically, the 1979 Convention on the Elimination of all Forms of Discrimination against Women. Similarly, despite the advances in recent years, references to non-discrimination still exclude LGBT considerations,[43] primarily at the insistence of various religiously-conservative States. Thus, to this extent, the Global Goals are a product and a representation of a conflicted international community as it both seeks to portray itself and, in reality, how it is.

It is thus both surprising (and simultaneously not surprising) to hear the UN Secretary General at the Human Rights Council in 2016 to say '[t]he 2030 Agenda for Sustainable Development is a major step forward for human rights.... The integrated, indivisible and universal nature of the 17 Sustainable Development Goals is deeply rooted in universal human rights'.[44] In a quixotic sense, the Global Goals are a manifestation of where human dignity leads, and what it obliges. But equally, as Alston noted so forcibly as regards the MDGs, 'language as well as context is important. The language of human rights cannot be systematically ignored if claims of human rights friendliness are to be accepted at face value'.[45] A similar argument could be made as regards the Global Goals; indeed, the international community does not seem to have moved on in the over 15 years since the inception of the MDGs.

---

[39] UN (2011).

[40] UNGA (2015), para. 19: 'We reaffirm the importance of the Universal Declaration of Human Rights, as well as other international instruments relating to human rights and international law. We emphasize the responsibilities of all States, in conformity with the Charter of the United Nations, to respect, protect and promote human rights and fundamental freedoms for all...'.

[41] For instance, Global Goal 16: Peace, Justice and Strong Institutions, which includes targets on violence and violence-related deaths, trafficking and torture of children, guaranteeing birth registration, and access to justice.

[42] Vogelstein (2015).

[43] http://www.stonewall.org.uk/sites/default/files/sdg-guide_2.pdf.

[44] http://www.un.org/apps/news/infocus/sgspeeches/statments_full.asp?statID=2946#.VzWxck10zIU.

[45] Alston (2005), p. 826.

4 The Global Goals and/as International Law: Hard, Soft or Re-imagined?

Transforming Our World is a paradoxical document when it comes to international law. On the one hand, it makes mention of—and with suitable deference to—international law.

> We will implement the Agenda for the full benefit of all, for today's generation and for future generations. In doing so, we reaffirm our commitment to international law and emphasize that the Agenda is to be implemented in a manner that is consistent with the rights and obligations of States under international law.[46]

This is one amongst a number of statements 'reaffirm[ing]', or highlighting that the Goals are 'guided by' or 'grounded in', international law or, more occasionally, certain named legal instruments.[47] But, as was noted above, a reference such as 'in a manner that is consistent with' both constrains as well as enables. It frames the available policy space without challenging the underlying structures. It is a phrase often used to deny or to discourage unilateralism, be that progressive or regressive in nature. It both provides continuity and assurance and, however implicitly, often a promise; a promise not to disturb the *status quo*. Development, if it is to occur, does so through a set pattern; characterised more often than not by aspirational yet self-interested voluntarism of the North, soft nudging of private enterprise and for the global South to follow certain demarcated policy pathways.

It is thus not surprising that the Global Goals are inherently political in nature; in the words of the document they are 'aspirational and global', thus it is left to each individual country to 'set[...] its own national targets guided by the global level of ambition but taking into account national circumstances'.[48] If there were any emerging view that the MDGs (limited as they were in number) were reflective of putative customary international law (and even as far back as 2005, Alston was prepared to go so far as to say that 'it can be observed that the case would be most easily made in relation to the first six of the Goals'[49]) it is difficult how the same could be said of the more numerous, and perhaps more disparate, Global Goals. Indeed, one of the criticisms of (some of) the goals is that they have lost much of the descriptive-cum-moral appeal in their attempt to be more inclusive.

How might one, for instance, understand, communicate, as well as reconcile, the various elements of Global Goal 9 ("To build resilient infrastructure, promote inclusive and sustainable industrialization and foster innovation")? The International Court of Justice in the *North Sea Continental Shelf Cases* noted that for something to be a rule of custom, it had to be of a 'fundamentally norm-creating

---

[46]UNGA (2015), para. 18.

[47]Instruments mentioned include the 1982 UN Convention on the Law of the Sea and the 2003 World Health Organization Framework Convention on Tobacco Control.

[48]UNGA (2015), para. 55.

[49]Alston (2005), p. 774.

character'.[50] While one might debate the extent of the State practice and *opinio juris* surrounding many of the MDGs, there was often at least a clarity of aim and purpose. It is less simply stated in respect of many of the Global Goals. To take Global Goal 9; what makes infrastructure 'resilient' or industrialisation 'inclusive and sustainable'?

And as regards those goals where the language would seem to at least allow for the possibility of greater normativity, at least at the "headline" level (e.g. Global Goals 14 and 15 on the conservation of maritime and terrestrial ecosystems), it would seem to be just that; a possibility. The Global Goals neither add to, nor detract, from broader debates on the customary status of environmental norms. Their inclusion as Global Goals may signal political importance in tackling the issues—heralded now not only as significant in and of themselves but as causes of poverty and underdevelopment—but the overt lack of legal commitment contained therein means they are a long way removed from indicating any extension of pre-existing normative obligations.

Some might point to the Goals to suggest a form of soft law being in evidence. For sure, not binding; but not completely optional either. If soft law as a workable concept is viewed as a means of incorporating objectives for States to work towards (and concurrently voluntary constraints upon discretionary State conduct) in a similar manner to, but distinct from, binding law,[51] do not the Global Goals have a similar effect? If one were to consider the monitoring and review mechanisms that developed around the MDGs,[52] with not dissimilar (with some hope stronger) processes to be established for the Global Goals, might not one see resonance with other soft law commitments? The level of accountability may fall short of that established by some international instruments—be that the reporting requirements under human rights law, the inspection/monitoring processes under such diverse regimes as anti-nuclear proliferation and certain environmental regimes, or the capacity of investor-state resolution under bilateral investment treaties (to name but three "types")—but soft law accountability by its very nature is often achieved as much through (the threat of) collective pressure as it is by formal scrutiny. Thus, when *Transforming Our World* talks of a 'robust, voluntary, effective, participatory, transparent and integrated' follow-up and review framework will make a vital contribution to implementation'[53]—a key part of which will be undertaken by the already established High-Level Political Forum on Sustainable Development (HLPF)[54]—surely it is not that different to how other soft law processes operate?

---

[50]ICJ, *North Sea Continental Shelf Cases* (1969) ICJ Rep 42.

[51]Boyle and Chinkin (2007), pp. 211–229.

[52]For general information see Millennium Development Goals Indicators, http://unstats.un.org/unsd/mdg/Host.aspx?Content=Indicators/About.htm.

[53]UNGA (2015), para. 72.

[54]The modalities for which were set out in UN A/RES/67/290 (2013), notably: 'that the high-level political forum, consistent with its universal intergovernmental character, shall provide political leadership, guidance and recommendations for sustainable development, follow up and review progress in the implementation of sustainable development commitments' (para. 2).

But notwithstanding the appearance of soft law, there is a significant stumbling block in the nomenclature of soft law in this instance. Soft law is not simply a non-binding way to achieve targets and to improve accountability, there is also something invariably iterative and transitional about soft law; it often requires a sense of movement towards, or at a least a contribution to, formal legality. As Boyle and Chinkin note, '[s]oft law is a multi-faceted concept, whose relationship to treaties, custom and general principles is both subtle and diverse. At its simplest soft law facilitates progressive evolution of international law'.[55] For instance, the development of soft codes of conduct that can be used as evidence of meeting a State's international obligations in international trade law, or litigating (for or against the use of) soft law principles in international courts and tribunals as nascent principles of customary international law, or utilising soft law instruments hoping that confidence will build to garner sufficient state endorsement to move to a legally binding agreement. Soft law may fall outside traditional descriptors of what is legally binding, but there is nevertheless an intention, however implicit, to regulate in the absence of law.

With the Global Goals, any contribution to formal legality, and any intention to regulate, is almost wholly missing. There are two quite contrary reasons for this. First, the rhetoric. The purpose of the Goals is—for want of a better phrase—to achieve the common good; they are neither prescriptive and regulatory (as much of soft law is) nor is there any obvious intention of moving towards such prescription and regulation. The numerous targets and indicators are certainly measurable (and thus there is a semblance of commonality between the Global Goals and soft law types) but the end-purpose is too idealised and idealistic to be captured by limited models of governance and regulation that soft law often acts as a proxy for. As *Transforming Our World* prosaically states

> In its scope, however, the framework we are announcing today goes far beyond the Millennium Development Goals. Alongside continuing development priorities such as poverty eradication, health, education and food security and nutrition, it sets out a wide range of economic, social and environmental objectives. It also promises more peaceful and inclusive societies.[56]

A second argument against soft law sits behind this, and is much more critical in nature. It is recognition that such Goals are not established to challenge the international community, but rather to make a 'rhetorical commitment'[57] for change. As Salomon comments as regards the MDGs, but the critique could—until contradicted—be held equally against the Global Goals: '[t]he Goals were not set up to address the structural conditions antagonistic to their achievement and they are now serving to advance the economic interests of wealthy states even under the guise of the humanitarianism of addressing world poverty'.[58] In short, the Goals

---

[55] Boyle and Chinkin (2007), p. 229.
[56] UNGA (2015), para. 17.
[57] Salomon (2008), p. 57.
[58] Idem.

are neither soft nor binding law not only because of the aspiration of their idealism but because of the politics of their construction and implementation. In short, to the extent that soft law merely foreshadows binding law, its application to the Global Goals is equally problematic.

But if the Global Goals were to be viewed, and were to be constructed, as legal norms, how might things look different? It is important to recognise that despite the mainstream rejection of legality, there is nevertheless a strongly held viewpoint prepared to acknowledge wider normative obligations on States in this area. This is achieved primarily by recognising, and giving meaningful effect, to the wording of such texts as the International Covenant on Economic, Social and Cultural Rights, Article 2(1) of which requires all States Parties 'to take steps, individually and through international assistance and cooperation, especially economic and technical, to the maximum of its available resources, with a view to achieving progressively the full realization of the rights recognized in the present Covenant by all appropriate means, including particularly the adoption of legislative measures'. This received further elaboration by the Committee on Economic, Social and Cultural Right's in which it was said

> The Committee wishes to emphasize that in accordance with Articles 55 and 56 of the Charter of the United Nations, with well-established principles of international law, and with the provisions of the Covenant itself, international cooperation for development and thus for the realization of economic, social and cultural rights is an obligation of all States. It is particularly incumbent upon those States which are in a position to assist others in this regard.[59]

Alston talked similarly in the midst of the MDGs of the emergence of an 'internationalization of responsibility'.[60] Nevertheless, whilst acknowledging the MDGs had the potential to change the tone of the debate, he was circumspect as to the likelihood, recognising that there is little practice, never mind consensus, to support the 'proposition that any given country is obligated to provide specific assistance to any other country'.[61] Of particular importance in this regard, but in equal measure controversial, was MDG 8, which required the elaboration of a global partnership for development. But again, the extent to which any such partnership between States and presumably other international actors could evolve from the cooperative to a level of compulsion is deeply problematic when viewed from both what States have said, and how they have historically agreed to work, on development.

Thus, we remain in the area of contested and putative legality. As de Serpa Soares notes, 'a major opportunity also exists for international law to engage at the conceptual heart of the matter'.[62] Though he does not do so, I want to propose two "re-imaginings"; neither of which are that far removed from mainstream

---

[59]CESCR (1990), para. 14.
[60]Alston (2005), p. 775.
[61]Alston (2005), p. 777.
[62]de Serpa Soares (2015), p. 5.

international law, but are nevertheless sufficiently distant from the present consensus to be worth creative consideration. The first is the work on the non-binding Maastricht Principles on the Extraterritorial Obligations of States in the Area of Economic, Social and Cultural Rights and secondly, is the work of the Independent Expert on Human Rights and International Solidarity. These are mere examples of where such normative arguments could in the future lead.[63]

4.1 Maastricht Principles on the Extraterritorial Obligations of State

The debate on respecting, protecting and fulfilling economic, social and cultural rights has been taken forward in a most interesting direction in recent years with the work of a group of experts in their personal capacity, leading to the 2011 Maastricht Principles on the Extraterritorial Obligations of States in the Area of Economic, Social and Cultural Rights.[64] Such principles build on other attempts, both within the Covenant system and elsewhere, to strengthen the implementation of such rights.[65] Key to the Principles is the conviction that States 'have repeatedly committed themselves to realizing the economic, social and cultural rights of everyone. This [is a] solemn commitment'.[66] There is insufficient space to outline in depth the Maastricht Principles in this paper, and the reader is encouraged to explore the Commentaries to the Principles. Nevertheless, certain of the fundamental propositions can be clearly outlined.

First, is the scope of jurisdiction, which is at the heart of the extraterritorial extension of duties owed to such rights. Relying on the jurisprudence of the International Court—if arguably not always directly on point—the Principles seek to demarcate the extraterritorial circumstances as to when a State may be under an obligation to secure socio-economic rights. As set down in Principle 9, quoted below:

Principle 9: Scope of Jurisdiction

A State has obligations to respect, protect and fulfil economic, social and cultural rights in any of the following:

---

[63] Note also de Serpa Soares himself who considers the institutional framework of international organisations as a key area for "growth" in international law, arguing that 'international law would help to ensure that development commitments are fulfilled by establishing institutions with mandates to assess compliance and generally-accepted set of criteria. Through such steps, international development law could move from the general and the technical to the operational – helping to fulfil the transformative development agenda' (de Serpa Soares 2015, p. 12).

[64] For the Principles and the Commentaries, see De Schutter, Eide, Khalfan, Orellana, Salomon, and Seiderman (2012) (hereinafter referred to as De Schutter et al.).

[65] For instance, the 1987 Limburg Principles on the Implementation of the International Covenant on Economic, Social and Cultural Rights (UN Doc. E/CN/4/1987/17/, Annex).

[66] De Schutter et al. (2012), preamble.

a) situations over which it exercises authority or effective control, whether or not such control is exercised in accordance with international law;

b) situations over which State acts or omissions bring about foreseeable effects on the enjoyment of economic, social and cultural rights, whether within or outside its territory;

c) situations in which the State, acting separately or jointly, whether through its executive, legislative or judicial branches, is in a position to exercise decisive influence or to take measures to realize economic, social and cultural rights extraterritorially, in accordance with international law.

Needless to say, while the Commentaries make every effort to substantiate the existence of such bases of jurisdiction, such circumstances are not without controversy. Even circumstance (a) (where a state 'exercises authority or effective control'), though this has been the subject of significant case law in recent years, and while it can be argued convincingly that in such a situation a State has obligations to respect and protect *all* rights, even here, most of the case law relied on is notably in the field of civil and political rights.[67]

Unsurprisingly, moving onto circumstances (b) and (c), these are much more contested. For instance, circumstance (b) applies to 'situations over which State acts or omissions bring about foreseeable effects'. While the Commentaries seek to rule out any outlandish or unworkable application of the scope of this circumstance, noting that '[b]ecause this element of foreseeability must be present, a state will not necessarily be held liable for all the consequences that result from its conduct',[68] nevertheless the Commentaries are notably lacking in state practice to justify jurisdiction in such context. Relying on *dicta* from international human rights courts and tribunals, it seems eminently true that there are situations in which States should—and must—promote and support the fulfilment of socio-economic rights of other populations in how they act, even where they are not in territorial or effective control. But what seems eminently true does not *per se* make it legally binding. One might, for instance, think of how national foreign aid programmes should be operated in a way to promote particular objectives (or, in reverse, not to apply it in a discriminatory manner); we might even argue that States have a duty of due diligence to have considered such issues in developing their programmes. But as a matter of jurisdiction, is international law sufficiently advanced to develop a proposition that the 'foreseeable effects' of such actions brings with it obligations? A legally binding good neighbour principle, as it were, writ-large?

---

[67]For instance, the Commentaries refer to the ICJ judgments in *Advisory Opinion on the Legal Consequences of the Construction of a Wall in the Occupied Palestinian Territory* (2004) and *Democratic Republic of the Congo v Uganda* (2005), both specifically relating to the International Covenant on Civil and Political Rights.

[68]De Schutter et al. (2012), p. 1109.

Similarly, circumstance (c) imposes jurisdiction when a state (by itself or in concert) is 'in a position to exercise decisive influence or to take measures to realize' such rights. Again, this may seem unquestionable from a moral point of view[69]; and to the extent that such obligations are tied to the general obligation on States under Article 2(1) ICESCR to cooperate there is clear treaty support for it. Nevertheless 'decisive influence' as a concept here seems unduly wide in scope, building on notions on economic capacity and, what the Committee on Economic, Social and Cultural Rights, sees as those states 'which are in a position to assist others'.[70] Moreover converting soft legal aspiration (as unfortunately many States see General Comments to be) into concrete legal obligations is a significant step.

It is important to be clear what I am not saying here. I am not dismissing these Principles out-of-hand. Nor am I suggesting they may not have a significant role to play. But rather to indicate the rather paradoxical linkage—and disconnect—from present international law. With all the best putative claims to international law, there is always significant coherence between new claims and the current law. Nevertheless, notwithstanding its foundation in binding human rights law, and the Principles own claim that they clarify the content of pre-existing law rather than being progressive development[71]—there is such a chasm between where States now lie and what the Principles enunciate that one but cannot consider them as *de lege ferenda* in many important respects, however worthy they in fact do appear.

The idea that States are under certain global responsibilities to ensure the human rights of all are protected and, in certain cases, fulfilled is not unreasonable, if however uncertain. The extraterritorial impact of policies and measures in the field of trade, investment and finance especially has long been recognised but little has been done to address the issues.[72] The usual territorial limitations on jurisdiction and a general unwillingness to accept responsibility for anything other than the direct consequences for direct State action (and even then, as the jurisprudence on the jurisdictional scope of the European Convention on Human Rights has revealed, in a rather piecemeal way[73]) has left a rather substantial vacuum at the heart of human rights law.

To that extent, the Maastricht Principles—of which a few more of its key provisions are set out below as mere exemplars of the scope of this ambition—invariably push forward an ambitious agenda of international obligations for both States and other international actors; or to use Alston's phrase (though unconnected with this work) the 'internationalisation of responsibility'.

---

[69] Cf. French (2009) 600.

[70] CESCR (1990), para. 14.

[71] Nevertheless, see the discussion on variations in State acceptance of such obligations in De Schutter et al. (2012), p. 1094.

[72] See, for instance, the work of the Human Rights Independent Expert on the effects of foreign debt and other related international financial obligations of States on the full enjoyment of all human rights, particularly economic, social and cultural rights (http://www.ohchr.org/EN/Issues/Development/IEDebt/Pages/IEDebtIndex.aspx).

[73] See Milanovic (2012).

Principle 20. Direct interference

All States have the obligation to refrain from conduct which nullifies or impairs the enjoyment and exercise of economic, social and cultural rights of persons outside their territories.

Principle 21. Indirect interference

States must refrain from any conduct which:

a) impairs the ability of another State or international organization to comply with that State's or that international organization's obligations as regards economic, social and cultural rights; or

b) aids, assists, directs, controls or coerces another State or international organization to breach that State's or that international organization's obligations as regards economic, social and cultural rights, where the former States do so with knowledge of the circumstances of the act.

Of particular interest also in the Maastricht Principles is the recognition that where obligations exist, so does accountability (Principle 36) and the necessity of effective redress (Principle 37). Together, they form a set of principles which seek to take a significant stride forward in how seriously States should take their social and economic international obligations, both domestically and extraterritorially.

Nevertheless, the Maastricht Principles are, at their heart, premised on traditional conceptions of human rights—recognising the singular importance of the individual and, in some cases, the group as the rights-holder—even if their application ranges beyond the normal scope of jurisdiction ordinarily envisaged, or perhaps more accurately, accepted. As an attempt to move the debate away from the increasingly sterile conversations around third generational rights, for instance the human right to development, and towards effective implementation of what already exists, the Principles are to be considered an important step forward.

For the purposes of the Global Goals, there is of course the fundamental issue of assimilation with human rights; are the Goals to be considered sufficiently equivalent to human rights to be equally worthy of extraterritorial protection? The Commentary to the Maastricht Principles is instructive on this point, referencing together—if not invariably equating—human rights and what it views as 'multilaterally agreed goals', in this case the MDGs.

> The *erga omnes* character of human rights may justify allowing the exercise by states of extraterritorial jurisdiction, even in conditions that might otherwise not be permissible, where such exercise seeks to promote such rights. Similarly, the realization of the MDGs is of interest to all states. Therefore, extraterritorial jurisdiction seeking to promote human rights, or the achievement of the MDGs, is not a case where one state seeks to impose its values on another state, as in other cases of extraterritorial jurisdiction.[74]

---

[74]De Schutter et al. (2012), p. 1142.

Critics might rightly point to a too easy conflation of treaty-based rights and political targets to make a somewhat startling claim to a settled basis of jurisdiction.[75] Nevertheless, it is without question that the domestic and regional implementation of many of the Goals will be affected by the actions of a number of, especially the most economically powerful, States. What the Maastricht Principles raise is the question of whether we should begin to attach much more directly formal responsibility and legal accountability to such actions to what Principle 9 refers to as such States' 'decisive influence'.

4.2 Global Solidarity as the Unspoken Ideal in Global Development

The second re-imagining of the Global Goals through (a particular lens of) international law is that whilst acknowledging the benefits, but also the limitations, of a traditional human rights approach to development (as ultimately the Maastricht Principles seeks to present), it is also possible to view things at an even higher (more macro-) level. Of course, this is likely to encounter much (if not more) of the same criticism, mentioned above, namely: codifying aspiration, indeterminacy and conflating political choices and normative obligations. Nevertheless, if one is to query the structure of the status quo, there is perhaps scope for deeper contestation of that which we take for granted? Of particular interest is the work of the Independent Expert on Human Rights and International Solidarity,[76] who has been working on a draft declaration on this matter to be put to the General Assembly. In its most recent formulation, international solidarity is defined as follows:

> International solidarity shall be understood as the convergence of interests, purposes and actions between and among peoples, individuals, States and their international organizations in order to preserve the order and ensure the very survival of international society and to achieve common goals which require international cooperation and collective action, based on the international normative system of duties which they implement and practise to foster peace and security, development and human rights.

> International solidarity shall be made evident in the collective actions of States that have a positive impact on the exercise and enjoyment of human rights by peoples and individuals within and outside of their respective territories, notably in the ratification of the United Nations international human rights treaties and international labour standards and the

---

[75]For a potentially interesting example of this already as regards the Global Goals and human rights law, see the 2016 Concluding Observations on the Committee on the Rights of the Child on the UK's fifth periodic report, in which rights under the relevant Convention and the Global Goals are grouped together. For instance, see para. 12: 'In accordance with article 4 of the Convention and Sustainable Development Goal 10, Targets 10.2 and 10.4, the Committee urges...'.

[76]See generally: http://www.ohchr.org/EN/Issues/Solidarity/Pages/IESolidarityIndex.aspx.

adoption of commitments and decisions agreed upon voluntarily between and among States at the regional and international levels.[77]

There are, of course, some notable similarities with the work of the Maastricht Principles, especially the obligations on States to work towards the good of all 'within and outside of their respective territories'. What is perhaps different is the purpose of that cooperation; not aimed at the attainment of individual rights *per se* but rather 'to preserve the order and ensure the very survival of international society and to achieve common goals'. It is a view of the international community that is to some unfathomable, whereas for others it is intrinsic to the values and purposes inherent within the United Nations. It is high rhetoric, and unsurprisingly finds deep connections with much of the preambular references in *Transforming Our World*; ideas of co-existence, collaboration and common good. If the Maastricht Principles bends previous understandings of human rights obligations to promote new ideas of jurisdiction, responsibility and accountability, solidarity is undoubtedly more societally transformative in outlook. Whilst not undermining sovereignty—which is part of the paradox that solidarity invariably contains (how to protect and maximise domestic space whilst simultaneously seeking to achieve a common purpose?)— these ideas nevertheless reflect a fundamental challenge to the present order.

More specifically, and for the purposes of re-imagining the normativity of the Global Goals this is vital, solidarity moves away from voluntarism towards a clearer sense of legal obligation and legal entitlement.

> International solidarity is a broad principle not limited to international assistance and cooperation, aid, charity or humanitarian assistance, and that it includes sustainability in international relations, especially international economic relations, the peaceful coexistence of all members of the international community, equal partnerships and the equitable sharing of benefits and burdens.[78]

This is a call-to-arms to revisit structural privileges and entrenched poverty. The Draft Declaration sees as one of its fundamental principles as being 'equitable, just and fair partnerships of States as the basis of international cooperation'.[79] Placing the Global Goals in the context of international solidarity, one is thus immediately struck by some of the similarity in ideas and words. This is particularly with reference to Global Goal 17, which focuses on "Partnerships for the Goals" just as the final Millennium Development Goal, MDG 8 sought to "[d]evelop a Global Partnership for Development". The targets associated with Global Goal 17 range widely but are broadly framed around finance, technology, capacity-building, and trade. Of course, international collaboration is to be found in all the Goals and not simply Global Goal 17. Particularly interesting are certain targets in Global Goal 10 ("Reducing Inequalities") and Global Goal 16 ("Peace, Justice and Strong Institutions"), which include, *inter alia*, targets on prioritising international aid, further implementing special and differential treatment for developing countries

---

[77]Dandan (2014), pp. 17–18.

[78]Dandan (2014), p. 16.

[79]Dandan (2014), p. 18.

(particularly towards least developed countries) on matters of trade, and tackling illicit financial flows and corruption.

Nevertheless, just as with MDG 8, the new goal of partnerships struggles with various innate tensions, arguably central to its attainment. First, how to balance global governance ('enhanc[ing] global macroeconomic stability, including through policy coordination and policy coherence'[80]) with sovereign discretion ('respect[ing] each country's policy space and leadership to establish and implement policies for poverty eradication and sustainable development'). Secondly, reconciling the public and regulatory objectives of Global Goal 17 with the more limited capacity of States to "nudge" the private and corporate interests behind many of these pressures. And thirdly, how to understand the role of civil society, which is both promoted within the Global Goals and is curiously muted (invariably as a response to various countries' domestic restrictive approaches to civil society involvement). It is within these tensions that the expected partnerships have already, and will continue, to operate.

But there is a more fundamental tension at play here. There would seem to be a discordance between the targets set—however worthy—and the goal itself. In short, Global Goal 17, just as with MDG 8, can be viewed as operating on two very distinct levels; with each level rhetorically, but only superficially substantively, actually connecting. On one level, are the targets set; for instance on the transfer of technology, capacity building and debt sustainability. To the extent that these undoubtedly further the Global Goals, they are instrumental in identifying and giving effect to particular means of implementation. But what they are not, and what they do not achieve, is the second level, which might be referred to, more conceptually, as a global partnership properly-conceived. Such targets, however utile, are far removed from guaranteeing what the Draft Declaration refers to as 'equitable, just and fair partnerships of States as the basis of international cooperation'—and arguably in their random selection are even some way from the slightly less aspirational title of Global Goal 17 itself. In short, the targets of Global Goal 17 have little connexion to securing the structural global change envisaged by the ambitious idealism inherent within international solidarity.

This is not the first attempt, of course, where claims have been made to establish a stronger *legal* basis for international partnership. In addition to the intergovernmental moves to establish a New International Economic Order, the International Law Association sought to promulgate legal principles which might provide a basis on which such a new understanding of international law would operate. Some of these principles included well-established rules of permanent sovereignty over natural resources and non-discrimination and other more aspirational notions of participatory equality, substantive equality and the principle of equity.[81] Similar ideas are at the heart of the current work on international solidarity. As I concluded

---

[80]Viewed as "Systemic Issues" under Global Goal 17.
[81]ILA (1986), pp. 1–11.

following a study of those principles, but it would seem to apply more generally to the theme of international solidarity;

> A sounder argument is to consider [such] documents...as containing useful pointers – if not, in some instances, also measurable signposts – towards the achievement of longer-term goals, in this case arriving 'at a just balance between converging and diverging interests and in particular between the interests of developed and developing countries', which must be considered foundational to the functioning not only of an equitable economic system but also, in the light of changing expectations, a sustainable international community, more generally. But being longer-term makes such objectives no less important.[82]

Nevertheless, realism is equally important. It is important to recognise that despite international solidarity having significant moral appeal, as a legal obligation much remains uncertain. Scobbie is particularly insightful when he notes: 'Can a sufficient solidarity easily be assumed, or would the rejection of a Vattelian worldview risk the emergence of a (greater) world-anarchy? Even within territorial units, would social cohesion be maintained?'.[83] Even if one were not to envisage crisis rather than harmony as the consequence of solidarity, progressive movement towards the goal requires confronting a conundrum as yet unresolved in international polity; 'whatever autonomous normative authority (be it even of a rhetorical kind) one may believe international law to possess – it does not yet have a mandate to coerce states to accept that to which they do not voluntarily subscribe'.[84]

5 Conclusion

The Global Goals would seem to be a momentous achievement for the international community. First, they are an endorsement of an approach to development that the UN has finally found some global traction—with member states, partner institutions and socially aware private enterprise, building on the overall, though by no means absolute, success of the MDGs. Secondly, the Global Goals themselves are notable in several key respects; in their creation, in their scope and in their scale of ambition. The UN has an aspirational agenda of huge proportions over the next 15 years; and, as noted above, unlike some of the MDGs which were achieved by proxy via improvements in GDP, most of the Global Goals are linked to more nuanced changes in policy, institutional structures and consumer and industrial behaviour. There are arguably fewer "quick fixes" in the Global Goals.

For the international lawyer, however, the Global Goals present something of a conundrum. They are not legally binding, nor are they written in legal text. They may, of course, involve changes, or require the implementation, of the law. But equally they may not. As noted above, law is often regarded as a fact—a fixed

---

[82] French (2008), p. 32, quoting ILA (1986), p. 5.
[83] Scobbie (2005), p. 312.
[84] French (2012), p. 701.

framework—through which the Goals must work; occasionally it might also be viewed as a useful tool. But in both cases, law is perceived in instrumental terms and for particular purposes. For those who want to envisage the Global Goals as having greater normative force in international law, the scope for discourse seems much more limited.

Of course, the clearest way to view the Global Goals as international law would be to argue that they have, or are working towards, customary status. Certainly, arguments of a similar kind were made towards the MDGs. Regardless of whether that was true of the previous goals, I am simply unconvinced that this is possible for many of the Global Goals. Setting aside, at present, how far States will actively and consistently work towards making such Goals a reality (the "State practice"), I have little sense that one would be able to deduce acceptance from what States do or how they discuss the Goals (the "*opinio juris*"). For me, looking for customary status is an interesting endeavour, but unlikely to be productive. Moreover, Global Goals are not like those general principles of international law or norms of *jus cogens*, which are invariably upheld in treaties, official documentation and speeches, and thus is said to compensate for variable State practice. The prohibition on torture, for instance. Global Goals are overtly, and remain, in the political sphere.

And for me, this also prevents an argument that such Goals are emerging as soft law. For proponents, soft law may appear a rather neat way to tackle the lack of present bindingness in the Global Goals, while still wanting to give them normative credence. But as I discuss, what makes soft law from a legal perspective is not *per se* the fact that it is official yet not binding, but that there is paradoxically an intention to regulate in the absence of law. Moreover, much soft law is on a journey to some form of "hardness"; it is invariably this transitional stage which makes soft law usable from a lawyer's perspective. In respect of both of these criteria, the Global Goals fall down. They are neither designed to be regulatory nor is it particularly apparent that they are progressing towards bindingness. Thus, the question becomes what relevance the nomenclature of soft law, other than a neat (if unhelpfully generalised) categorisation?

This leaves open a range of possibilities; to abandon law or to embrace alternatives. Above, the paper poses two re-imaginings—both putative in nature; developing the extraterritorial extent of the present law and, more radically, embracing a normative approach to international solidarity. As identified, neither are susceptible to providing easy solutions to global problems. Not only because they raise questions of positive law—which is surely inherent in the nature of a re-imagining—but also because they can be questioned as to how practicable they might turn out to be. For developed States, in particular, where voluntarism determines much development activity, it is extremely unlikely that either more expansive interpretations of pre-existing obligations (Maastricht Principles) or a more holistic account of global partnership (international solidarity) will find favour. Nevertheless, what both do—in their own way—is to force us to question the relevance of international law in the pursuit of development. Why is international law not viewed as an acceptable conduit and process for advancement of global development? International lawyers are still some way off from formulating—and persuading others of—a convincing response to this question; and perhaps we need to do this before we enter into our own (often internal and self-referential) dialogues of which of the differing "routes" to legality are found to be the more persuasive.

But in being cautious moving forward, let us not reject such re-imaginings as the stuff of childish things. As Allott has so forcefully argued:

> we found within ourselves another capacity, the capacity to form the idea of the ideal — the idea of a better human future which we can choose to make actual...To overcome the tyranny of the actual, to overcome the ignorant and infantile belief that the actual self-organising of humanity is necessary and inevitable, we need only recall and recover our extraordinary power constantly to re-conceive the ideal, in order yet again to choose to make it actual.[85]

Acknowledgments I thank the editors of the Yearbook, the anonymous reviewers and Dr. Graham Melling for the insightful observations on a draft of this paper.

References

Allott P (1999) The concept of international law. Eur J Int Law 10:31–50
Alston P (2005) Ships passing in the night: the current state of the human rights and development debate seen through the lens of the millennium development goals. Hum Rights Q 27:755–829
Alston P (2015) Report of the Special Rapporteur on extreme poverty and human rights (4 August 2015) UN Doc. A/70/274
Amin S (2006) The millennium development goals: a critique from the south. Mon Rev 57. http://monthlyreview.org/2006/03/01/the-millennium-development-goals-a-critique-from-the-south/
Boas M, McNeill D (eds) (2003) Global institutions and development: framing the world? Routledge, London
Boyle A, Chinkin C (2007) The making of international law. Oxford University Press, Oxford
CESCR (1990) General Comment 3 ('The Nature of States Parties Obligations (Art. 2 par. 1)') (14 December 1990) UN Doc. E/1991/23
Committee on the Rights of the Child (2016) Concluding observations on the fifth period report of the United Kingdom of Great Britain and Northern Ireland (3 June 2016) UN CRC/C/GBR/CO/5
Dandan V (2014) Report of the Independent Expert on human rights and international solidarity (1 April 2014) UN Doc. A/HRC/26/34
Darrow M (2003) Between light and shadow: the World Bank, the International Monetary Fund and international human rights law. Hart, Oxford
De Schutter O, Eide A, Khalfan A, Orellana M, Salomon M, Seiderman I (2012) Commentary to the Maastricht principles on extraterritorial obligations of states in the area of economic, social and cultural rights. Hum Rights Q 34:1084–1169
de Serpa Soares M (2015) Room for growth: the contribution of international law to development. Chin J Int Law 14:1–13

---

[85] Allott (1999), p. 50.

French D (2008) 'From Seoul with love': the continuing relevance of the 1986 Seoul ILA declaration on progressive development of public international law relating to a new international economic order. Neth Int Law Rev 55:3–32

French D (2009) Global justice and the (ir)relevance of indeterminacy. Chin J Int Law 8:593–619

French D (2012) International development law in the spirit of solidarity: a personal view on the "International Law of the Ordinary". In: Morin M, Cordonier Segger M-C, Gélinas F, Gehring M (eds) Responsibility, fraternity and sustainability in international law. LexisNexis, Ontario, pp 687–701

French D (2015) Editorial: the 2015 global goals: the (present) world is not enough. Environ Liabil 23:77–79

Green M (2015) Just getting richer is not going to get us to the global goals. http://www.theguardian.com/global-development-professionals-network/2015/oct/08/just-getting-richer-is-not-going-to-get-us-to-the-global-goals-economic-growth

Hickel J (2015) The problem with saving the world. https://www.jacobinmag.com/2015/08/global-poverty-climate-change-sdgs/

ILA (1986) Declaration on the progressive development of principles of public international law relating to a new international economic order. International Law Association (ILA), London

IMF (2014) Strengthening the contractual framework to address collective action problems in sovereign debt restructuring. http://www.imf.org/external/np/pp/eng/2014/090214.pdf

Meagher R (1979) International redistribution of wealth and power: a study of the charter of economic rights and duties of states. Pergamon Press, New York

Milanovic M (2012) Al-Skeini and Al-Jedda in Strasbourg. Eur J Int Law 23:121–139

Millennium Development Goals Indicators. http://unstats.un.org/unsd/mdg/Host.aspx?Content=Indicators/About.htm

Ruggie J (2006) Interim report of the special representative of the secretary-general on the issue of human rights and transnational corporations and other business enterprises (UN Doc. E/CN.4/2006/97)

Rühmkorf A (2015) Corporate social responsibility, private law and global supply chains. Edward Elgar, Cheltenham

Salomon M (2007) Global responsibility for human rights: world poverty and the development of international law. Oxford University Press, Oxford

Salomon M (2008) Poverty, privilege and international law: the millennium development goals and the guise of humanitarianism. Ger Yearb Int Law 51:39–74

Scobbie I (2005) Slouching towards the Holy City: some weeds for Philip Allott. Eur J Int Law 16:299–313

UN (2011) Guiding principles on business and human rights: implementing the United Nations "Protect, Respect and Remedy" Framework (UN Human Rights Office of Human Rights Commissioner) UN Doc. A/HRC/17/31 (endorsed by the Human Rights Council in HRC resolution 17/4 (16 June 2011))

UN (2015) Addis Ababa Action Agenda of the third international conference on financing for development. https://sustainabledevelopment.un.org/index.php?page=view&type=400&nr=2051&menu=35

UNDP (1994) Human development report: new dimensions of human security. http://hdr.undp.org/en/content/human-development-report-1994

UNGA (1986) Declaration on the Right to Development (4 December 1986). UN Doc. A/RES/41/128

UNGA (2000) United Nations Millennium Declaration (8 September 2000). UN Doc. A/RES/55/2 UNGA

UNGA (2015) Transforming our world: the 2030 agenda for sustainable development (21 October 2015) UN Doc. A/RES/70/1

Various (2011) Five decades of development debate on sustainability. Development 54:271–281

Vogelstein R (2015) Gender equality and the global goals. http://blogs.cfr.org/women-around-the-world/2015/10/06/gender-equality-and-the-global-goals/

Wendt N (1999) 50th anniversary of the World Bank and the IMF prompts criticisms. Transl Law Contemp Probl 9:149–162
World Commission on Environment and Development (1987) Our common future. Oxford University Press, Oxford
WTO (2015) Nairobi Ministerial Declaration. https://www.wto.org/english/thewto_e/minist_e/mc10_e/mindecision_e.htm

Duncan French is Head of School and Professor of International Law, University of Lincoln, United Kingdom.

Developing Countries Under the International Climate Change Regime: How Does the Paris Agreement Change Their Position?

Olivia Woolley

Abstract The article considers how the Paris climate change agreement of December 2015 alters the position of countries regarded as 'developing' under the international climate change regime. It does this by comparing their position (both as contributors to the global response to climate change and as recipients of support under the Framework Convention on Climate Change and the Kyoto Protocol) with that under the Paris Agreement in the main areas of action by the international community to combat climate change. The article finds that there has been little change in some respects with the obligations of developing states to mitigate climate change and of developed states for the provision of climate finance and technology transfer not having altered significantly. Where the position of developing countries has changed markedly is in the clear expectation, expressed in several non-binding statements, that they should contribute to mitigating climate change alongside their developed counterparts with their contribution increasing progressively in line with the aspirational collective mitigation goal of zero net emissions during the second half of this century; and in the imposition of more exacting obligations to report on their actions with greater potential for pressure from peers and civil society to improve on their contributions as a result. In addition, adaptation, loss and damage, and capacity building are all given a higher profile in line with developing country demands during climate change negotiations that they should be given more weight.

1 Introduction

The international climate change regime was established in 1992 by the adoption by a large majority of the world's states of the United Nations Framework Convention on Climate Change (hereafter 'the Convention').[1] The Convention places high level

---

[1] United Nations Framework Convention on Climate Change (adopted on 29 May 1992, entered into force on 21 March 1994) 1771 UNTS 107 (FCCC).

O. Woolley (✉)
School of Law, University of Aberdeen, Aberdeen, UK
e-mail: olivia.woolley@abdn.ac.uk

obligations on its parties to mitigate and contribute in other respects to efforts to combat climate change.[2] Their generality reflects the need to achieve compromise between parties calling for detailed commitments on emissions reduction and those accepting the need to respond to climate change but preferring flexibility when deciding on how to do so.[3] It was quickly recognised that the vague obligations for cutting emissions placed on the mostly developed country parties listed in Annex I of the Convention by Article 4(2) of the Convention would have to be strengthened to make a meaningful contribution to the Convention's goal of preventing dangerous anthropogenic interference with the climate.[4] Resulting negotiations led to the adoption of the Kyoto Protocol (hereafter 'the Protocol') in 1997 under which the Convention's Annex I states (included in Annex B in the Protocol) made commitments to achieve specified levels of greenhouse gas emission reductions within the commitment period 2008–2012.[5]

Both the Convention and the Protocol distinguish sharply between states regarded as developed and developing. The former bear obligations exclusively for achieving overall cuts in emissions, and are expected to lead the way on responding to climate change in light of their historic responsibility for significantly increasing risks of climate change from two centuries of economic growth based on fossil fuel consumption, and to the possession of the financial resources required to combat climate change as a result of this.[6] The developing country parties also have obligations to mitigate climate change, but are not bound to make overall cuts in emissions. Indeed, as discussed in greater depth in Sects. 2 and 3 below, they have an ill-defined licence to increase their greenhouse gas emissions in connection with economic and social development.

This split in responsibilities for mitigating climate change was grudgingly accepted by developed states when the Convention and Protocol were negotiated, but became increasingly unacceptable to many of them, particularly the U.S., because of the rapid fossil fuel driven economic growth of some developing states, most notably China, India, Mexico, Indonesia, South Korea and Brazil. This placed them in the ranks both of the world's largest economies and its leading greenhouse gas emitters, but without obligations to achieve overall emissions cuts or to contribute to the global climate change response in other respects.[7] Discontent with the allocation of responsibilities for combating climate change manifested

---

[2] For an overview of the Convention and its provisions see Sands et al. (2012), pp. 276–283.
[3] Ibid., pp. 275–276.
[4] Ibid., 283–284.
[5] Kyoto Protocol to the United Nations Framework Convention on Climate Change (adopted on 10 December 1997, entered into force on 16 February 2005) FCCC/CP/1997/7/Add.1 (Kyoto Protocol).
[6] For fuller discussion of reasons for differentiation between the obligations of developed and developing country parties under the international climate change regime see Cullet (2010), pp. 168–170 and Rajamani (2015), pp. 1–2.
[7] Cullet (2010), pp. 175–177; Andresen (2014), pp. 27–28.

itself in the refusal by the U.S. to ratify the Kyoto Protocol,[8] and in problematic climate change negotiations for a successor agreement to the Protocol including the ill-tempered Copenhagen Conference of Parties to the Convention in 2009.[9] It is also apparent in the refusal by most of the world's large emitters to commit to absolute emissions cuts under the second commitment period of the Kyoto Period (2012–2020) that was agreed at the Doha Conference of Parties to the Convention in 2012,[10] and from the fact that the agreed amendments to the Protocol creating the second commitment period are not yet in force and seem unlikely to become effective at the present rate of ratification before the second commitment period concludes.[11] Despite these deep divisions, parties to the Convention were able to agree at the Durban Conference of Parties to the Protocol in 2011 that renewed efforts should be made to reach an agreement between them to which all parties could adhere.[12] The process initiated by this agreement, known as the Ad Hoc Working Group on the Durban Platform for Enhanced Action, was given the mandate to explore possibilities for reaching a new climate change agreement by 2015 that would come into effect from 2020 as a successor to the Protocol. It was agreed that the new agreement would be in the form of "a Protocol, another legal instrument or agreed outcome with legal force", and, importantly given developed country objections to existing arrangements, that it would be "applicable to all Parties".[13]

Negotiations leading up to the Paris climate change conference in December 2015 gave little cause for confidence that the Durban Platform for Enhanced Action's goals would be achieved, with associations of states adhering to entrenched and seemingly irreconcilable positions on how burdens for mitigating climate change and addressing its consequences should be shared.[14] The group of like-minded developing countries (LMDC) was insistent on a continuation of the approach under which the states listed in Annex I of the Convention have more exacting obligations for mitigating climate change than other states.[15] The LMDC group argued that these states should continue to take the lead on combating climate change and its adverse effects because of their responsibility for its occurrence and greater ability, because of decades of fossil fuel driven economic growth, to finance responses to this global problem. States with developed economies, represented by

---

[8]Sands et al. (2012), p. 284.

[9]Ibid., pp. 293–299; Christoff (2016), pp. 766–768; Bodansky (2016), pp. 291–294.

[10]Bothe (2014), pp. 8–11; Rajamani (2012), pp. 512–515.

[11]Article 20(4) of the Protocol advises that an amendment to it enters into force only after three quarters of its parties (144 states) have submitted an instrument of acceptance. As of 23 September 2016, only 70 parties to the Protocol had formally accepted the amendments establishing the second commitment period. For further information see UNFCCC, 'Status of the Doha Amendment', available at <http://unfccc.int/kyoto_protocol/doha_amendment/items/7362.php>.

[12]UNFCCC, 'Decision 1/CP.17 Establishment of an Ad Hoc Working Group on a Durban Platform for Enhanced Action, 2011' (15 March 2012) FCCC/CP/2011/9/Add.1.

[13]Ibid., para 2.

[14]Aldson (2015), p. 21; Rajamani (2014), p. 721.

[15]Rajamani (2014), p. 731; Obergassel et al. (2015), pp. 245–246.

the Umbrella Group amongst others, took a contrary position. They were no longer prepared to bear the weight of achieving emissions cuts alone in view of seismic shifts in the global economy which, as noted above, had seen some states labelled as 'developing' in 1992 having become wealthier and higher emitters than some of the Convention's Annex I states.[16] The developed states required that a new agreement should abandon the strict separation between states based on their economic situations in the early 1990s in favour of a more dynamic approach to burden sharing reflecting changing circumstances and capacities to contribute to the international mitigation effort.

It came as a welcome surprise in view of this inauspicious backdrop that the parties were able to reach an agreement which, although it left much detail to be negotiated, far exceeded expectations.[17] Compromise was made possible by what has been described as a "historical U-turn" by the parties on distributing the burden of responding to climate change.[18] The LMDC group accepted that the strong differentiation in favour of developing states under the Convention and Protocol should be replaced by an agreement under which all states make self-determined contributions to international action on climate change. Developed state groups made corresponding concessions that the principle of common and differentiated responsibilities, which lay at the heart of the bifurcated approach of the Convention and the Protocol, should be restated in the new agreement although in the context of allowing states to self-differentiate rather than by placing stronger obligations on the developed state parties. The acquiescence of developing states was also secured by the repetition and expansion of developed state commitments under the Convention to support them, particularly through finance and technology transfer, both in their efforts to shift to lower carbon emitting ways of living and to adapt to climate change.

The Paris Agreement is widely regarded by commentators as a significant departure from the pre-existing interstate relationships under the international climate change regime.[19] Bodansky describes it as "potentially pivotal because it completes the paradigm shift from the bifurcated world of the Kyoto Protocol...to the common global framework that began to emerge in the Copenhagen Accord".[20] Streck et al. similarly refer to the agreement as representing "a turn from distributive bargaining strategies" to an attempt to find solutions "on the basis of trust and commonly agreed principles".[21] In this article, I consider whether the evolution in the nature of the international climate change regime is as radical as these

---

[16]Rajamani (2014), pp. 731–732; Obergassel et al. (2015), p. 244.

[17]UNFCCC, 'Decision 1/CP.21 Adoption of the Paris Agreement' (29 January 2016) FCCC/CP/2015/10/Add.1, Annex (Paris Agreement).

[18]Savaresi (2016), p. 22.

[19]Savaresi (2016), pp. 22–23; Bodansky (2015), p. 188; Streck et al. (2016), pp. 26–27; Rajamani (2016), p. 493.

[20]Bodansky (2015), p. 189.

[21]Streck et al. (2016), p. 27.

commentators have suggested. In particular, I explore how and the extent to which the position of developing countries has changed. I do so by identifying the key features of the developed/developing world relationship under the Convention and Protocol and comparing them to the position under the Paris Agreement. The Agreement entered into force on 4 November 2016, having met the double threshold of ratification by at least 55 parties to the Convention and by states collectively responsible for an estimated 55% of global greenhouse gas emissions on 5 October 2016.[22] The U.S., China and India were among the early ratifiers.

Comparative analysis of these features reveals that the substantive obligations of developing countries have not changed significantly. They are required to take action to mitigate and respond to climate change, but by how much and over what timescale is a matter for each state to decide on. The Paris Agreement differs strikingly from the Convention however in the international consensus it records that developing countries should enhance their mitigation efforts progressively, proceeding more slowly than developed states, but moving to a point where they too will be able to undertake absolute emissions cuts. Responsibility for supporting efforts by developing countries to mitigate and adapt to climate change financially and technologically remain primarily with the developed states, but the altered economic situation of some developing states is apparent in encouragement for other parties to get involved with this. Finally, developing countries have fuller obligations to report on their mitigation actions than under the Convention and are again encouraged to provide information in other areas. This greater transparency may turn out to be the most significant alteration to the position of developing countries under the Paris Agreement with increased scrutiny from the international community and from the Agreement's various review mechanisms having the potential to prompt progressive improvements in their contributions.

It is important to bear in mind when comparing the Agreement with the Convention that the former is adopted under the latter rather than replacing it. The Agreement is described in Article 2 as "enhancing the implementation of the Convention". This raises questions about the relationship between the two instruments with the Agreement often taking a different approach or placing different obligations on parties than the Convention. The generality of provisions under both instruments may allow interpretation in a way that avoids conflict between them.[23] However, it is conceivable that disputes on the applicable legal position will arise once the Paris Agreement takes effect on matters where it and the Convention point in different directions.

---

[22]Paris Agreement (n 17) Article 21(1).
[23]Rajamani (2016), pp. 506–507.

1.1 Developed and Developing Countries

The term 'developed state' is used in this article to mean those states that were given additional responsibilities for mitigating climate change and targets for achieving emissions cuts by their inclusion in Annex I and Annex B of the Convention and Protocol respectively. The term 'developing state' is used to mean all states party to the Convention who were not included in the Annexes. I make this clarification as neither term is defined in the Convention or the Protocol. The terms are reused in the Paris Agreement, but again without definition as developed states were keen to avoid an official differentiation of parties' duties by reference to the historic Annex I/non-Annex I split which they considered did not correspond with economic realities or responsibility for climate change in the present.[24] The membership of these groups under the Paris Agreement is not completely clear as a result. This is not problematic under provisions that place burdens on all parties, but could raise questions about who is legally bound to act under provisions that distinguish between developed and developing states when conferring obligations (e.g. adaptation, finance, technology transfer, capacity building, and transparency).

Two sub-groups of developing states are used in the Agreement to clarify the applicability of obligations or to indicate parties to whom specific support should be provided. The term 'Least Developed Countries' (LDCs) is not defined in the Agreement, but is used to refer to a group of countries identified by the Committee for Development Policy of the United Nations applying criteria related to gross national income, human assets, and economic vulnerability.[25] Forty-eight states were included in this category as of May 2016.[26] The Small Island Developing States (SIDS) are recognised as a group by the United Nations with their 38 state members (with some overlaps with the LDCs) corresponding to the Alliance of Small Island States climate change negotiating group.[27] The distinction between these groups and other developing states is significant as their interests are not always aligned. LDCs and SIDS demanded stronger mitigation actions by all large emitters in the negotiations leading up to the Paris Agreement, and enjoyed success in raising the Agreement's level of ambition including through inclusion of the pursuit of efforts to limit the global temperature increase to 1.5 °C as an objective of the Agreement.[28]

---

[24]Obergassel et al. (2015), pp. 245–246; Bodansky (2015), pp. 188–189.

[25]United Nations Development Policy and Analysis Division.

[26]United Nations Development Policy Committee (2016).

[27]United Nations Office of the High Representative for the Least Developed Countries, Landlocked Developing Countries and Small Island Developing States.

[28]Obergassel et al. (2015), pp. 245–246.

2 Obligations to Mitigate Climate Change

Developing country parties to the Convention *are* obliged, contrary to the impression that references given by the strong split of responsibilities under the climate change regime may give, to contribute to mitigation efforts by the international community. All parties commit under Article 4(1)(b) to "[f]ormulate, implement, publish and regularly update national and, where appropriate, regional programmes containing measures to mitigate climate change...". The division of responsibilities is stronger in respect of obligations to achieve absolute economy wide emission reductions. The Convention advises that developed country parties should aim to return to their 1990 levels of greenhouse gas emissions by 2000.[29] The Kyoto Protocol is more definite, requiring the parties listed in Annex I of the Convention (Annex B under the Protocol) to cut overall emissions by specified amounts within the commitment period 2008–2012.[30] The Protocol makes little reference to developing countries' contribution to mitigating climate change apart from reconfirming their commitments under the Convention.[31] Neither legal instrument places obligations on developing countries to achieve absolute emissions cuts in the present or suggests that they should do so in the future.

The Paris Agreement has been lauded for moving beyond the divide between developed and developing states. In practice, this change has been achieved with regard to mitigation by replacing the express obligation on developed states to achieve emissions cuts with a non-binding statement of expectation that they will do so rather than by formally increasing the share of the burden borne by developing states for avoiding dangerous anthropogenic interference with the climate.[32] Instead, all states take on a lowest common denominator obligation of self-determining their contribution to mitigation efforts.[33] Article 4(2) echoes the 'communicate and implement' obligation under the Convention by requiring each party to "prepare, communicate and maintain successive nationally determined contributions that it intends to achieve". This provision could even be said to place a lower level of expectation than the Convention on developing countries in that it requires parties only to "pursue domestic mitigation measures with the aim of achieving the objectives of" their nationally determined contributions rather than the unqualified requirement under the Convention to implement the programmes of measures communicated by them periodically.

Where the Paris Agreement does depart from its predecessors in its treatment of developing country (and other) parties is by introducing a more structured approach for periodic re-evaluation of their contributions to mitigating climate change in connection with the submission of new national proposals by parties every 5 years.

---

[29]FCCC (n 1), Art. 4(2)(b).

[30]Kyoto Protocol (n 5), Art. 3.

[31]Ibid., Art. 10.

[32]Paris Agreement (n 17), Art. 4(4).

[33]Ibid., Art. 4(2).

Procedures have been agreed by the Conference of Parties to the Convention for the regular submission of national communications on climate change policy, but no indication is made either in the Convention or the Protocol about the trajectory that parties' stated contributions to the global response should follow.[34] Indeed, the only guidance that the Convention provides on how parties' efforts should evolve is the suggestion that developing states may be excused from strengthening their response to climate change where this would conflict with developmental policy goals.[35] In contrast, the clear expectation of the international community under the Paris Agreement is that parties' contributions will become progressively stronger from the starting point of their initial nationally determined contribution. This is in line with the 'no-backsliding' principle around which a consensus emerged during the negotiations.[36] Article 3 advises that "the efforts of all Parties will represent a progression over time". Article 4(3) similarly advises that each party's nationally determined contribution "will represent a progression beyond the Party's then current national determined contribution and reflect its highest possible ambition". In addition, Article 4(4) advises developing country parties that they should "continue enhancing their mitigation efforts", and that they are encouraged to move "over time towards economy-wide emission reduction or limitation targets in the light of different national circumstances". These provisions make normative statements rather than imposing legally binding obligations. The legal position is therefore no different to that under the Convention with parties having no formal obligation to improve their climate change responses. Even so, it is clear that states are expected to strengthen their contributions regularly unless justification can be provided for not doing so.

Acceptance by developed states that the principle of common but differentiated responsibilities and respective capabilities should continue to inform thinking on how the burden of responding to climate change should be shared will affect the nature and extent of commitments that developing country parties are willing to make in their nationally determined contributions.[37] Article 2 of the Agreement advises that it should be implemented to reflect this principle, and other obligations and expectations for developing country parties are qualified by reference to it.[38] The possibility remains open therefore for developing states to justify lower levels of contribution than what they are capable of on grounds that the lion's share of responsibility for exposing the world to risks of dangerous climate change still lies with the developed Annex I states because of their historic actions. However, it is going too far to say that the principle provides a "get-out clause" for developing

---

[34]Information on national reporting requirements under the Convention and Protocol can be found at the UNFCCC website at the following address: http://unfccc.int/national_reports/items/1408.php.

[35]FCCC (n 1), Art. 4(7).

[36]Lawson (2015), p. 237.

[37]Rajamani (2016), pp. 507–509.

[38]Paris Agreement (n 17), Arts. 4(3) and 4(19).

country parties from contributing to the global mitigation effort.[39] For one, the principle operates in the different context of expected progression from that of the Convention. Whilst the details of the transparency mechanism (discussed at Sect. 6 below) are yet to be fleshed out, it seems likely in view of international consensus on the need for constant enhancement that this will provide a backdrop to appraisals of parties' contributions, and that those contributing less than they are capable of without adequate justification will come under peer pressure to improve their positions.

Secondly, the principle as it appeared in the Convention is modified in the Agreement by addition of the phrase "...in the light of different national circumstances".[40] This wording was included at the behest of the US and other developed states to make clear that the principle should be interpreted dynamically rather than being understood as maintaining the division between Annex I and non-Annex I states.[41] It has been argued with some merit that the additional wording is an unnecessary duplication in that the phrase 'respective capabilities' already permits states to consider their particular situations.[42] Even so, it does reinforce the message that parties should reappraise and, by implication, strengthen their climate change mitigation activities in line with economic growth and increasing responsibility in the present for consuming what is left of the 'safe' climate space.[43] The additional wording also serves to differentiate responsibilities within the developing state group. This can no longer be viewed as a homogenous collective. Instead, states such as China, India and Qatar, enjoying substantial growth both as economies and polluters, should bear a greater burden than the least developed countries whose ability to address climate change and responsibility for this are still at a low level.[44]

In summary, the legal obligations for developing states to mitigate climate change under the Agreement are not substantially different from those held by them under the Convention. The main change lies in the clear expectation that the contributions of developing country parties to mitigating climate change will be progressively enhanced to the fullest extent possible within their capabilities and subject to valid justification for a lower level of ambition by reference to the principle of common but differentiated responsibility. Whether or not this consensus on appropriate standards of behaviour will be adhered to will depend, in view of the lack of obligation, on the willingness of individual states to make self-imposed constraints on the emissions attributable to them as influenced by the prospect (or lack of it) of peer pressure from the international community for a failure to do the right thing.

---

[39] Lawson (2015), p. 237.
[40] Paris Agreement (n 17), Art. 2(2).
[41] Obergassel et al. (2015), p. 749.
[42] Streck et al. (2016), p. 7; Rajamani (2015).
[43] Streck et al. (2016), p. 7; Rajamani (2016), pp. 507–509.
[44] Cullet (2010), pp. 175–177.

3 Development and Emissions Trajectories

The Convention was negotiated contemporaneously with the Rio Declaration on Environment and Development, a major statement by the international community on how states should act with a view to making development sustainable.[45] The sustainable development concept was formulated to overcome a stand-off between states, typically already developed, who argued for stronger international rules on environmental protection and developing states with the latter group objecting to the imposition of legal constraints in ways that would restrict their opportunities to pursue economic growth and social improvement at the request of those who had already benefitted from exploiting natural resources to the detriment of others.[46] The concept espouses an approach to development which seeks to balance the pursuit of economic, social and environmental objectives.[47] Particular emphasis is placed on the right of developing states to enjoy economic growth and of the need to eradicate poverty notwithstanding the reduced scope for attaining these objectives due to the consequences of developed states activities in the preceding centuries.[48]

The influence of the development agenda on the Convention is apparent in provisions which accept that developing state parties should be permitted to pursue economic growth even where this would result in their greenhouse gas emissions increasing as a result. The preamble to the Convention notes that the share of "per capita emissions in developing countries are still relatively low and that the share of global emissions originating in developing countries will grow to meet their social and development needs". It also advises that consideration of how responses to climate change should be coordinated with social and economic development should consider "the legitimate priority needs of developing countries for the achievement of sustained economic growth and the eradication of poverty". The text of the Convention confirms this licence for developing countries to prioritise these goals where they would conflict with their climate change responsibilities with Article 4(7) noting that the extent to which they will effectively implement them "will take fully into account that economic and social development and poverty eradication are the first and overriding priorities of the developing country parties". This provision does not exonerate developing country parties from contributing to climate change mitigation, but affords them much scope to argue when putting forward proposals for mitigating climate change that these priority matters prevent them from observing their mitigation obligations under Article 4(1) fully.

The Paris Agreement recognises that the ability to pursue economic and social development is no less important to many of its parties than it was when the Convention was negotiated. The statement of the Agreement's objectives makes clear that its goals are pursued "in the context of sustainable development and

---

[45]Rio Declaration on Environment and Development (1992), ILM 31, 874.
[46]Ross (2012), pp. 11–16.
[47]French (2010), pp. 51–52.
[48]Holder and Lee (2007), pp. 237–243.

efforts to eradicate poverty...".[49] The ultimate aim of common mitigation efforts, to achieve a balance between emissions and removals by sinks[50] in the second half of the century, is also to be furthered within these contexts.[51] These provisions may provide a basis for developing country parties to justify lower levels of climate mitigation than would be otherwise achievable by them. However, they are much less strident than the corresponding provisions under the Convention with no suggestion being made that it would automatically be legitimate for developing states to prioritise economic and social objectives over their climate change responsibilities. Instead, the Agreement adopts a subtler tone, recognising that it would be appropriate for parties to consider sustainable development and poverty eradication in the preparation of their nationally determined contributions, but encouraging the pursuit of development goals in ways which are compatible with rather than antagonistic to climate change action. The preamble emphasises the "intrinsic relationship that climate change actions, responses and impacts have with equitable access to sustainable development and eradication of poverty", and recognises the role that "sustainable lifestyles and sustainable patterns of consumption and production..." may have on addressing climate change. Sustainable development (as opposed to economic and social development alone) is also identified as an objective of the various cooperation mechanisms that are to be established under the agreement, of the global goal on adaptation, and of technology transfer.[52]

In common with the Convention, the Agreement recognises that the emissions of developing country parties are likely to increase initially. Article 4(1) notes that it will take longer for developing countries to reach a point where their growth in emissions peaks. Similarly, they are only encouraged "to move over time towards economy-wide emission reduction or limitation targets" in contrast to developed states who the Agreement advises should reduce overall emissions as their default approach.[53] The Agreement does differ from the Convention however in envisaging that developing states will work towards a point where their total emissions will start to decline. It is implicit in the observation that it will take longer for the emissions of developing countries to peak that this is something which they should aim for.[54] No indication is given as to how quickly this should occur, but the unabated growth of developing country emissions is unlikely to be compatible with the Agreement's goal of achieving a balance between global emissions by source

---

[49]Paris Agreement (n 17), Art. 2(1).

[50]Article 1(8) of the Convention defines a "sink" as "any process, activity or mechanism which removes a gas, an aerosol or a precursor of a greenhouse gas from the atmosphere". Examples of sinks include the sequestration through photosynthesis of atmospheric carbon by forests and by oceanic phytoplankton.

[51]Ibid., Art. 4(1).

[52]Ibid., Arts. 6(4), 7(1) and 10(5).

[53]Ibid., Art. 4(4).

[54]Ibid., Art. 4(1).

and removals by sinks during the twenty-first century even if developed countries are able to transition to low carbon economies during the coming decades.[55]

In summary, the legal position of developing countries with regard to emissions trajectory has not changed in substance under the Paris Agreement. The dictates of economic growth and poverty eradication continue to provide a basis for developing states to temper their contributions to mitigating climate change. Again however, the context for developing mitigation proposals has altered with the silence on the expected contribution of developing states under the Convention being replaced by a clear signal that mitigation actions, even before peaking, should be designed in a way that moves them towards this goal. Whether or not these considerations affect a state's behaviour will variously depend, as discussed in Sect. 2 above, on its willingness to pursue a different developmental pathway than it may otherwise have followed, on the extent to which the state concerned is influenced by international opinion (assuming that this favours a different approach to that which the state would otherwise have pursued), and, as discussed in the following section, on the support it receives from developed and wealthier developing states for its mitigation efforts.

4 Financial and Technological Support for Mitigation

The third defining feature of the Convention and Protocol is that developed country parties are obliged to provide financial and technological support to developing countries to enable them to comply with their obligations to mitigate. They must meet the agreed costs of measures taken by developing states to implement Article 4(1) of the Convention, and are required in doing so to consider "the need for adequacy and predictability in the flow of funds" from the developed to the developing world.[56] They are also required to "take all practicable steps to promote, facilitate and finance, as appropriate, the transfer of, or access to, environmentally sound technologies and know-how" to states in general, but particularly to developing states.[57] The necessity of such support for the active participation of developing states in mitigating climate change is underlined by Article 4(7) which makes the effective implementation by them of their obligations under the Convention conditional on the effective implementation by developed country parties of their commitments "related to financial resources and transfer of technology".

The strength of these provisions in favour of developing countries reflects the clarity of the ethical position in 1992: that parties that had enjoyed the financial benefits of altering the atmosphere but which now wished to prevent a worsening of risks already posed by their activities should use accrued resources to provide

---

[55] Ibid.
[56] FCCC (n 1), Art. 4(3).
[57] Ibid., Art. 4(5).

developing states with the low carbon technologies required to enjoy economic growth and improvements in living standards despite the scope for them to enjoy a fossil fuel driven economic expansion without causing dangerous anthropogenic interference with the climate having been much eroded. Financial support is the necessary price for developing countries to undergo a more rapid trajectory of decarbonisation, and perhaps even to avoid a fossil fuel stage of development completely, rather than to take a similar economic path to that followed by developed states with attendant environmental consequences.

This trade-off between developed state support in return for developing states' forbearance from acting in ways that would worsen the environmental situation is simply expressed in the Convention. However, financial and technological transfers have always been controversial in practice under the international climate change regime with developed country parties showing increasing levels of reluctance to offer hard financial support for developing countries, and particularly those which have become competitors since the early 1990s.[58] In view of this unwillingness by developed states to comply with their financial obligations under the Convention, developing countries fought hard for more definite commitments in the Paris Agreement.[59] Their demands were ultimately traded off however for concessions in other respects (some of which are discussed in Sect. 5 below) with the result that the position of developing states as beneficiaries of support for mitigation is little changed under the Paris Agreement from that under the Convention. The commitment by developed states to provide financial resources is repeated, but the level of support that they should provide is not quantified.[60] Hard figures are given only in the non-binding decision of the Conference of Parties to the Convention that accompanies the Paris Agreement (hereafter 'the Paris Decision').[61] This restates the existing intention by developed states to mobilise $100 billion support a year up to 2025 and advises that the Conference of Parties to the Paris Agreement will agree on a new annual amount to take effect from 2025 with $100 billion as a starting point for negotiations.[62] The provision on technology transfer under the Agreement, although it is more explicit about the objectives of this support, does not otherwise go beyond the already established position in the Convention that developing country parties should receive financial support to enable them to participate in the exchange of technology and related knowledge.[63] The fleshing out of the more substantive commitments is left to future discussions by the Conference of Parties to the Convention and by future meetings of the parties under the Paris Agreement when it enters into force.[64]

---

[58] Obergassel et al. (2015), p. 257.
[59] Ibid.; Streck et al. (2016), pp. 19–20.
[60] Paris Agreement (n 17), Art. 9(1).
[61] UNFCCC, 'Decision 1/CP.21 Adoption of the Paris Agreement' (29 January 2016) FCCC/CP/2015/10/Add.1 (Paris Decision), para 54.
[62] Ibid.
[63] Paris Agreement (n 17), Art. 10(6).
[64] Paris Decision (n 61), paras 66–71.

Surprisingly given the emphasis placed by them in negotiations on the receipt of support, it is more in the position of developing states as providers rather than recipients of finance and technology transfer that the Paris Agreement differs from the Convention. Firstly, the provision of backing is no longer presented as the exclusive responsibility of developed states. In a reflection of the altered economic situation of some developing states since 1992, the agreement encourages "[o]ther parties...to provide or continue to provide such support voluntarily".[65] This changed situation is also apparent in the Paris Decision which notably distinguishes monies to be mobilised by developed states up to 2025, prolonging an agreement made at the Conference of Parties held in Cancun in 2010, from the quantified goal which is due to replace it.[66] This is described as 'collective', suggesting that all parties will potentially be involved with generating funding for the financing mechanism.[67] A similar change in emphasis can be seen in the technology transfer provision with the obligation to support developing countries in this regard being placed not on developed states alone but on all parties, presumably with those developing parties which are now technologically advanced and capable of supporting technology transfer themselves in mind.[68]

Secondly, compliance by developing states with their obligations under the Convention is not made conditional on the performance by developed states of their commitments to provide finance and to enable technology transfer. The self-determination by parties of what they will contribute to the global response to climate change affords scope for developing states to take account of perceived inadequacy in the support received from others. However, it does not excuse them automatically from contributing to climate change mitigation irrespective of their capacity to do so.

In summary, the Paris Agreement moves beyond the blunt distinction in the Convention between developed states and developing states as the providers and recipients of support respectively with action by the latter contingent on performance by the former. The expectation remains that wealthier parties will provide financial and technological support, but the agreement envisages, in contrast to the Convention, that developing states may offer, as well as benefit from backing. The Paris Agreement is also less clear that a failure by developed countries to comply with their financing obligations would excuse developing countries from acting to mitigate climate change. As Article 4(5) makes clear, backing by the former and action by the latter remain linked, but not to the degree that inadequate performance would justify developing states from withholding efforts to combat climate change completely.

---

[65]Paris Agreement (n 17), Art. 9(2).
[66]Paris Decision (n 61), para 54.
[67]Ibid.
[68]Paris Agreement (n 17), Art. 10(b).

5 Adaption, Loss and Damage and Capacity Building

Analysis of the Paris Agreement's provisions on mitigation reveals a shift in expectation, although not in obligation, over the contribution of developing countries to reducing emissions.[69] This shift was secured, in part, by developed and other party concessions on matters relating to the consequences of a changing climate with the LDCs and SIDS groups being particularly vocal on the need for a rebalancing of efforts under the international regime not only to prevent climate change, but also to address its effects.[70]

The first fruit of this negotiating dynamic can be seen in a raised profile for the adaptation agenda. Relevant obligations are present in the Convention with all parties being required to include measures to facilitate adequate adaptation to climate change in their programmes and to cooperate in preparing for adaptation to its impacts.[71] Developed country parties also commit to assist "developing country Parties that are particularly vulnerable to the adverse effects of climate change in meeting costs of adaptation to those adverse effects".[72] Commitments made in the Paris Agreement by states on supporting efforts to adapt by other parties do not go far beyond those made two decades previously. The obligation for parties to engage in planning for and to implement adaptation actions adds detail on the types of steps that should be taken, but does not otherwise go beyond what Article 4(1)(b) of the Convention requires parties to undertake.[73] Indeed, inclusion of the words "as appropriate" could be said to water down the provision by allowing states to self-differentiate on whether or not they regard themselves as obliged to plan for adaptation and, if they do, to what extent. The requirement to provide continued and enhanced international support to developing country parties for the implementation of their adaptation programmes is broader than the corresponding provision under the Convention, but its force is weakened by a failure to quantify the support to be provided.[74]

Similarly to the position with mitigation, where the Agreement differs markedly from the Convention is in the emphasis placed in non-binding provisions on the need for adaptation to be given greater weight. An adaptation goal is included for the first time.[75] Its call for "enhancing adaptive capacity, strengthening resilience and reducing vulnerability to climate change" has been called "largely symbolic" because of its generality,[76] but the requirement for a five yearly review on overall progress made towards the goal as part of the regular global stocktake indicates that

---

[69] See Sects. 2 and 3 above.
[70] Obergassel (2015), pp. 243–244; Streck et al. (2016), p. 18.
[71] FCCC (n 1), Arts. 4(1)(b) and 4(1)(e).
[72] Ibid., Art. 4(4).
[73] Paris Agreement (n 17), Art. 7(9).
[74] Ibid., Art. 7(13).
[75] Ibid., Art. 7(1).
[76] Lawson (2015), p. 239.

it is meant to be taken seriously as a benchmark against which adaptation actions by all parties will be judged.[77] The Agreement also goes beyond the Convention in expressing the view that communications on adaptation should be made as part of or at the same time as nationally determined contributions on mitigation. Finally, the provisions on financial resources and technology transfer make clear that support for adaptation, previously the poor relation in financing, should be balanced with that for mitigation.[78] Support provided by developed countries for adaptation should be communicated to the Conference of Parties along with information on mitigation in line with Article 13(9). The exposure resulting from this combination of reporting and review against an agreed standard may prompt parties to enhance their support for adaptation although the generality of the obligations mentioned above, coupled with the lack of quantification of overall funding required, would make it difficult to challenge them if they do not.

The second area in which negotiating demands of developing country parties bore fruit is in the inclusion of a provision concerned with the consequences of climate change, grouped under the heading 'loss and damage', that cannot be addressed satisfactorily through adaptation actions.[79] This proposal was controversial due to developed state concerns that it could provide a bridgehead for future calls on them to compensate for climate damage,[80] and its inclusion in the Agreement was only made possible by including a statement in the Paris Decision "that Article 8 of the Agreement does not involve or provide a basis for any liability or compensation".[81] The provision is highly general as a result, imposing no obligation on parties and noting only the desirability of interstate cooperation and facilitation of pertinent action and support including the establishment of early warning systems, emergency preparedness plans and the availability of risk insurance.[82] Importantly, the agreement extends the authority of the Warsaw International Mechanism for Loss and Damage as the vehicle established under the Convention for collaboration on responding to the unavoidable impacts of global warming.[83] The non-binding and therefore more acceptable arena of the Paris Declaration allows fleshing out of the mechanism's tasks which include the establishment of "a repository for information on insurance and risk transfer", and the development of "recommendations for integrated approaches to avert, minimize and address displacement related to the adverse impacts of climate change".[84] Establishment of the latter met a key demand of developing countries in the negotiation.[85]

---

[77]Paris Agreement (n 17), Arts. 7(10) and (11).

[78]Ibid., Arts. 9(4) and 10(6).

[79]Paris Agreement (n 17), Art. 8.

[80]Obergassel et al. (2015), pp. 256–257; Streck et al. (2016), pp. 18–19.

[81]Paris Decision (n 61), para 52.

[82]Paris Agreement (n 17), Art. 8(4).

[83]Ibid., Arts. 8(2) and 8(3).

[84]Paris Decision (n 61), paras 49 and 50.

[85]Savaresi (2016), pp. 23–24; Obergassel et al. (2015), pp. 256–257.

A third respect in which developing country demands were met in negotiations for the Paris Agreement was through the inclusion of a section on support for capacity building to enable developing countries to implement their obligations under the climate change regime.[86] The provision itself is weak, making positive noises about the benefits of capacity building and how this should be conducted, but placing no obligation on developed or other states to finance this. The only formal requirement is for parties that take measures to enhance the capacity of developing states to communicate their actions to the Conference of Parties.[87] As with loss and damage, the most tangible contribution of the Agreement on capacity building is to call for the creation of institutional arrangements under which continued consideration will be given to how the capacity of developing states to mitigate and adapt to climate change can be enhanced.[88] The Paris Decision responds to this by establishing the Paris Committee on Capacity Building, the stated aim of which is to "address gaps and needs...in implementing capacity-building in developing country Parties..."[89]

6 Transparency

The transparency framework of the Agreement is considered latterly as its purpose is to underpin performance of the substantive obligations considered in earlier sections. However, it is arguably the most important aspect of an Agreement under which parties have a large measure of discretion over their contribution with their choices informed by normative statements of preferred behaviour rather than by legally binding and enforceable obligations. Progress under such an arrangement depends on the availability of full information concerning a party's emissions and conduct to meet its obligations, and on its accessibility to other parties and the public, creating the potential for states and other actors to criticise and exert pressure where a party's contributions are not judged to be sufficient. The establishment of mechanisms for the review of parties' submissions may aid the process by flagging up respects in which they are insufficient and areas where scope arises for enhancement. It is also in respect of transparency that the most significant changes have occurred in the position of developing country parties on a comparison of the Convention and the Agreement. Under the former, the developing country parties have lighter reporting responsibilities than other parties, reflecting the assumption that their contribution to reducing global greenhouse gases would be limited in the near term compared to developed states which would take the lead

---

[86]Paris Agreement (n 17), Art. 11.
[87]Ibid., Art. 11(4).
[88]Ibid., Art. 11(5).
[89]Paris Decision (n 61), para 72.

on cutting emissions. These extend only to the submission of national inventories of emissions and general descriptions of steps taken or envisaged to implement the Convention.[90] Developed state parties are separately required to present much fuller accounts of how they have complied with their obligations.[91] In addition, the compliance by developing states with their reporting obligations is made subject to the provision by developed country parties of financial resources to cover the agreed costs of compliance.[92]

The first difference under the Agreement on reporting obligations is that the distinction between levels of information on mitigation activities to be provided by developed and developing states is abandoned. All parties are prima facie obliged to provide "[i]nformation necessary to track progress made in implementing and achieving" their nationally determined contributions alongside national inventories of emissions.[93] This should be made available at least every 2 years.[94] The Agreement recognises that the depth and quality of reporting can be expected to vary according to the differing capacities of each party. It advises that the transparency framework should provide flexibility in the implementation of the provisions of Article 13 to those developing country parties that need it in the light of their capacities.[95] Paragraph 90 of the Paris Decision explains further that flexibilities shall be provided on matters including "the scope, frequency and level of detail of reporting, and in the scope of review".[96] A concession is also made in the Paris Decision to the LDCs and SIDS who may submit information required under Article 13 "at their discretion", but are not required to do so.[97] The basic position apart from for LDCs and SIDs however is that all parties, subject to whatever adjustment their circumstances may justify, should have the same responsibility for submitting information on their contributions to mitigating climate change. In this regard, the Conference of Parties to the Convention seeks to support developing country parties in improving their ability to meet their transparency requirements by establishing a capacity-building initiative.[98] Recourse to this initiative is voluntary, but a failure by states to avail themselves of its aid may undermine claims that they are unable to meet the Agreement's requirements on openness about their actions.

The second difference is that reporting by developing country parties is not made conditional on the provision of funds by developed states. The flexibility for implementing Article 13 depending on a party's capacity allows an inability to

---

[90] FCCC (n 1), Art. 12(1).
[91] Ibid., Art. 12(2).
[92] Ibid., Arts. 4(3) and 12(5).
[93] Paris Agreement (n 17), Art. 13(7).
[94] Paris Decision (n 61), para 91.
[95] Paris Agreement (n 17), Art. 13(2).
[96] Paris Decision (n 61), para 90.
[97] Ibid., para 91.
[98] Ibid., para 85.

finance data gathering and publication to be considered when determining what level of transparency a party should be able to attain. Several references in the transparency section of the Paris Declaration to the Global Environment Facility suggest that financial, as well as practical assistance, may be made available to support the capacity building exercise.[99] However, there is no express suggestion that developed states should meet the costs of developing state's transparency efforts directly or that a failure to provide finance would justify non-compliance.

Third, the Agreement complements the encouragement of developing country parties to provide financial support, including for technology transfer and capacity building, by inviting parties other than developed states to provide information on financial, technological and capacity building support provided by them to developing country parties.[100] Article 13 also advises developing country parties that they should provide information on support needed by them, a sensible proposal for making the provision of financial and technological support more effective, and one which limits scope for developing countries to argue that they are unable to contribute to climate change mitigation because of inadequate support without having provided information about the assistance that they require.[101]

The introduction of structured processes for the review of information is a departure for all parties to the climate change regime with the Convention having conferred only a general power on the Conference of Parties to assess "on the basis of all information made available to it...the implementation of the Convention by the Parties".[102] The Agreement establishes three layers of review. Information submitted by all parties on mitigation and support is to undergo technical expert review, the purpose of which is to facilitate improvement by providing non-binding guidance on "areas of improvement" for parties.[103] Second, each party is required to participate in a facilitative multilateral consideration of progress with respect to the provision of financial support, and concerning "its respective implementation and achievement of its nationally determined contribution".[104] Nothing further is said either in the Agreement or the Paris Declaration about this process, but such an institutional arrangement could play a vital role in bringing peer pressure to bear on parties whose contributions to climate change mitigation, adaptation and financing are perceived to be inadequate.

Third, the collective contribution of parties to achieving the purpose of the Agreement and its long-term goals (presumably the objectives stated in Article 2 although this is not stated expressly) is to be reviewed every 5 years by the Conference of Parties of the Agreement in a global stocktake.[105] The outcome of

---

[99]Ibid., paras 7–9.
[100]Paris Agreement (n 17), Art. 13(9).
[101]Ibid., Art. 13(10).
[102]FCCC (n 1), Art. 7(2)(e).
[103]Paris Agreement (n 17), Arts. 13(11) and 13(12).
[104]Ibid., Art. 13(11).
[105]Ibid., Art. 14.

this process is intended to inform parties in updating and enhancing their nationally determined contributions.[106] A first stocktake under the Agreement will be held in 2023 and every 5 years thereafter.[107] The parties to the Convention have also agreed to convene an earlier 'facilitative dialogue' in 2018 that will "take stock" specifically of progress towards the goal of zero net emissions during the second half of the century.[108]

The mechanisms for review apply to all parties, but are particularly significant for developing states as their contributions to mitigation, adaptation and financing climate change have not previously been subjected to close scrutiny. The extent to which they serve to stimulate an uplift in contributions is also particularly relevant to developing countries that have fewer hard obligations under the Agreement. Exposure to external review and comment will be a key driver for improved performance by them if they do not enhance their contributions to meeting the Agreement's goals of their own volition. The effectiveness of these arrangements may therefore make the difference between a continuation in practice of limited developing state efforts to mitigate and of a gradual increase in ambition of developing states responses to global warming under the stimulus of assessment against the Agreement's normative expectations of state behaviour and peer pressure from the international community.

7 Conclusion

This article examines how the Paris Agreement alters the position of developing countries under the international climate change regime. It finds that their formal legal responsibilities are little changed with developing states having general obligations to mitigate but no binding requirements under either instrument on how to go about this. In addition, obligations to provide financial and technological support for mitigation efforts continue to fall predominantly on developed states although the availability of funding is no longer made an express precondition for developing state action to mitigate climate change. The Agreement differs substantially from the Convention on paper in its several non-binding statements of expectation that developing country parties will progressively enhance their mitigation activities with a view to moving towards making absolute economy-wide emission cuts and which encourage them to enhance their contributions with regard to adaptation, support and reporting. Whether or not these normative statements will make any difference to their actions in practice will depend on the political will of individual states to make serious efforts to combat climate change with their resolve backed up by the knowledge that fuller information must be submitted on

---

[106] Ibid., Art. 14(3).
[107] Ibid., Art. 14(2).
[108] Paris Decision (n 61), para 20.

their contributions and that they will be exposed to greater scrutiny than under the Convention and Protocol as a result. The various review mechanisms reinforce the potential for reporting on emissions, on mitigation actions and voluntarily on other matters to influence developing state behaviour positively. The key additional stimulus that the agreement makes to a strengthened developing country involvement with responding to global warming therefore lies in the operation of the transparency and review mechanisms. The fuller detailing of how they will operate in advance of the Paris Agreement's entry into force by the Ad Hoc Working Group on the Paris Agreement will be of central importance to its effectiveness.

Acknowledgement I am grateful for the very helpful comments on the draft article made by two anonymous peer reviewers and by Dr Zeray Yihdego, the Editor-in-chief of the Ethiopian Yearbook of International Law.

References

Aldson F (2015) Key issues in the current COP 21 climate change negotiations. Environ Law Manage 27:21–24
Andresen S (2014) The climate regime: a few achievements, but many challenges. Clim Law 4:21–29
Bodansky D (2015) Is the Paris Agreement historic? Thoughts the day after the Agreement was adopted. Environ Law Manage 27:188–189
Bodansky D (2016) The Paris climate change agreement: a new hope? Am J Int Law 110:288–319
Bothe M (2014) Doha and Warsaw: reflections on climate law and policy. Clim Law 4:5–20
Christoff P (2016) The promissory note: COP21 and the Paris climate change agreement. Environ Polit 25:765–787
Cullet P (2010) Common but differentiated responsibilities. In: Fitzmaurice M, Ong D, Merkouris P (eds) Research handbook on international environmental law. Edward Elgar, Cheltenham, pp 161–180
French D (2010) Sustainable development. In: Fitzmaurice M, Ong D, Merkouris P (eds) Research handbook on international environmental law. Edward Elgar, Cheltenham, pp 51–68
Holder J, Lee M (2007) Environmental protection, law and policy, 2nd edn. Cambridge University Press, Cambridge
Lawson F (2015) Key features of, and the occasional surprise in, the Paris Agreement. Environ Law Manage 27:237–242
Obergassel W, Arens C, Hermwille L, Kreibich N, Mersmann F, Ott H, Wang-Helmreich H (2015) Phoenix from the ashes: an analysis of the Paris Agreement to the United Nations Framework Convention on Climate Change – Part I. Environ Law Manage 27:243–262
Rajamani L (2012) The Durban Platform for Enhanced Action and the future of the climate regime. Int Comp Law Q 61:501–518
Rajamani L (2014) The Warsaw climate negotiations: emerging understandings and battle lines on the road to the 2015 climate agreement. Int Comp Law Q 63:721–740
Rajamani L, C2ES (2015) Differentiation in a 2015 climate agreement. Available at: http://www.c2es.org/docUploads/differentiation-brief-06-2015.pdf
Rajamani L (2016) Ambition and differentiation in the 2015 Paris Agreement: interpretive possibilities and underlying politics. Int Comp Law Q 65:493–514
Ross A (2012) Sustainable development law in the UK: from rhetoric to reality? Earthscan, Abingdon

Sands P, Peel J, Fabra A, Mackenzie R (2012) Principles of international environmental law, 3rd edn. Cambridge University Press, Cambridge

Savaresi A (2016) The Paris Agreement: a new beginning? J Energy Nat Resour Law 34:16–26

Streck C, Keenlyside P, von Unger M (2016) The Paris Agreement: a new beginning. J Eur Environ Plan Law 13:3–29

United Nations Development Policy and Analysis Division, 'Identifying least developed countries', available at: http://www.un.org/en/development/desa/policy/cdp/ldc/ldc_criteria_id.shtml

United Nations Development Policy Committee, 'List of Least Developed Countries (as of May 2016)', available at http://www.un.org/en/development/desa/policy/cdp/ldc/ldc_list.pdf

United Nations Office of the High Representative for the Least Developed Countries, Landlocked Developing Countries and Small Island Developing States, 'About the Small Island Developing States', available at: http://unohrlls.org/about-sids/

Olivia Woolley is a lecturer in renewable energy law and environmental law at the University of Aberdeen. She is the author of 'Ecological Governance: Reappraising Law's Role in Protecting Ecosystem Functionality' (Cambridge University Press, 2014).

Part III
Current Development

The Declaration of Principles on the Grand Ethiopian Renaissance Dam: An Analytical Overview

Salman M.A. Salman

Abstract The Nile has been plagued by major disputes between the different riparians since the beginning of last century, with the demand by Egypt and Sudan for recognition by other riparians of their existing uses and rights being the central one. The Grand Ethiopian Renaissance Dam (GERD) which Ethiopia started constructing in 2011 exacerbated such disputes by challenging this demand. The article traces and follows the developments regarding the GERD, and discusses the incremental approach through which Ethiopia succeeded in making the GERD a *fait accompli*. It discusses how this reality has been bolstered 4 years later, in 2015, through the signature by the three countries of two instruments—the Declaration of Principles and the Khartoum Document. The article examines the new Nile legal order emanating therefrom, and concludes with an examination of the opportunities forgone as a result of the riparians' unilateral development plans, and those to be gained through cooperation.

1 Introduction

One of the main features of the Nile River is the large number of dams that have dotted the Basin since the end of the nineteenth century, and the fact that all these dams are unilateral development projects for the exclusive use of the riparian country building it. The old Aswan Dam in Egypt that was built between 1898 and 1902 was the first dam on the Nile River. It was followed by the Sennar dam in the Sudan in 1925, and then in 1937 by the Jebel Aulia dam in the Sudan for the exclusive uses and benefits of Egypt. Uganda entered the dam-building fray in 1949 when it started building the Owen Falls dam. The Aswan High Dam (AHD) in Egypt (completed in 1970), and the Roseiris and Khashm El-Girba dams in the Sudan (completed in 1966 and 1964, respectively), were the results of the bilateral 1959 Nile Waters Agreement that the two countries concluded on November 8, 1959, excluding all the other Nile riparians.

S.M.A. Salman (✉)
International Water Resources Association (IWRA), Khartoum, Sudan
e-mail: salmanmasalman@gmail.com

Ethiopia was the last of the Nile Basin countries to enter the dam building competition. Ethiopia started with the Fincha dam—a small dam on the Blue Nile that was completed in 1973 for generation of hydropower. It was followed by two other small dams, the first and second Tis Abbay projects, on Lake Tana for generation of hydropower also. However, at the beginning of this century Ethiopia moved forward on the fourth Nile dam, the largest and most significant of all. That was the Tekeze dam on the Atbara River (the north most, and the last tributary to join the Nile River in the Sudan) which was started in 2002, and was completed in 2010, for generation of more than 360 MW of hydropower. The reservoir behind the dam stores more than nine Billion Cubic Meters (BCM). Concurrently Ethiopia also built the Tana-Beles project that connected the Beles River (a tributary of the Blue Nile) with Lake Tana, and generated hydropower at that connecting point.

What is common on all the Egyptian, Sudanese, Ugandan, and Ethiopian dams, as stated above, is the fact that these projects are all unilateral development projects, for the exclusive use and benefits of the state building the dam, with no attempts for a joint cooperative action or benefit sharing with another Nile riparian.[1] This approach deepened the suspicion, distrust, and disputes among the Nile riparians, especially from those Nile states which are not yet parties to the dam-building fray.

Moreover, the Ethiopian dam projects, particularly the Tekeze dam, paved the road and prompted Ethiopia to move in the direction of the largest dam, to date, on the Nile, and the tenth largest in the world—the Grand Ethiopian Renaissance Dam (GERD) in 2011. As expected, the GERD resulted in a major dispute, initially between Sudan and Egypt with Ethiopia. However, Sudan started moving slowly away from Egypt on this issue, and 2 years later, in December 2013, Sudan declared its full support for the GERD.

Fifteen months later Egypt joined the Sudan in accepting the GERD. The three states signed on March 23, 2015, the Declaration of Principles on the Grand Ethiopian Renaissance Dam (DoP), whereby Egypt explicitly accepted the GERD, and Sudan reconfirmed its support for the GERD.

Many factors pushed Egypt in that direction. By the end of 2016, the dam was more than 60% complete, and had clearly become a *fait accompli*. Most of the close allies of Egypt either supported the GERD, or have simply kept quiet. Egypt closest ally in the Nile, Sudan, broke ranks with Egypt on the GERD, and then started raising other issues with Egypt, particularly the dispute on the Hala'ib triangle in the north-east corner of the Sudan that Egypt annexed unilaterally in 1995. Egypt has clearly under-estimated, and keeps under-estimating, the role of the Hala'ib dispute in the overall Egyptian Sudanese relations.[2]

Moreover, Egypt itself has been occupied by its own internal crisis following the January 2011 revolution that toppled former President Mubarak in February of that

---

[1]For more discussion of these dams see Salman (2016), p. 512.

[2]'Press conference to address the Hala'ib Triangle land dispute between Sudan and Egypt' Boundary News (2016).

year. The unrest that followed resulted in General El-Sisi coup that toppled the Islamists' government of Dr. Mursi in July 2013, and Mr. El-Sisi taking over as president in June 2014. Thousands of Egyptian Islamists, including the leaders of the movement, have been put in jail, followed by hurried trials that have passed harsh sentences on many of the Islamists' leaders. The Islamists vowed to, and are fighting back, resulting in more turmoil that has engulfed Egypt. Furthermore, and as discussed below, the Nile Agreements of 1902 and 1959 that Egypt tried to rely on in its rejection of the GERD have not really helped Egypt much.

The purpose of this article is to give an analytical overview of the DoP, after a brief discussion of the legal and political background to the DOP, and an overview of the developments regarding the GERD. The article concludes with some observations regarding the GERD, the DoP, and the future relations between the three states, and among the eleven Nile River riparians, as well.

2 The Nile Agreements

Treaties are the mechanisms that states conclude to resolve their disputes and institutionalize cooperative action for the benefit of the parties to each such treaty. However, this basic fact has been completely absent in the case of the Nile. Three Nile agreements—the 1902, 1929 and 1959 agreements—have been very contentious, and a cause of major disputes between the Nile Basin countries.

The 1902 Agreement was concluded between Britain and Ethiopia.[3] Egypt argues that it has succeeded Britain to the Agreement, and claims that the Agreement, which is valid and binding, gives Egypt veto power over the Nile projects in Ethiopia. Egypt has been arguing that under the 1902 Agreement Ethiopia cannot start any infrastructure project on the Nile before notifying Egypt and receiving Egypt's consent. Ethiopia, on the other hand, claims that Egypt is not a party to the Agreement, and adds that this agreement was not ratified by any organ of the Ethiopian government. Ethiopia further claims that the English and Amharic versions read differently on this matter, and thus the 1902 Agreement is neither valid nor binding on Ethiopia. Ethiopia argues further that Egypt and Sudan have not notified Ethiopia of any of their projects on the Nile River, and as a matter of international water law and reciprocity, Ethiopia is under no obligation to notify either country of its projects on the Nile.[4] Additionally, Ethiopia argues that, as the country that is the source of 86% of the Nile waters, Ethiopia is entitled to its

---

[3]Treaty between Ethiopia and the United Kingdom, relative to the frontiers between the Anglo-Egyptian Sudan, Ethiopia, and Eritria (1902). The Treaty states in Article III that Emperor Menelik II of Ethiopia "engages himself towards the Government of His Britannic Majesty not to construct, or allow to be constructed, any work across the Blue Nile, Lake Tsana, or the Sobat which would arrest the flow of their waters into the Nile, except in agreement with His Britannic Majesty's Government and the Government of the Sudan."

[4]For a discussion of this issue see Degefu (2003), pp. 96–99.

equitable and reasonable share of such waters, in accordance with the basic principles of international water law.[5] Thus, the dispute over this agreement dominated the Egyptian Ethiopian relations until the DoP was concluded in March 2015.

Another treaty that is a source of major contention is the 1929 Nile Agreement between Egypt and Britain representing the Nile countries of Sudan, Kenya, Uganda and Tanganyika (later Tanzania) which were under the control of Britain at that time.[6] Similar to the 1902 Agreement, Egypt argues that the Agreement gives it veto power over any project on any of the Nile tributaries in any of these four countries. Upon gaining independence in the early 1960s, the three countries of Tanzania, Kenya, and Uganda, adopted a strategy, later called the Nyerere Doctrine, which gave the 1929 Agreement 2 years, during which it would either be replaced by another treaty, or it would simply lapse.[7] Because no other agreement was concluded to replace the 1929 Agreement, the three countries announced that the Agreement lapsed in 1962. Egypt rejected that position, and still claims that, like the 1902, the 1929 Agreement is valid and binding on the three countries. It should be clarified that Ethiopia is not a party to this agreement.

A third agreement that is a major source of contention and resentment is the bilateral Nile Waters Agreement concluded by Egypt and Sudan on November 8, 1959.[8] Through this Agreement the two countries divided the entire Nile flow of 84 BCM measured at Aswan between them, to the exclusion of all the remaining riparians. Egypt received 55.5 BCM, and Sudan 18.5 BCM, while the remaining 10 BCM are lost annually to evaporation at the huge reservoir of the Aswan High Dam (AHD).

After allocating the entire flow of the Nile between themselves and evaporation, Egypt and Sudan noted that other riparians of the Nile may claim a share in the Nile waters, and agreed to study together these claims and adopt a unified view thereon. If such studies result in the possibility of accepting the request of one or more of the riparians, and allotting an amount of the Nile waters to one or the other of these riparians, Egypt and Sudan agreed that the value of this amount as at Aswan shall be

---

[5] See Yihdego and Rieu-Clarke (2016), p. 528.

[6] Exchange of Notes between Great Britain and Northern Ireland and Egypt in Regard to the Use of the Waters of the River Nile for Irrigation Purposes (1929) Paragraph 4 (ii) of the Agreement states: "Except with the prior consent of the Egyptian Government, no irrigation works shall be undertaken nor electric generators installed along the Nile and its branches nor on the lakes from which they flow if these lakes are situated in Sudan or in countries under British administration which could jeopardize the interests of Egypt either by reducing the quantity of water flowing into Egypt or appreciably changing the date of its flow or causing its level to drop."

[7] See Mekonnen (1984).

[8] Agreement between the United Arab Republic and the Republic of the Sudan for the full utilization of the Nile waters (1959). Note that title of the Agreement refers to "the full utilization of the Nile waters." Egypt and Syria united as one country in 1958, and the new country was called "United Arabic Republic."

deducted in equal shares from the share of each of the two countries. The two countries further agreed that the Permanent Joint Technical Committee, established by the two of them under the 1959 Agreement,[9] shall make arrangements for control and checking of the agreed amounts of the Nile water so allocated by Egypt and Sudan to this Nile riparian country.[10]

The Agreement also stipulated that in case any question connected with the Nile water needs negotiations with the governments of any riparian territories outside the Republic of Sudan and Egypt, the two Republics shall agree beforehand on a unified position in accordance with the investigations of the problem by the Committee. This unified position shall then form the basis of instructions to be followed by the Committee in the negotiations with the governments concerned.

Ethiopia had repeatedly demanded participation in the 1959 negotiations, but Egypt and Sudan ignored those requests. Consequently, Ethiopia sent a number of memoranda rejecting the Agreement, and Kenya, Uganda and Tanzania followed the same route. Egypt and Sudan now claim that their shares of Nile waters under the 1959 Agreement have become an established and acquired right, and the other riparians are obliged under international law not to interfere with it, as this would cause significant harm to Egypt and Sudan. On the other hand, the other riparians demand their equitable and reasonable share of the Nile waters, and raise the principle of equality of all the riparians of the shared watercourse as the basic principle of international water law. Indeed, this is the issue that resulted in the collapse of the negotiations over the Nile Basin Cooperative Framework Agreement, as discussed below.

The Nile Basin Cooperative Framework Agreement (CFA) 2010 has been one major outcome of the Nile Basin Initiative (NBI).[11] Negotiations on the CFA started in 1999, following the establishment of the Nile Basin Initiative (NBI) early that year, and broke down in 2010 mainly over Egypt and Sudan's claim to what they termed their existing uses and rights of the Nile waters. The two countries demanded recognition of these uses and rights in the CFA under "water security", but this demand was vehemently rejected by the other Nile riparians.[12] The CFA has become a source of a bitter dispute between Egypt and Sudan on the one hand, and other members of the Nile Basin riparians, and has resulted in a major setback to the NBI.

---

[9]The details regarding the Committee are spelled out in the Protocol concerning the establishment of the Permanent Joint Technical Committee (1960).

[10]This paragraph of the 1959 Agreement actually makes the allocation of some Nile waters by Egypt and Sudan a donation by Egypt and Sudan to the other Nile riparian, rather than as a right under international water law for such a riparian, as discussed later in this article.

[11]The Nile Basin Initiative (NBI) is an inter-governmental partnership of ten Nile Basin countries (Eritrea is an observer) that was established in 1999. The shared vision objective of the NBI is "to achieve sustainable socio-economic development through the equitable utilization of, and benefit from, the Nile Basin resources." For more on the NBI see Nile Basin Initiative (2016).

[12]For a critical analysis of the concept of water security, see Mekonnen (2010), p. 421.

The CFA has been signed, thus far, by six riparians: Ethiopia, Tanzania, Rwanda, Kenya, Uganda and Burundi,[13] and the first three countries have already ratified the CFA.[14] The CFA needs six instruments of ratification to enter into force and effect.[15]

Hence, the Nile Basin has gained another unique feature—disputes among the riparians over the existing agreements. The validity of the 1902 and 1929 agreements is being challenged by one or more of the parties to each of these agreements, while the other party, Egypt, is insisting on such validity.[16] Similarly, what Egypt and Sudan claim as their uses and rights under the 1959 Agreement is totally rejected by the other Nile riparians.[17] These differences have been carried over, and are the basis for the differences over the CFA 2010. It is with this turbulent legal and political background, and the unilateral development projects on the Nile, that the GERD and the DoP should be viewed and analyzed.

3 The Grand Ethiopian Renaissance Dam (GERD)

The studies conducted by the United States Bureau of Reclamation in the 1960s indicated that the hydropower potential of Ethiopia exceeds 45,000 MW, with 30,000 from the Nile.[18] The studies recommended a number of dam projects on the Nile, including the Border dam on the Blue Nile, close to the frontiers with the Sudan. The study for this dam was later updated, and in March 2011 Ethiopia announced its plans to construct a dam on the Blue Nile, about 20 km from the Sudanese borders. This dam became known as the Millennium Dam, and later its name was changed to the Grand Ethiopian Renaissance Dam (GERD).

Construction of the GERD commenced at the beginning of April 2011, a few days after the official announcement about the dam was made at the end of March 2011. At that time, Egypt was completely immersed in its January 2011 revolution that toppled President Hosni Mubarak in February of that year.

The GERD is a large dam, with a storage capacity of 74 Billion Cubic Meters (BCM)—close to the total Nile flow of 84 BCM measured at Aswan, as per the

---

[13]The Republic of South Sudan became an independent nation on July 9, 2011. South Sudan has declared its support of the CFA, but has neither signed nor acceded to the CFA. For a discussion of this issue see Salman (2011b), p. 154.

[14]Agreement on the Nile River Basin Cooperative Framework (2010) (Entebbe Treaty).

[15]For a detailed discussion of the CFA and the reasons for its rejection by Egypt and Sudan see Salman (2013b), p. 17.

[16]For a detailed analysis of those agreements and the positions of the different riparians, as well as other agreements on the Nile concluded during the colonial era, see Okidi (1994), p. 110.

[17]For a detailed discussion of these agreements see Garretson (1967), p. 256.

[18]Ethiopia sought and received the assistance of the United States of America Bureau of Reclamation following the conclusion of the Nile Waters Agreement between Egypt and Sudan (1959), and the heavy involvement of the Soviet Union in the financing and construction of the Aswan High Dam.

1959 Nile Agreement. The installed capacity of the GERD is 6000 MW, with 16 turbines, each expected to generate 375 MW (increased recently to 6,450 megawatts). This is almost three times the electricity being generated by the AHD of 2100 MW.

Egypt and Sudan reacted immediately after the Ethiopian announcement was made, protesting and denouncing the Ethiopian decision, and declaring their strong opposition to the GERD. Both countries contended that the GERD will decrease considerably the amount of Nile waters reaching Sudan and flowing thereafter to Egypt. Egypt further claimed that the GERD will turn large areas of its irrigated lands into desert, and will result in a considerable decrease of the hydropower generated by the AHD. Both countries demanded that the different studies for the GERD be provided to them so they can assess the harm that the GERD will cause each of them. Sudan was also concerned about the safety of the GERD, and the extensive harm Sudan could suffer if the GERD were to crack, fail, or collapse.

However, the Sudanese position began to witness some gradual, but steady changes, and a large number of experts and politicians argued that Sudan will actually benefit from the GERD. They explained that the benefits to Sudan include the entrapment of the huge sediments that the Blue Nile carries and brings annually to the Sudan, which have caused the Sennar and Roseiris dams to lose more than half of their storage and electricity generating capacity. The benefits also include regulation of the flow of the waters of the Blue Nile, and putting an end to the recurrent flooding, and the destruction to property and crops, caused by the seasonal flow of the river. Regulation of the flow, it is further argued, will help Sudan increase its crop rotations to two or even three a year, from the current single rotation because of the seasonality of the flow of the waters of the river. This would also help the replenishment of groundwater throughout the year.

It should be added that Sudan is one of the countries with the lowest amount of water stored (about 10 BCM in its four dam reservoirs, compared to 162 BCM for Egypt in AHD). It should be added that Sudan uses only 12 BCM of the 18.5 BCM allotted to it under the 1959 Nile Waters Agreement with Egypt. Sudan's unused portion of 6.5 BCM has been crossing the northern Sudanese borders to Egypt annually and regularly since 1959.[19] Sudan could thus negotiate the storage of some of its Nile waters in the GERD reservoir.[20]

The sale of the GERD electricity to Sudan, as well as to Egypt, which is cheaper than the electricity generated by either country, has also been cited as one major additional benefit to both countries, which face huge deficit in electric power.

---

[19]Salman (2015a).

[20]Some Sudanese suggested that Sudan could sell to Ethiopia its unused portion of the Nile waters under the 1959 Agreement in exchange for electricity from the GERD. However, this suggestion was not carried further because of Sudan's realization that Ethiopia has always refused to recognize the 1959 Agreement, and thus will not agree even to negotiate this suggestion because it will mean its recognition of the Agreement.

Those arguing in favor of the GERD for Sudan have pointed out that the only two issues of concern for Sudan should be the safety of the dam, and the length of the period during which the reservoir will be filled.

On the other hand, some Sudanese technocrats and politicians opposed the GERD. They raised the issues of the loss of sediments, the decrease of the flow of the Blue Nile during the period in which the reservoir will be filled, and the risks associated with the failure of the dam which is only 20 km from the Sudanese borders.[21]

However, the President of Sudan put an end to this debate, and announced in December 2013 in clear and unequivocal language the support of the Sudan for the GERD. This announcement created a major crack in the Egypt/Sudan Nile water alliance that was born as a result of the conclusion of the Nile Waters Agreement on November 8, 1959, and the establishment of the Permanent Joint Technical Committee.

As discussed above, this change in Sudan's position, together with the other compelling factors, pushed Egypt in the direction of accepting the GERD, and the conclusion on March 23, 2015 the DoP. Egypt's acceptance of the GERD came about gradually, and through an incremental approach during the recurrent trilateral meetings of the ministers of water resources that started in 2013. The ministers of water resources were later joined by the ministers of foreign affairs in these meetings, creating two tracks for negotiations—technical and political.

The earlier tripartite meetings took place in Khartoum, but were later moved to both Addis Ababa and Cairo. After 2 years, the meetings resulted in the "Agreement on Declaration of Principles between the Arab Republic of Egypt, the Federal Democratic Republic of Ethiopia and the Republic of the Sudan" (DoP). The DoP was signed on March 23, 2015 in Khartoum by the three top political figures in the three countries—Presidents Abdel Fattah El-Sisi of Egypt, and Omer Hassan Ahmed El-Bashir of Sudan, and Prime Minister Hailemariam Desalegn of Ethiopia.

4 Agreement on Declaration of Principles on the GERD

The DoP consists of a preamble and ten principles, four of which relate to the GERD, while the other six deal with some basic principles of international water law.[22]

The preamble pointed to the rising demand of the three countries on their transboundary water resources, and noted the significance of the Nile River as the source of livelihood and a significant source to the development for the people of the three countries. Thus, unlike the previous agreements discussed above, the DoP

---

[21]For a detailed discussion of these issues see Salman (2011a).

[22]For a detailed discussion of the DoP, see Salman (2016), p. 512.

has restated and recognized the basic principle of international water law—the equality of all the riparians in the sharing and uses of the common river.

Article 1 of the DoP dealt with the principle of cooperation, based on common understanding, mutual benefits, good faith, and the principles of international law, as well as understanding upstream and downstream water needs in its various aspects. This is also another major break with the past agreements that made no reference at all to riparian cooperation, or to the rights of the other riparians. Recognition of the need for cooperation, though late, is a major, and first step to a basin-wide approach, starting with the Eastern Nile.

Indeed, cooperation is the cornerstone of international water Law. The United Nations Convention on the Law of the Non-Navigational Uses of International Watercourses (UN Watercourses Convention)[23] is based on cooperation,[24] and uses the word "cooperation" and its derivatives about fifteen times. The CFA specifies cooperation as the first of a number of principles for the protection, use, conservation and development of the Nile Basin. Thus, the DoP has walked in the footsteps of the UN Watercourses Convention and the CFA on this vital aspect of international water law.

Article 2 stipulated clearly the recognition of Egypt and Sudan of the purpose of the GERD as power generation, contribution to economic development, promotion of transboundary cooperation and regional integration through generation of reliable and sustainable energy. Thus, the article has brought Egypt in line with the Sudan in the support of the GERD, and has recognized the right of Ethiopia to use the Nile waters for economic development. Indeed, the DoP reconfirmed the basic principle of international water law of the equality of the riparians of the shared watercourse. Henceforth, the idea of the GERD is no longer in dispute; only the details.

Article 3 obliged the three parties to take all appropriate measures to prevent the causing of significant harm in utilizing the Blue and the Main Nile. The Article goes on to state that where significant harm nevertheless is caused to one of the countries, the state whose use causes such harm shall, in the absence of agreement to such use, take all appropriate measures, in consultations with the affected state, to eliminate or mitigate such harm and, where appropriate, to discuss the question of compensation. Article 3 is based largely on Article 7 of the UN Watercourses Convention, and Article 5 of the CFA.

Article 4 dealt with the principle of equitable and reasonable utilization. It stated that the three countries shall utilize their shared water resources in their respective territories in an equitable and reasonable manner, and lays down the same factors, set forth in the UN Watercourses Convention and the CFA, for ensuring such equitable and reasonable utilization, namely:

---

[23]The UN Watercourses Convention was approved by the UN General Assembly on May 21, 1997, and entered into force on August 17, 2014; see Salman (2015b), p. 1.
[24]McCaffrey (2007), p. 408.

a. Geographic, hydrographic, hydrological, climatic, ecological and other factors of a natural character;
b. The social and economic needs of the Basin States concerned;
c. The population dependent on the water resources in each Basin State;
d. The effects of the use or uses of the water resources in one Basin State on other Basin States;
e. Existing and potential uses of the water resources;
f. Conservation, protection, development and economy of use of the water resources and the costs of measures taken to that effect;
g. The availability of alternatives, of comparable value, to a particular planned or existing use.

In addition, the DoP included two more factors which are specified in the CFA, but not in the UN Watercourses Convention, namely:

i. The contribution of each Basin State to the waters of the Nile River system; and
ii. The extent and proportion of the drainage area in the territory of each Basin State.

It is noteworthy that, unlike the UN Watercourses Convention and the CFA, the DoP dealt with the obligation not to cause Significant harm in Article 3, before dealing with the principle of equitable and reasonable utilization, which is addressed in Article 4. The UN Watercourses Convention and the CFA both dealt first with the principle of equitable and reasonable utilization, followed by the obligation not to cause significant harm. The reversal of order of the two articles in the DoP, *vis-a-via* the UN Watercourses Convention and the CFA, was, perhaps, a concession to Egypt which had built its entire legal case on the Nile on the obligation not to cause harm.

However, this reversal of order cannot alter the fact that under international water law, the UN Watercourses Convention, and the CFA, and now the DoP, the obligation not to cause significant harm is subordinate to the principle of equitable and reasonable utilization. With regards to the DoP this conclusion is based on a close reading of Articles 3 and 4 of the DoP.[25]

As stated above, Article 4 enumerated a number of factors for determining equitable and reasonable utilization. These factors include (i) "the effects of the use or uses of the watercourse in one watercourse State on other watercourse States," and (ii) "existing and potential uses of the watercourse." These same factors will also need to be used, with other factors, to determine whether significant harm is caused to another riparian, because harm can be caused by depriving other riparians of the water flow and thereby affecting their existing uses. Thus, Article 3 of the DoP has used the suffering of harm as a factor for determining equitable and reasonable utilization under Article 4 of the DoP.

---

[25]Salman (2016).

Moreover, Article 3 of the DoP obliged the three parties to take all appropriate measures to prevent the causing of significant harm in utilizing the Blue/Main Nile. Where significant harm nevertheless is caused to another watercourse state, then Article 3 of the DoP required the state causing the harm to "take all appropriate measures, in consultation with the affected State, to eliminate or mitigate such harm, and where appropriate, to discuss the question of compensation." Although Article 3, unlike the UN Watercourses Convention and the CFA, does not require giving due regard to the Article on equitable and reasonable utilization, it does indicate that the causing of significant harm (and not just harm) may be tolerated in certain cases such as when the harm can be mitigated, and furthermore, when the possibility of compensation may be considered.

Accordingly, a careful reading of Articles 3 and 4 of the DoP should lead to the conclusion that the obligation not to cause significant harm has been subordinated to the principle of equitable and reasonable utilization, in line with the UN Watercourses Convention and the CFA. Indeed, the principle of equitable and reasonable utilization has been firmly established as the guiding principle of international water law.

Professor Charles Bourne, confirming this line of thinking, opined "[t]oday, however, the doctrine of prior appropriation has almost been universally rejected in favour of the doctrine of equitable utilization. Under the latter doctrine, a state is always entitled to 'a reasonable and equitable share in the beneficial uses of the waters of an international drainage basin,' and 'the past utilizations of the waters of the basin, including in particular existing utilization' is only one of the many other factors to be taken into account in the determination of its share."[26]

Professor Lucius Caflisch went further and stated that the main users of international watercourses have usually been lower riparians because of the typical topography of most river basins—mountainous in upper riparians, and leveled plains in downstream riparians. In his view, if the no-harm rule were to prevail over the principle of equitable and reasonable utilization, it would heavily advantage lower riparians and disadvantage upstream states, and "the economic and social growth of any newcomer, in particular upstream countries, would be stunted."[27]

Commenting on the relationship between the two principles, Professor McCaffrey stated that "...while the no-harm principle does qualify as an independent norm, it neither embodies an absolute standard nor supersedes the principle of equitable utilization where the two appear to conflict with each other. Instead, (the no-harm principle) plays a complementary role, triggering discussions between the states concerned and perhaps, in effect, proscribing certain forms of serious harm."[28]

---

[26]Bourne and Wouters (1997), p. 158.

[27]Caflisch (1998), p. 6.

[28]McCaffrey (2007), p. 408.

The International Court of Justice (ICJ) in the Gabcikovo-Nagymaros case (Hungary/Czechoslovakia) that was decided in September 1997, discussed the relationship between the principle of equitable utilization and the obligation not to cause harm.[29] The ICJ addressed the issue of harm suffered by one riparian, and attributed that to the deprivation of such a riparian of the right to an equitable and reasonable utilization of the shared watercourses. The ICJ stated that it "...considers that Czechoslovakia, by unilaterally assuming control of a shared resource, and thereby depriving Hungary of its right to an equitable and reasonable share of the natural resources of the Danube .... failed to respect the proportionality which is required by international law." The ICJ went further and emphasized the concept of equitable and reasonable utilization when, referring to the project under consideration, it directed that "the multi-purpose programme, in the form of a co-ordinated single unit, for the use, development and protection of the watercourse is implemented in an equitable and reasonable manner." It is worth noting that the ICJ made no reference to the obligation not to cause harm to other riparians. These principles have been reconfirmed by the ICJ in 2010 in the Pulp Mills case.[30]

The ICJ emphasized the principle of equitable and reasonable utilization further by linking it to the concept of equality of all the riparian states. It quoted from the 1929 judgment by its predecessor, the Permanent Court of International Justice (PCIJ), where the PCIJ stated "[the] community of interest in a navigable river becomes the basis of a common legal right, the essential features of which are the perfect equality of all riparian States in the user of the whole course of the river and the exclusion of any preferential privilege of any one riparian State in relation to the others."[31]

As discussed above, Article 4 of the DoP added two more factors for determining equitable and reasonable utilization, copied from the CFA, dealing with (i) the contribution of each state to the waters of the Nile River, and (ii) the extent and proportion of the drainage area in the territory of each Basin State. These two factors certainly weigh in favor of Ethiopia which contributes about 86% of the Nile waters, and is third, after Sudan and South Sudan, in the size of the Nile drainage area in its territories.

It should be added and clarified that harm is actually a two-way matter. Just as upstream riparians can harm downstream riparians, the downstream riparians can also harm the upstream ones. It is obvious, and clearer, that the downstream riparians can be harmed by the physical impacts of water quantity and quality changes caused by use by the upstream riparians. The quantity of water flow can be decreased by the upstream riparians through construction of dams, canals and pipelines, and through

---

[29]ICJ, *Case Concerning the Gabčíkovo-Nagymaros Project (Hungary v. Slovakia)*, Judgment, (1997), ICJ Rep 1997.

[30]ICJ, *Case Concerning Pulp Mills on the River Uruguay (Argentina v, Uruguay)*, Judgment, (2010), ICJ Rep 156.

[31]PCIJ, *Case Relating to the Territorial Jurisdiction of the International Commission of the River Oder, (United Kingdom, Czechoslovakia, Denmark, France, Germany and Sweden v. Poland)*, (1929), Judgment No. 16.

the storage and diversion of the waters of the shared rivers. The quality of the water of the shared rivers can be affected by the upstream riparians through pollution caused by industrial waste, sewage or agricultural run-off.

It is much less obvious, and generally not realized, that the upstream riparians can be affected, or even harmed, by the potential foreclosure of their future use of water, caused by the prior use, and the claiming of rights to such water by the downstream riparians. Projects on shared rivers in the downstream riparian states would help those riparians in acquiring, and later claiming, rights to the water abstracted under those projects. The availability and use of such waters in future by the upper riparians would have already been foreclosed by the downstream riparians. Such downstream riparians would usually invoke the principle of acquired rights and the obligation not to cause harm in the face of claims by the upstream riparians.[32] The upstream riparians' claims to part of the waters of the shared watercourse under the principle of equitable and reasonable utilization would be countered by claims of historic rights and existing uses, and the obligation against causing harm by affecting them.[33] Thus, as Ethiopia is under obligation not to cause significant harm to Egypt and the Sudan, Egypt and the Sudan are equally obliged not to cause significant harm to Ethiopia through foreclosure of Ethiopia's future uses.[34]

Article 5 of the DoP dealt with the principle to cooperate in the first filling and operation of the dam. It called on implementation of the recommendations of the International Panel of Experts (Panel),[35] and for respect of the outcomes of the

---

[32] For a more detailed analysis of this matter see Salman (2010), p. 3.

[33] Ethiopia indicated its understanding of the concept of foreclosure of future uses in its Note Verbale of 20 March 1997, addressed to Egypt, on the Toshka or New Valley Project which Egypt was constructing and which draws water from the Nile River. The Note Verbale stated: "Ethiopia wishes to be on record as having made it unambiguously clear that it will not allow its share to the Nile waters to be affected by a *fait accompli* such as the Toshka project, regarding which it was neither consulted nor alerted." For more discussion on the Note Verbal *see* Waterbury (2000), p. 84.

[34] One treaty which addressed the concept of foreclosure of future uses is the Senegal River Water Charter which was concluded by Mali, Mauritania and Senegal in May 2002, and which Guinea became a party to in 2006. Article 4 of the Charter enumerates a number of principles for allocation of the waters of the Senegal River among the riparians. These principles include "the obligation of each riparian state to inform other riparian states before engaging in any activity or project likely *to have an impact on water availability, and/or the possibility to implement future projects.*" (Italics added). This paragraph clearly protects all the riparians of the Senegal River, both downstream and upstream; with the upstream riparians, Guinea and Mali, receiving a clear and explicit reference in the Water Charter to the protection of their rights from the lower riparians, namely Senegal and Mauritania. For the Senegal River Water Charter see 'Water Charter of the Senegal River Basin' OMVS (2002).

[35] The International Panel of Experts was established in November 2011 and consisted of ten members, two from each of the three countries, and four from outside the Nile Basin countries. The Terms of Reference of the Panel included identifying any negative impacts of the GERD on Sudan and Egypt, and recommending ways of mitigating such impacts. See International Panel of Experts (2013).

Tripartite National Committee (TNC)[36] final report on the joint studies recommended by the Panel throughout the different phases of the dam project. Article 5 also required the three countries, in the spirit of cooperation, to utilize the final outcomes of the studies to agree on the guidelines and rules for the first filling of the GERD.[37] However, the Article clarified that this will take place "in parallel with the construction of the GERD." The Article also asked the three parties to agree on guidelines and rules for the annual operation of the GERD, but subjected this to adjustments which the owner of the dam may take from time to time. It then required Ethiopia to inform the two other countries of any unforeseen circumstances requiring adjustments in the operation of the GERD.

Article 5 also addressed the issue of cooperation and coordination of the operation of the GERD with downstream reservoirs, and asked the three countries to set up, through the line ministries, appropriate coordination mechanisms among them within 15 months from the inception of the studies recommended by the Panel.[38]

Article 6 dealt with the issue of confidence building and stipulated that priority would be given to the downstream countries in the purchase of power generated by the GERD. It is noteworthy that the article does not oblige Ethiopia to sell any portion of the power generated by the GERD to either Sudan or Egypt, nor does it oblige Sudan or Egypt to purchase such hydropower.

Article 7 addressed the issue of exchange of data and information, in good faith and in a timely manner, between the three parties for carrying out the studies recommended by the Panel, and to be carried out by the TNC. It is worth noting that the article does not deal with the concept of notification; only with exchange of data and information.[39]

Article 8 dealt with the issue of the dam safety. The Article underscored the appreciation of the three countries to the efforts undertaken thus far by Ethiopia in implementing the recommendations of the Panel with regards to the dam safety, and called on Ethiopia to continue to implement in good faith these recommendations.[40]

---

[36]The Tripartite National Committee (sometimes referred to as National Technical Committee—TNC) is the executive organ of the three ministers of water resources of the three countries, and consists of an equal number of experts from each of the three countries.

[37]For possibilities in the filling of the reservoirs of the GERD see Zhang et al. (2016), p. 593. See also, Wheeler et al. (2016), p. 611.

[38]This part of Article 5 of the DoP has perhaps been the result of a report prepared by Massachusetts Institute of Technology (MIT) (2014). The report made three main recommendations, the first of which stated "Need for an agreement on the coordinated operation of the GERD with the Aswan High Dam."

[39]It should be added that Ethiopia opposed including any provisions on notification in the CFA, and the final signed version of the CFA 2010 made no mention of notification, only exchange of data and information. Thus, the DoP walked on the foot path of the CFA on this issue. For more details of the differences over the CFA see Salman (2013a), p. 360.

[40]It is interesting to note that Article 8 deals with the appreciation of "the three countries", rather than the appreciation of Sudan and Egypt. For an analysis of the legal issues concerning dam safety see Bradlow et al. (2002).

Article 9 returned to the concept of cooperation, and required the three parties to cooperate based on sovereign equality, territorial integrity, mutual benefit, and good faith to attain the optimal utilization and adequate protection of the Nile River.[41] It is worth noting that this article is a reiteration of the first paragraph of Article 3 of the CFA which required the parties of the CFA to cooperate "on the basis of sovereign equality, territorial integrity, mutual benefit and good faith in order to attain optimal utilization and adequate protection and conservation of the Nile River Basin ..."

In turn, Article 3 of the CFA is based on Article 8 of the UN Watercourses Convention which stated "[w]atercourse states shall cooperate on the basis of sovereign equality, territorial integrity, mutual benefit and good faith in order to attain optimal utilization and adequate protection of an international watercourse." The reiteration of the concept of cooperation, and the copying of the provisions of both the UN Watercourses Convention and the CFA, is certainly worth noting.[42]

Article 10, the last Article of the DoP, dealt with the principle of peaceful settlement of disputes. It required the three countries to settle any disputes arising out of the interpretation or implementation of the agreement amicably through consultation or negotiation in accordance with the principle of good faith. Failing that, the parties may jointly request conciliation or mediation, or refer the matter for consideration of the heads of states/governments. Thus, the DoP does not include a resort to arbitration or to the International Court of Justice.

Thus, Egypt finally joined the Sudan in accepting the GERD as a reality and sought through the DoP to share in the benefits of the GERD, namely the huge amount of electricity that the GERD is expected to generate.

Acceptance by Egypt and the Sudan of the GERD, and of the principles enunciated in the DoP, was reconfirmed 9 months later. The fourth tripartite meeting of the ministers of water resources and the ministers of foreign affairs of the three countries took place on December 27 and 28, 2015 in Khartoum. After 2 days of intensive discussions on the studies recommended by the Panel, the six ministers signed a document titled "Summary and the Outcomes of the Meeting" (referred to as the "Khartoum Document").

The Khartoum Document consisted of six articles and three annexes.[43] The second paragraph of the Preamble reconfirmed "the sincere and full commitment of the three countries to adhere to the Agreement on Declaration of Principles (DoP)" putting an end to the rumors about Egypt's imminent move to withdraw

---

[41]Tawfik (2016), p. 574.

[42]Cascao and Nicol (2016), p. 550.

[43]The six ministers of the three countries agreed through the Khartoum Document to the recommendation of the TNC to select the consulting firms of BRLi and Artelia to undertake the two studies recommended by the Panel. Artelia replaced Deltares which was selected by the TNC earlier, but withdrew because of some differences over its role in the studies. Annex C to the Khartoum Document stated that the contracts with the two consulting firms and TNC would be signed on February 1, 2016. However, the contracts were signed on September 20, 2016, more than 7 months from the originally agreed date.

from the DoP. Furthermore, in Article 3 of the Document, the three countries "reiterated their full commitment to implement the provisions of the Agreement on Declaration of Principles signed in Khartoum on the 23rd of March, 2015." Ethiopia also reiterated its commitment to implement Article 5 of the DoP on coordination of the operation of the GERD with the downstream reservoirs. Article 3 of the Khartoum Document also dealt with cooperation stating that "In the spirit of cooperation and trust building, Ethiopia extended a cordial invitation to Egypt and Sudan to conduct visits to the GERD site."[44] Article 5 of the Khartoum Document dealt with "Enhancement of Confidence Building", and stated that "The three countries agree to support and encourage efforts aimed at promoting confidence building measures so as to enhance people to people relations of the three countries. Ethiopia invites parliamentarians, the media and public diplomacy groups of both Egypt and Sudan to visit the GERD."

Thus, the DoP received a major boost, and a clear and unequivocal reconfirmation of its provisions, through the Khartoum Document that was signed by both: the ministers of foreign affairs and the minister of water resources of the three countries, 9 months after the DoP was concluded and signed by the three top political figures in the three countries. The GERD has indeed become a reality that is explicitly accepted and endorsed by Egypt and Sudan through these two instruments. Not only this, but Egypt and Sudan are now seeking to share in the huge hydropower the GERD will generate.[45]

5 Conclusion

The DoP is no doubt a landmark development in the history of the Nile Basin. Egypt and Sudan which divided the entire flow of the Nile between them under the 1959 Agreement, and asked the other riparians to apply to them for any share of the Nile waters, have finally recognized the equality of all the Nile states. They have also acknowledged the right of these states to utilize the waters of the Nile River for the sustainable development of their people. The playing fields have clearly been levelled for the first time in the history of the Nile Basin.

By accepting the GERD, and the right of Ethiopia to an equitable share in the Nile waters, and by making no reference in the DoP to the 1902 agreement, Egypt and Sudan have basically accepted the position of Ethiopia regarding the 1902

---

[44]In fact, the three ministers had previously visited the GERD dam site. The visit took place on September 25, 2014, following the end of the tripartite meeting of the ministers of water resources in Addis Ababa, Ethiopia on September 23 and 24, 2014.

[45]Sudan has started purchasing power from Ethiopia in December 2013, and 250 megawatts are now delivered to the Sudan through the power lines connecting the two countries that were inaugurated in December 2013. The power lines were financed by through a grant from the donors as part of the NBI projects in the Eastern Nile (Blue Nile and Atbara River). Thus, it is expected that Sudan will purchase more hydropower from Ethiopia once the GERD is completed.

agreement. Indeed, the failure of Egypt and Sudan to refer to the 1902 Agreement, or to their existing uses and rights as per the 1959 agreement, carry with it a clear acceptance by the two countries of the new legal order established by and resulting from the DoP.[46] This acceptance is in sharp contrast to the rejection by Egypt and Sudan of the CFA in 2010, because it failed to include explicit provisions on their existing uses and rights. As noted above, insistence of Egypt and Sudan on the inclusion of such provisions, and the rejection of other riparians to this demand, have been the main reasons for the refusal of Egypt and Sudan to sign the CFA.

By repeatedly underscoring the need for cooperation, the parties may be opening a new chapter in the history of the Nile Basin that may eventually put an end to the unilateral approach adopted by the Nile Basin riparians for the last century of infrastructure projects on the Nile.[47] Indeed, the GERD (or a larger Border Dam) should have been built in the 1960 as a joint project by Egypt, Ethiopia, and the Sudan, in lieu of the Aswan High Dam and the Roseiris Dam. That would have saved the extensive fertile land, in both Egypt and Sudan, submerged under the huge reservoir of the AHD, and the heavy evaporation losses of 10 BCM from the reservoir of the AHD (as opposed to two Billion Cubic Meters from the GERD reservoir). It would have also saved the huge financial costs incurred in the construction of these two dams, and averted the involuntary resettlement of more than 120,000 Egyptian and Sudanese Nubians whose towns and villages were submerged under the reservoir of the AHD. The benefits of the AHD and the Roseiris Dam of irrigation water, water storage, power generation, and ending of the periodic floods, would have certainly been achieved by the larger Border Dam, without these huge costs of the two dams.

That approach would have also sown the seeds of cooperation on the Nile as early as 1960. With that opportunity forgone, the GERD should have been jointly owned, financed, and operated by the three countries, as Ethiopia initially offered in 2011. That was another missed opportunity, as Egypt and Sudan ignored the offer when it was made. Regrettably, time seems to have clearly bypassed that offer, as the GERD is now more than 60% complete.

Now that Egypt and Sudan are no longer insisting on their existing uses and rights of the Nile waters, and instead have accepted the principle of equality with the other Nile Basin countries in the sharing and uses of the Nile waters, the logical and consequential step is for the two countries to join the other six Nile countries and to accede to the CFA. The road to the CFA becoming an inclusive instrument for all the Nile riparians is not that difficult, and would involve a simple compromise. Egypt and Sudan would drop their insistence on a reference in the CFA to their existing uses and rights (as well as dropping any reference to the 1902 and 1929 Agreement), and Ethiopia and the other Nile riparians would agree to the inclusion in the CFA of provisions on notification, similar to those of the UN

---

[46]Yihdego et al. (2016), p. 503.
[47]Berndtsson et al. (2017), p. 251.

Watercourses Convention. That would address the concerns of both sides to the dispute on the CFA.

Indeed, the logical and consequential step after the DoP, and concurrent with joining the CFA, is for all of the Nile riparians, particularly Egypt, Ethiopia and the Sudan, to become parties to the UN Watercourses Convention.[48] After all, the Convention called in Article 1, as have done the CFA and DoP more than a decade later, on all states to "cooperate on the basis of sovereign equality, territorial integrity, mutual benefit and good faith in order to attain optimal utilization and adequate protection of an international watercourse."

References

Berndtsson R et al (2017) The Grand Ethiopian Renaissance Dam: conflict and water diplomacy in the Nile Basin. In: Islam S, Madani K (eds) Water diplomacy in action: contingent approaches to managing complex water problems. Anthem Press, Boston, pp 253–263

Bourne C, Wouters P (eds) (1997) International water law—selected writings of Professor Charles Bourne. Kluwer Law International

Bradlow D, Palmieri A, Salman S (2002) Report, regulatory frameworks for dam safety – a comparative study. http://documents.worldbank.org/curated/en/785201468763768736/Regulatory-frameworks-for-dam-safety-a-comparative-study

Caflisch L (1998) Regulation of the uses of international watercourses. In: Salman SMA, Boisson de Chazournes L (eds) International watercourses—enhancing cooperation and managing conflict. The World Bank

Cascao AE, Nicol A (2016) GERD: new norms of cooperation in the Nile Basin? Water Int 41:4

Degefu GT (2003) The Nile – historical, legal and developmental perspectives. Trafford, Victoria

Garretson AH (1967) The Nile Basin. In: Garretson AH, Hayton RD, Olmstead CJ (eds) The law of international drainage basins. Oceana Publications, New York

International Panel of Experts (2013) Report, Grand Ethiopian Renaissance Dam Project. http://www.scidev.net/filemanager/root/site_assets/docs/international_panel_of_experts_for_ethiopian_renaissance_dam-_final_report.pdf

Massachusetts Institute of Technology (MIT) (2014) Report, The Grand Ethiopian Renaissance Dam: an opportunity for collaboration and shared benefits in the Eastern Nile Basin – an *Amicus Brief* to the Riparian Nations of Ethiopia, Sudan and Egypt, from the Eastern Nile Working Group (convened at the Massachusetts of Technology on 13–14 November 2014). https://jwafs.mit.edu/sites/default/files/documents/GERD_2014_Executive_Summary.pdf

McCaffrey S (2007) The law of international watercourses, 2nd edn. Oxford University Press, Oxford

Mekonnen Y (1984) The Nyerere doctrine of state succession and the new states of East Africa. Eastern Africa Publications, Arusha

---

[48]None of the Nile countries is actually a party to the UN Watercourses Convention, nor has any of them signed the Convention. Sudan and Kenya voted for the Convention during the UN General Assembly vote on May 21, 1997; Egypt, Ethiopia, Rwanda and Tanzania abstained, each for its own reasons; The Democratic Republic of Congo, Eritrea, and Uganda did not participate in the vote; while Burundi voted against the Convention (together with China and Turkey). See Salman (2015b).

Mekonnen DZ (2010) The Nile Basin Cooperative Framework Agreement negotiations and adoption of a 'Water Security' paradigm: flight into obscurity or a logical Cul-de-Sac? Eur J Int Law 21:2

Okidi O (1994) History of the Nile and Lake Victoria Basins through treaties. In: Howell PP, Allan JA (eds) The Nile: sharing a scarce resources. Cambridge University Press, Cambridge

'Press conference to address the Hala'ib Triangle land dispute between Sudan and Egypt' (2016) Boundary News (14 January 2016). https://www.dur.ac.uk/ibru/news/boundary_news/?id=26799&itemno=26799

Salman SMA (2010) Downstream riparians can also harm upstream riparians – the concept of foreclosure of future uses. Water Int 35:4

Salman SMA (2011a) Grand Ethiopian Renaissance Dam – challenges and opportunities. Center for Infrastructure Protection University of George Mason, School of Law 10:4

Salman SMA (2011b) The New State of South Sudan and the hydro-politics of the Nile Basin. Water Int 36

Salman SMA (2013a) Mediation of international water disputes – The Indus, the Jordan and the Nile Basins Interventions. In: Boisson de Chazourens L, Leb C, Tignino M (eds) International law and freshwater: the multiple challenges. Edward Elgar Publishing Ltd, Cheltenham

Salman SMA (2013b) The Nile Basin Cooperative Framework Agreement – a peacefully unfolding African spring? Water Int 38

Salman SMA (2015a) Sudan continues relinquishing a growing portion of the Nile waters. Available at http://www.salmanmasalman.org/sudan-continues-relinquishing-a-growing-portion-of-nile-water-share/

Salman SMA (2015b) Entry into force of the UN Watercourses Convention – why should it matter? Int J Water Resour Dev 31

Salman SMA (2016) The Grand Ethiopian Renaissance Dam: the road to the declaration of principles and the Khartoum document. Water Int 41

Tawfik R (2016) The Grand Ethiopian Renaissance Dam: a benefit-sharing project in the Eastern Nile. Water Int 41:4

The Nile Basin Initiative (NBI) (2016) http://www.nilebasin.org/

Waterbury J (2000) The Nile Basin—national determinants and collective action. Yale University Press

Wheeler K et al (2016) Cooperative filling approaches for the Grans Ethiopian Renaissance Dam. Water Int 41:4

Yihdego Z, Rieu-Clarke A (2016) An exploration of fairness in international law through the Blue Nile and the GERD. Water Int 41

Yihdego Z, Rieu-Clarke A, Cascao AE (2016) How the Grand Renaissance Dam changed the legal, political, economic and scientific dynamics in the Nile Basin. Water Int 41

Zhang Y et al (2016) Filling the GERD: evaluating hydroclimatic variability and impoundment strategies for Blue Nile Riparian Countries. Water Int 41

Salman M.A. Salman worked until 2009 as the Water Law Advisor with the World Bank in Washington DC. Currently he is the Editor-in-Chief of International Water Law Journal (Brill); and is a Fellow with the International Water Resources Association (IWRA).

The South Sudan Crisis: Legal Implications and Responses of the International Community

Jasmin Hansohm and Zeray Yihdego

Abstract South Sudan, which gained independence in 2011, has been engulfed in violence and conflict periodically since that time. The Intergovernmental Authority on Development (IGAD) has played a major role in brokering peace talks between the respective parties. This role, as well as the role of the United Nations Mission in South Sudan (UNMISS), which recently authorised, through Security Council Resolution 2304, the deployment of a 4000-member Regional Protection Force (RPF) to Juba is discussed. This piece aims to provide an insight into some of the challenges and legal developments associated with ensuring lasting peace, addressing (and preventing) the allegations of widespread violations of international law, as well as the internal armed conflict affecting South Sudan, in light of the nature of responses from the international community.

1 Introduction

The security and humanitarian challenges that South Sudan, its people and the region face are extremely grave. The outbreak of armed violence that began on 8 July 2016 in South Sudan's capital, Juba, alone resulted in the deaths of around 300 people over 4 days,[1] and signalled the end of a tenuous peace agreement that had been signed by the warring parties less than a year earlier.[2] The most recent

---

[1] 'UN mission 'extremely concerned' over increased incidents of violence across South Sudan' UN News Centre (2016); see also 'Gang rape of aid workers in South Sudan is a turning point' NPR (2016).

[2] Agreement on the Resolution of the Conflict in the Republic of South Sudan (17 August 2015). https://unmiss.unmissions.org/sites/default/files/final_proposed_compromise_agreement_for_south_sudan_conflict.pdf.

J. Hansohm (✉)
University of Aberdeen, Aberdeen, Scotland, UK

Queen Mary, University of London, London, UK
e-mail: jasmin.hansohm@gmail.com

Z. Yihdego
University of Aberdeen, Aberdeen, Scotland, UK
e-mail: Zeray.yihdego@abdn.ac.uk

figures emerging from South Sudan indicate that the humanitarian conditions are critical. At the time of writing one and a half million people are displaced within the country, with more than 200,000 seeking shelter within UN compounds in the country under the control of the United Nations Mission in South Sudan (UNMISS). In addition, more than 600,000 people are refugees in Kenya, Uganda, and Ethiopia.[3] In terms of food availability, 4.8 million people are considered to be at emergency levels of food insecurity.[4]

This should be put into historical context. Sudan, which then included today's South Sudan, gained its independence from British rule in 1956. But this was also the time when the first Sudanese civil war, which lasted from 1955 to 1972, was already underway between the central government and the southern Sudanese region.[5] The Addis Ababa Peace Agreement of 1972[6] ended the civil war and provided the southern region with autonomous powers. The peace resulting from the Addis Ababa Agreement lasted for a decade, when war erupted again in 1983 following the discovery of oil in Bentiu, southern Sudan. This time, the war was waged between the central government and the rebel forces organised under the helm of the Sudan People's Liberation Movement/Army (SPLM/A). Nearly two million people are estimated to have died over the course of the second civil war alone.[7] At the time the Comprehensive Peace Agreement (CPA)[8] was signed in 2005, conflict had become almost a continuous state for the country.

The international community, and in particular the Intergovernmental Authority on Development (IGAD),[9] played an instrumental role in bringing the central government and the SPLA together and ensuring that a peace deal was agreed.[10] This influence continues to play a major role in South Sudanese affairs today. The central goal of the CPA was to make "unity of the Sudan an attractive option

---

[3]OHCHR (2016), p. 6; see 'South Sudan situation – Information sharing portal (2016) WFP (1 November 2016) http://data.unhcr.org/SouthSudan/regional.php for the most recent refugee figures.

[4]WFP (2016) provides this estimate as of June; see also UN (2016) Report of the Secretary-General on South Sudan, covering the period from 1 April to 3 June 2016, paras 19–24.

[5]'Sudan: Independence through Civil Wars, 1956–2005' The Enough Project (2011).

[6]Later incorporated into the *Interim National Constitution of the Republic of the Sudan*, 2005. http://www.refworld.org/pdfid/4ba749762.pdf.

[7]'Sudan: Independence through Civil Wars, 1956–2005' The Enough Project (2011).

[8]*The Comprehensive Peace Agreement Between The Government of The Republic of The Sudan and The Sudan People's Liberation Movement/Sudan People's Liberation Army*, signed on 9 January 2005 http://unmis.unmissions.org/Portals/UNMIS/Documents/General/cpa-en.pdf. The process was led or encouraged by the Intergovernmental Authority on Development (IGAD) and IGAD-partners from western donor countries.

[9]IGAD was founded in 1996, and includes in its membership Djibouti, Eritrea, Ethiopia, Kenya, Somalia, South Sudan, Sudan and Uganda. The strategic purpose of the organisation is to create a holistic framework for regional cooperation amongst the countries in key policy areas, see 'The IGAD region' IGAD (2016) for more details.

[10]'Sudan: Independence through Civil Wars, 1956–2005' The Enough Project (2011).

especially to the people of South Sudan",[11] and at the end of an interim period of 6 years a referendum was to take place to determine whether the southern region would separate from the rest of the country.[12] Numerous protocols within the CPA dealt with diverse issues including the international monitoring of the ceasefire,[13] the restructuring of the political system over a 6-year 'interim period' before the referendum was to take place,[14] the sharing of oil revenues,[15] and determining the status of Abyei.[16]

The result of the southern Sudanese referendum was overwhelmingly in favour of independence for South Sudan, with 99% of votes in support of the creation of a new state.[17] In legal terms, the people of South Sudan exercised their right to self-determination to establish their own state separate from Sudan.[18] Normally (external) self-determination is exercised in the context of colonisation, racial rule and foreign occupation,[19] although some arguably invoke the existence of remedial secession[20] from an existing state outside such an external context if there is exceptional repression and discrimination by a state against certain groups of its own people. Without going into the intricacies of the colonial history of Sudan and South Sudan and the application of remedial secession to the case of South Sudan, however, it is appropriate to note that the emergence of South Sudan as a state is well recognised under international law, as it was a by-product of a consensual undertaking[21] between the Sudan and its southern region.

This short piece aims to provide an insight into some of the challenges and legal developments associated with ensuring lasting peace, addressing (and preventing) the allegations of widespread violations of international law, as well as the internal armed conflict affecting South Sudan, in light of the nature of responses from the international community.

---

[11]Comprehensive Peace Agreement (2005), The Machakos Protocol (2002) Section 1.5.5.

[12]Comprehensive Peace Agreement (2005), The Machakos Protocol (2002) Section 2.5.

[13]Comprehensive Peace Agreement (2005), The Agreement on Security Arrangements (2003) Section 2.

[14]Comprehensive Peace Agreement (2005), The Machakos Protocol (2002) Section 2.

[15]Comprehensive Peace Agreement (2005), The Agreement on Wealth Sharing (2004) Section 1.2, 3.

[16]Comprehensive Peace Agreement (2005), Abyei Protocol (2004) Section 1.2–1.3.

[17]Malwal (2015), pp. 1–65; LeRiche and Arnold (2012).

[18]Vidmar (2012), p. 559. He concluded that 'South Sudan's path to independence was rooted in the legal arrangement provided for by the 2005 Comprehensive Peace Agreement 126 and the subsequently adopted Interim Constitution of Sudan. In accordance with these legal instruments, South Sudan became a self-determination unit with a constitutionally guaranteed right to secession. This right was operationalized by the 2009 Referendum Act'.

[19]*Declaration on the Granting of Independence to Colonial Countries and Peoples*, Adopted by General Assembly resolution 1514 (XV) of 14 December 1960; Crawford (2012), pp. 141–142.

[20]*Reference re Secession of Quebec*, [1998] 2 S.C.R. 217.

[21]Vidmar (2012), p. 546.

2 Internal Armed Conflict

Following the establishment of an independent South Sudan in 2011, internal conflict erupted in the new country on 15 December 2013. Tensions had been rising between factions aligned with President Salva Kiir, and those aligned with (former) Vice President Riek Machar.[22] It is beyond the scope of this paper to consider extensively the political issues between the two main actors in the conflict, but it is important to recognise that this political rivalry has a long and complex history.[23] While the conflict was originally limited to the political rivals and their close supporters, it has since manifested itself as a more general ethnic conflict between different groups. Atrocities have been committed in particular against civilians of the two largest ethnic groups in the country, the Nuer and the Dinka,[24] a subject that will be treated separately later. Furthermore, despite the intervention of foreign troops in the conflict[25] (outside the UN process), the war is primarily of an internal character.[26]

IGAD, the regional political and trading bloc in which South Sudan has participated as a member since independence, continues to play a major role in the peace negotiations to resolve this conflict. Supported politically and financially by the US, UK and Norway, amongst other developed country partners,[27] IGAD has brought the parties to the conflict together multiple times to make commitments towards peace. On several occasions, however, the parties have missed deadlines brokered by IGAD to reach a lasting solution, including those set for 6 March 2015 and 17 August 2015.[28] One criticism that has been levelled against IGAD in this respect is that it has not taken action when violation of the agreements took place.[29] For example, regional monitors posted to South Sudan provided evidence of multiple violations of the Cessation of Hostilities agreement of 23 January 2014, which resulted in none of the stated consequences for those responsible.[30]

The regional consequences of continued hostilities in South Sudan are further exacerbated by the increasing threat of famine[31] which led to a growing number of

---

[22] 'Conflicts in South Sudan' The Enough Project (2014); Rolandsen (2015), pp. 163–174.
[23] OHCHR (2016), para. 8.
[24] 'Conflicts in South Sudan' The Enough Project (2014).
[25] Johnson (2014), pp. 300–309.
[26] Mulukwat (2015), pp. 414–442; for distinguishing non-international and international armed conflict see Yihdego (2009), pp. 37–40.
[27] Communique of the heads of state and government of the IGAD Plus on the situation in South Sudan (2016a, b).
[28] Jok (2015), p. 11.
[29] Crisis Group (2015).
[30] 'Conflicts in South Sudan' The Enough Project (2014).
[31] Ibid.

refugees moving to neighbouring countries.[32] Direct (or indirect) military intervention from neighbouring countries—e.g. Uganda[33]—in the civil war is also an issue, a topic outside the scope of this piece. The issues raised and the evidence provided here show that the security crisis in South Sudan has the potential to become a regional security crisis unless swiftly addressed. However, the armed violence at issue goes beyond the question of peace and security.

3 Humanitarian Law and Human Rights Violations

The conflict has spread beyond political infighting and become an inter-ethnic conflict, with atrocities documented against civilians of both the Nuer and Dinka ethnic groups. The extent of some of the violence has led to warnings by the UN and other actors that it may amount to war crimes and genocide.[34]

The UN Office of the High Commissioner for Human Rights (OHCHR), Human Rights Watch, and UNMISS, amongst other organisations, have reported human rights violations, which suggest that the situation may amount to systematic and widespread intentional crimes against civilians. In December 2013 at the start of the civil war, UNMISS recorded the deliberate killing of Nuer civilians, as well as unarmed or captured Nuer soldiers between 15 and 20 December 2013 by SPLA soldiers and other security forces. Given their distinctive facial scarring, language and separated communities, members of the Nuer ethnic group are relatively easily identifiable.[35] In the same period, between two hundred and four hundred Nuer men were alleged to have been killed after being detained at the Joint Operations Centre in eastern Juba.[36] In another Juba neighbourhood, a further 200 Nuer men were detained for questioning, with only eight returning; according to the OHCHR, witnesses heard shots, suggesting that the remaining Nuer were killed.[37] Many Nuer sought refuge in UN compounds, where they remain to this day for safety reasons.[38]

Following these incidences of violence against the Nuer in Juba, reports indicate that Nuer factions of the SPLA in another South Sudanese town, Bor, captured and killed Dinka civilians, soldiers, and government officials in a similar pattern of

---

[32]According to data from UNHCR (as of 1 November 2016), the following countries in particular host South Sudanese refugees: Ethiopia hosts more than 250,000 South Sudanese refugees, Kenya hosts 50,000, Sudan hosts almost 250,000, and Uganda hosts 480,000 refugees, 'South Sudan situation – Information sharing portal (2016) WFP (1 November 2016) http://data.unhcr.org/SouthSudan/regional.php.
[33]Johnson (2014), p. 171.
[34]See OHCHR (2016), para 1.1.
[35]Ibid, para 145.
[36]UNMISS (2014), para 70–78.
[37]OHCHR (2016), para 147.
[38]See figures in footnote 3.

violence.[39] UNMISS determined that an estimated fifty-six prison staff affiliated with the government were killed in Bor prison, while numerous civilians were also killed.[40] They established that 525 people were buried in two mass graves in the town following the fighting.[41]

Further deaths were documented in the towns of Malakal and Bentiu,[42] and killings of civilians were also reported in places with special status under international (humanitarian) law including places of worship, hospitals, and UN compounds.[43]

Reports of sexual and gender-based violence have also been widespread during the course of the conflict. Both the African Union's Commission of Inquiry[44] and UNMISS found evidence of rape committed against women and girls.[45] Reports indicate that the rapes committed were widespread, and possibly systematic in nature, and UNMISS determined it may amount to a crime against humanity.[46]

In this respect it is useful to consider how international criminal law treats widespread and large-scale rape of this nature. The International Criminal Tribunal for the former Yugoslavia (ICTY) ruled on this issue in its judgment against *Kunarac, Kovač and Vuković*, three ethnic Serbs, who were accused of crimes against humanity for acts committed during the Balkans conflict.[47] This historic judgment, which closely followed the precedent set by the International Criminal Tribunal for Rwanda (ICTR) in the *Akayesu* case,[48] determined that systematic rape constitutes a crime against humanity, as well as genocide (provided that the intent element is there), and although the Trial Chamber determined that there was insufficient evidence to characterise rape as a "weapon of war", in the sense that it was a "concerted approach or an order given to the Bosnian Serb armed forces", it was used as an "instrument of terror", with the army free to use it "whenever and against whomsoever they wished".[49] Most recently, the ICC in the *Katanga*[50] case confirmed the connection *inter alia* between systematic rape and crimes against humanity. In terms of the violence in South Sudan, the reports discussed previously

---

[39]OHCHR (2016), para 148.
[40]UNMISS (2014), para 88–94.
[41]Ibid.
[42]OHCHR (2016), para 150–152.
[43]Ibid, para 153–159.
[44]AU COI Report (2014), para 809.
[45]UNMISS (2014), para 8.
[46]UNMISS (2014), para 8.
[47]ICTY, *Kunarac, Kovač and Vuković* (IT-96-23 & 23/1), 2001; see also ICTR Statute, Art. 3 (g).
[48]The ICTR previously recognised rape 'as an instrument of genocide and as a crime against humanity' in *Prosecutor v Jean-Paul Akayesu* (ICTR-96-4-T), 1998. See also Haffajee (2006), pp. 203–204.
[49]ICTY, *Kunarac, Kovač and Vuković* (IT-96-23 & 23/1), 2001; however, the 1945 London Charter of the International Military Tribunal (Nuremberg Charter), under Article 6 (g) listed rape as one conduct of crimes against humanity. See also The Rome Statute (2000), Arts. 7 (1) (g).
[50]ICC, *Prosecutor v. Germain Katanga*, Judgment Trial Chamber II, ICC-01/04-01/07, para. 999, and paras 958–972. See also *The Rome Statute* (2000), Arts. 7 (1) (g).

suggest that a similar pattern of widespread, systematic and targeted rapes may well have occurred.

Further incidences of violence against children including unlawful and arbitrary detention have been recorded by the UN and AU in South Sudan.[51] The UN Secretary-General Report covering the period between 1 April to 3 June 2016, for example documented that:

> 84 incidents affecting 1,605 children were reported, while the Monitoring and Reporting Mechanism Country Task Force verified 62 of those incidents, affecting 1,139 children. Denial of humanitarian access and the recruitment and use of children accounted for the majority of verified incidents, many of which were reported in Jonglei, Unity and Upper Nile.[52]

These incidents, subject to the presentation of sufficient and comprehensive evidence against the alleged perpetrators of the crime, as required by international law,[53] may amount to war crimes, as widely recognised in case law[54] and humanitarian law treaties. Additional Protocol II to the Geneva Conventions 1977, in Article 4(3)(c), provides that "children who have not attained the age of fifteen years shall neither be recruited in the armed forces or groups nor allowed to take part in hostilities."[55] This principle has attained customary international law status.[56]

Given the reports emerging that humanitarian law and human rights abuses may have occurred during the course of the conflict, the August 2015 Peace Agreement makes provisions for accountability for the perpetrators of past crimes.[57] This includes the creation of a hybrid tribunal backed by the African Union, and with the authority to try serious crimes including war crimes, crimes against humanity and genocide.[58] Under the August 2015 Peace Agreement, a transitional government is to be formed and tasked with creating a truth and reconciliation commission within 6 months to "establish a record of violations of human rights since the start of the conflict and a compensation and reparations authority".[59] It is not clear whether establishing a hybrid tribunal or a truth and reconciliation commission was the predominant intention of the August 2015 Agreement. While establishing a

---

[51]OHCHR (2016) and AU COI Report (2014), for example para 16.

[52]UN (2016) Report of the Secretary-General para. 40.

[53]This is notwithstanding the minimum guarantees accorded to an accused, including the burden of proof imposed on the prosecutor, and the right to an impartial and fair trial as provided for in the *International Criminal Court Statute* (ICC Statute) (2010) Art. 67(1) (a)-(i).

[54]See e.g. the landmark ICC, *Prosecutor v. Thomas Lubanga Dyilo* (ICC-01/04-01/06), 2012. Also relevant are earlier Special Court for Sierra Leone decisions including SCSL, *Prosecutor v. Alex Tamba Brima, Brima Bazzy Kamara*, and *Santigie Borbor Kanu* (SCSL-04-16-T), 2007.

[55]1125 *UNTS* 609.

[56]ICRC (2015), p. 482; see also Helle (2000), p. 797. See also Yihdego (2009), pp. 37–69.

[57]Agreement on the Resolution of Conflict in South Sudan (26 August 2015), chapter V.

[58]Agreement on the Resolution of Conflict in South Sudan (26 August 2015), chapter V(3).

[59]OHCHR (2016), p. 7.

hybrid tribunal to try suspected offenders could be a crucial step to rendering justice for the victims of the conflict, a truth and reconciliation commission[60] with the aim of repairing damages, compensating victims, and ultimately fostering peace is ultimately a different approach to the issue. If both were to be used they might contradict each other, but they can be made to co-exist[61] if a comprehensive strategy is established.

Although reports that analyse these incidences do not address the most recent outbreak of violence, the initial reports from July 2016 indicate that violence against civilians may have continued beyond the crimes reported since December 2013. One notable example, which suggests a further milestone in the violence, was the reported kidnapping and rape of foreign aid workers in a residential compound in Juba,[62] a well-established war crime under international law.[63] The aid workers in question contacted the nearby UN compound, as well as the US embassy in Juba and private security firms for help during the attack to no avail. This calls into question the UN mandate to protect civilians, in this conflict and in others. An inquiry by an independent body established that UNMISS had failed to sufficiently protect civilians in and around UN compounds during the fighting, and the Under-Secretary-General for UN Peacekeeping Operations announced on 3 November 2016 that a task force would be established to create greater accountability for the UNMISS leadership.[64]

In the most recent Security Council Resolution 2327 (2016), the UN body:

> Condemns the clash that took place in Malakal in February 2016 and the fighting in Juba in July 2016, and urges the UN to continuously incorporate lessons learned to conduct reforms across UNMISS to better enable it to implement its mandate, in particular regarding the protection of civilians, and to improve Mission chain of command, increase the effectiveness of UNMISS operations, strengthen safety and security of personnel, and enhance UNMISS' ability to manage complex situations.[65]

4 The Fragile Peace Deal and International Responses

These widespread crimes and violations of international law can be halted only by reinstating peace and stability in the country. On 26 August 2015, the warring parties concluded the Agreement on the Resolution of Conflict in South Sudan. Given that the Agreement came about under considerable pressure from the

---

[60] Keetch (2016).

[61] For a general discussion on the subject see Totten (2009), pp. 1–33.

[62] 'Gang rape of aid workers in South Sudan is a turning point' NPR (2016).

[63] Yihdego (2009), pp. 37–69.

[64] UN News Centre (2016).

[65] Oper Para 20. It was a USA proposed resolution with 35 operative paragraphs aiming at extending UNMISS mission, imposing potential suctions and rectifying the UN Mission's shortcomings https://www.un.org/press/en/2016/sc12634.doc.htm (accessed 7 December 2016).

international community, many issues are yet to be resolved, which is perhaps best reflected in the most recent eruption of conflict.[66] The UN, IGAD and others may, however, justify their pressure based on the continued atrocities happening in the country and their frustration given the seeming lack of genuine commitment of the two rivals to achieve a peaceful settlement.[67] This subject, and in particular the role of the international community in responding to the conflict, is dealt with later when applying the Responsibility to Protect doctrine to the conflict.

The main issues addressed in the August 2015 Agreement include provisions establishing a lasting ceasefire, on political inclusivity of the various parties involved through the creation of a transitional government of national unity, humanitarian aid, and provisions on transitional justice. The latter in particular were discussed previously in relation to the alleged extensive human rights and humanitarian law breaches that had occurred. The Agreement provides that the transitional government is to continue until the next election.[68] One major goal of the drafters was to promote inclusivity, not only in terms of the government, and the armed opposition fighters under Riek Machar, but also including other political parties in the process.[69] This was an issue during the negotiation process, particularly in terms of how much executive power the rivals would each have.

The status of the military forces was also a major issue in the negotiating process; there are an estimated 200,000 fighters on both sides, and there were questions about how to integrate the forces, with Riek Machar advocating a policy of keeping the forces apart for some time until integration is possible.[70] Ultimately, the peace deal determined that the forces would be unified within 18 months of signing the agreement.[71] With the latest outbreak of violence and Riek Machar vowing to resume fighting against his rival, the status of the peace agreement remains uncertain. Generally, such agreements entered into between rivals within the confines of a state are not legally binding under international law,[72] unless the terms of the agreement emanate from, or are imposed by, the United Nations Security Council (UNSC) based on chapter VII of the Charter. UNSC Resolution 2252 (2015), adopted under Chapter VII, 'endorsed' the 2015 Agreement, and 'calls for immediate and full implementation of the Agreements by the parties, and expresses its intention to consider all appropriate measures' where there is

---

[66] Jok (2015); see also 'U.N. council in South Sudan to press government to cooperate or face arms embargo' Reuters (2016).

[67] 'Remarks by Ambassador Samantha Power and Ambassador Fodé Seck at a Joint Press Availability Upon the UN Security Council's Arrival in Juba, South Sudan' United States Mission to the United Nations (2016).

[68] Agreement on the Resolution of Conflict in South Sudan (26 August 2015), Art. 1.4.

[69] Agreement on the Resolution of Conflict in South Sudan (26 August 2015), Art. 3.

[70] Jok (2015), p. 12.

[71] Agreement on the Resolution of Conflict in South Sudan (26 August 2015), Art. 7.1.

[72] Consider, the ICJ, *Armed Activities on the Territory of the Congo*, 2005; Permanent Court of Arbitration, *Abyei arbitration*, ICGJ 422, 2009; and Special Court for Sierra Leone, *Prosecutor v Morris Kallon,* SCSL 4, 2004.

non-compliance with the Agreement. Arguably, this suggests that the agreement is still valid and the parties to the Agreement are under a positive duty to comply with its terms as far as international law is concerned.

Following the eruption of violence in July 2016, an IGAD Summit on the crisis[73] established that there was a need for a regional protection force (RPF) to protect, in particular, civilians in Juba. On 5 August, the UNSC passed Chapter VII based Resolution 2304 calling for a 4000 member RPF to be deployed to Juba to protect civilians and use "all necessary means to carry out its tasks".[74] The Resolution reiterated the Council's 'grave alarm and concern regarding the political, security, economic, and humanitarian crisis' and 'strongly condemning all human rights violations and abuses and violations of international humanitarian law' there, determining 'that the situation in South Sudan continues to constitute a threat to international peace and security in the region'. The RPF is authorised to protect civilians, UN personnel and humanitarian actors, amongst others, which effectively makes it a peace enforcement (rather than a peacekeeping) force.[75]

The overarching mandate of the RPF is to secure and contain the violence in Juba, and if necessary, outside the capital. More specifically it is mandated with ensuring "safe and free movement into, out of, and around Juba", protecting the airport and key infrastructure within the city, and importantly, "promptly and effectively engag[ing] any actor that is credibly found to be preparing attacks, or engages in attacks, against United Nations premises, United Nations personnel, international and national humanitarian actors, or civilians".[76] This is especially relevant given the most recent bouts of violence, where the UN has been criticised of playing too passive a role. The RPF will operate under the umbrella of UNMISS, and will report to the Mission force commander.[77]

Resolution 2304 also extends the mandate of UNMISS until December 2016,[78] which is not superseded by Security Council Resolution 2327 (2016) adopted on 16 December, which extended the Mission's mandate until 15 December 2017. While the Mission's initial mandate ranges from protecting civilians, to monitoring respect for human rights, facilitating dialogue among the parties, and maintaining public safety and security, it is also authorised under chapter VII 'to use all necessary means' for discharging its duties.

---

[73]IGAD Communique of 16 July 2016 establishes need for deployment of an RPF.

[74]UNSC Res 2304 (2016) [on extension of the mandate of the UN Mission in South Sudan (UNMISS) until 15 December 2016)] S/RES/2304, operative para 5. The resolution was passed by 11 votes in favour, with none against, and 4 abstentions. It authorises the deployment of a RPF until at least 15 December 2016, with the possibility of extension where necessary.

[75]Thakur (1994), pp. 387–410.

[76]Agreement on the Resolution of Conflict in South Sudan, Art. 10 (a)-(c).

[77]UNSC Res 2304, operative para 8.

[78]Agreement on the Resolution of Conflict in South Sudan, Art. 4. For the mandate of UNMISS see UNSC Res 2155 (2014) [on extension of the mandate of the UN Mission in South Sudan (UNMISS) until 30 Nov. 2014)], S/RES/2155.

In Resolution 2327 UNMISS was tasked to protect civilians (a) at risk of violence with emphasis on women and children, (b) 'to deter violence against civilians, including foreign nationals', (c) 'to implement a mission-wide early warning strategy', (d) 'To maintain public safety and security of and within UNMISS protection of civilians sites', (e) 'To deter and prevent sexual and gender-based violence within its capacity and areas of deployment', (f) 'To exercise good offices, confidence-building, and facilitation in support of the mission's protection strategy' and (g) 'to foster a secure environment for the eventual safe and voluntary return of IDPs and refugees including through monitoring of, [and] ensuring respect for human rights'.[79] Moreover, protecting and investigating human rights and their violations, facilitating humanitarian assistance and the implementation of the Peace Agreement[80] are among its mandates.

UNMISS appears to have a primarily peacekeeping mandate, but includes an enforcement component. With the authorisation of deploying the RPF under its auspices, however, it will now grow to up to 17,000 personnel, if the deployment of the RPF materialises.

Numerous challenges have arisen with respect to the creation of the RPF. The South Sudanese government is unhappy to admit troops from neighbouring countries to form part of the force at best, or unwilling to accept deployment of the RPF at worst.[81] This creates the dilemma of whether to honour the traditional requirement of consent of the host state prior to the deployment of peacekeeping forces or whether to enforce international law and order irrespective of such consent. In the on-going South Sudan crisis' case the Security Council seems to have wanted both at the same time. In its Resolution 2327 The Council requested the UN Secretary-General to report from time-to-time on:

> whether the TGNU (Transitional Government of National Unity) has maintained its consent in principle to deployment of the RPF and not imposed any political or operational impediments to operationalizing the RPF or obstructed UNMISS in the performance of its mandate, and requests the Secretary-General to review needs on the ground, and provide an updated assessment of the RPF's operations, deployment, and future requirements, as well as any political or operational impediments to operationalizing the RPF and obstructions to UNMISS in performance of its mandate.[82]

However, assuming that the RPF will be deployed in time, given the pressure exerted by the international community, some have questioned whether its mandate is realistic, for example, considering the size of the force in comparison with the large number of vulnerable people currently seeking shelter in UN bases in Juba alone.[83] The precarious working relationship between the UN and the government

---

[79] Res 2327 (2016) opera para 7 (a) (i)-(vii).

[80] Ibid, opera para 7 (b)-(d).

[81] 'UN peacekeeping chief says S Sudan deliberately delaying protection force' Radio Tamazuj (2016).

[82] Res 2327 (2016) opera para 31.

[83] An estimated 30,000 people are currently seeking shelter in UNMISS in Juba.

of South Sudan adds further complexity to the situation.[84] Following the alleged evacuation of Riek Machar by the UN in the aftermath of recent violence, government officials questioned the neutrality of the organisation,[85] although the UN or other actors may justify the decision on humanitarian and/or conflict resolution grounds.[86] Nevertheless, such suspicions on the part of South Sudanese authorities raises a key question often arising in peacekeeping and arguably peace enforcement issues. The issue is the neutrality of international organisations from internal politics and rivalry. Gaining the trust and confidence of all sides to the conflict in South Sudan would thus be a challenge to the RPF and in effect to UNMISS.

It is worth stressing that any sovereign state, including South Sudan, has legal rights in times of conflict, including protection from foreign military intervention under international law. According to the Responsibility to Protect doctrine,[87] however, each state has the primary responsibility to protect its citizens.[88] South Sudan is no exception. This is why UNSC Resolution 2304 (2016) emphasised that 'South Sudan's Transitional Government of National Unity bears the primary responsibility to protect its populations from genocide, war crimes, ethnic cleansing, and crimes against humanity'.[89] However, where a 'state is unable or unwilling to fulfil this responsibility, or is itself the perpetrator...it becomes the responsibility of the international community to act in its place'.[90] The fact that the UNSC acted based on Chapter VII to deploy the RPF and reinforce the UNMISS mandate in South Sudan to discharge its primary responsibility for the maintenance of international peace and security, underpins the collective legal response to the South Sudan crisis which prevails over the will of the South Sudanese government.

---

[84] For example, Hilde Johnson, the former head of UNMISS was accused of links with the rebel movement; 'UN boss denies links with South Sudanese rebels' Sudan Tribune (2014).

[85] 'President Kiir accuses UN of taking Machar's side for regime change' Sudan Tribune (2016).

[86] In Res 2327 (2016) opera para 17, for example, the Council '[E]ncourages UNMISS to ensure that any support provided to non-United Nations security forces is provided in strict compliance with the HRDDP (United Nations Human Rights Due Diligence Policy) on United Nations Support to non-United Nations security forces'.

[87] ICISS (2001); Despite strides in recognising this doctrine internationally in recent years its effectiveness and even application to all conflicts are questionable. The doctrine has not yet applied to the Syrian conflict. More relevant here is that across the border, in Sudan, the atrocities committed in Darfur have continued, seemingly unchecked for more than a decade although Responsibility to Protect was Invoked in UNSC Res 1706 (2006) Reports of the Secretary-General on the Sudan, S/RES/1706 on Darfur see Evans (2009), p. 15.

[88] Ibid, paras 2.14, 2.15.

[89] See UNSC Res 1706 (2006) Reports of the Secretary-General on the Sudan, S/RES/1706, on Darfur; and UNSC Res 1970 (2011) [on establishment of a Security Council Committee to monitor implementation of the arms embargo against the Libyan Arab Jamahiriya] contained similar language.

[90] Ibid, para 2.29. The Commission underlined that 'the responsibility to protect acknowledges that the primary responsibility in this regard rests with the state concerned, and that it is only if the state is unable or unwilling to fulfill this responsibility, or is itself the perpetrator, that it becomes the responsibility of the international community to act in its place'.

In fact, some argue that an alternative approach is necessary given the current situation in which the government is alleged to be one of the perpetrators of violent crimes against its civilians.[91] In this respect, the UN has taken some action against top leaders, with the UN Sanctions Committee Chair stating in support of targeted sanctions, "top South Sudan officials directed or knew about acts of violence".[92] The same must be applied when addressing the alleged role of opposition leaders in orchestrating violent crimes, or failing to prevent such crimes committed by their fighters as expressly required by customary international law.

5 Conclusion

Given this background, it is clear that the international community has played an important role in South Sudan since the creation of the state in 2011. IGAD in particular has had a long history of bringing together the parties to the respective conflicts and engaging them in peace talks, and has in fact played a vital role in the creation of the South Sudanese state. Despite frequent international intervention, South Sudan has been plagued by conflict, and this has had a devastating effect on civilians. The current policies of the UN and IGAD (plus) parties seem to be founded on enforcement and pressure. While a more appropriate strategy would be centred on winning over the hearts and minds of the key actors, the current climate suggests that the key leaders are unable or unwilling to protect the population and restore peace, and as such effective enforcement action appears necessary to find a lasting solution. Protecting civilians in South Sudan is, and should be, classified as a priority, and justice must be served to the victims of the alleged international crimes in the country. Given that the crisis has a strong regional dimension, particularly in terms of refugee flows across borders, and the potential (and actual) spill over of armed violence into neighbouring countries, which is a cause for sub- regional tension, a comprehensive regional effort, supported by global partners, should be the focus of efforts to address the crisis and ensure that South Sudan experiences peace, paving the path to prosperity.

References

African Union Commission of Inquiry (2014) Report, Report of the African Union Commission of Inquiry on South Sudan (15 October 2014). http://www.peaceau.org/uploads/auciss.final.report.pdf

---

[91]Williams (2016).

[92]'Top South Sudan officials directed or knew about acts of violence in war-torn nation, sanctions committee chair tells Security Council' UN News Centre (2016).

Communique of the heads of state and government of the IGAD Plus on the situation in South Sudan (2016a) Relief Web (5 August 2016). http://reliefweb.int/report/south-sudan/communique-heads-state-and-government-igad-plus-situation-south-sudan-5-august. Accessed 22 Oct 2016

Communique of the heads of state and government of the IGAD Plus on the situation in South Sudan (2016b) (IGAD) (16 July 2016). https://paanluelwel2011.files.wordpress.com/2016/07/communique-igad-plus-on-south-sudan.pdf

Conflicts in South Sudan (2014) The Enough Project (1 October 2014). http://www.enoughproject.org/conflicts/sudans/conflicts-south-sudan. Accessed 20 Oct 2016

Crawford J (2012) Brownlie's principles of public international law, 8th edn. Oxford, Oxford University Press

Declaration on the Granting of Independence to Colonial Countries and Peoples, Adopted by General Assembly resolution 1514 (XV) of 14 December 1960

Evans G (2009) The responsibility to protect: ending mass atrocities once and for all. Brookings Institution Press, Washington

Gang rape of aid workers in South Sudan is a turning point (2016) NPR (23 August 2016). http://www.npr.org/sections/goatsandsoda/2016/08/23/491057541/gang-rape-of-aid-workers-in-south-sudan-is-a-turning-point. Accessed 15 Oct 2016

Haffajee RL (2006) Prosecuting crimes of rape and sexual violence at the ICTR: the application of joint criminal enterprise theory. Harv J Law Gender 29

Helle D (2000) Optional Protocol on the involvement of children in armed conflict to the Convention on the Rights of the Child. Int Rev Red Cross 82(839):797

ICISS (2001) Report, the responsibility to protect (December 2001). http://responsibilitytoprotect.org/ICISS%20Report.pdf

ICRC (2015) Study, customary international humanitarian law. https://www.icrc.org/eng/assets/files/other/customary-international-humanitarian-law-i-icrc-eng.pdf

Interim National Constitution of the Republic of the Sudan, 2005. http://www.refworld.org/pdfid/4ba749762.pdf. Accessed 4 Dec 2016

Johnson DG (2014) Briefing: the crisis in South Sudan. J East Afr Stud 9:1

Jok JM (2015) Negotiating an end to the current civil war in South Sudan. Inter-Press Service/Berghof Foundation. http://ips-project.org/wp-content/uploads/2015/11/IPS-paper-16-Negotiating-an-End-to-the-Current-Civil-War-in-South-Sudan.pdf. Accessed 18 Oct 2016

Keetch P (2016) To guarantee peace in South Sudan, truth and reconciliation is the way forward. Harv Int Rev, July 5. http://hir.harvard.edu/guarantee-peace-south-sudan-truth-reconciliation-way-forward/. Accessed 05 Dec 2016

LeRiche M, Arnold M (2012) South Sudan: from revolution to independence. Hurst & Co, London

Malwal B (2015) Sudan and South Sudan - from one to two. Palgrave Macmillan, Basingstoke

Mulukwat KHL (2015) Challenges of regulating non-international armed conflicts – an examination of ongoing trends in South Sudan's civil war. J Int Humanitarian Leg Stud 6:2

OHCHR (2016) Report, assessment mission by the Office of the United Nations High Commissioner for Human Rights to improve human rights, accountability, reconciliation and capacity in South Sudan: detailed findings (10 March 2016). http://www.ohchr.org/EN/NewsEvents/Pages/DisplayNews.aspx?NewsID=17207&LangID=E

President Kiir accuses UN of taking Machar's side for regime change (2016) Sudan Tribune (14 September 2016). http://www.sudantribune.com/spip.php?article60221. Accessed 5 Nov 2016

Reference re Secession of Quebec, [1998] 2 S.C.R. 217

Remarks by Ambassador Samantha Power and Ambassador Fodé Seck at a Joint Press Availability Upon the UN Security Council's Arrival in Juba, South Sudan (2016) United States Mission to the United Nations (2 September 2016). http://usun.state.gov/remarks/7410. Accessed 1 Nov 2016

Rolandsen ØH (2015) Another civil war in South Sudan: the failure of Guerrilla Government? J East Afr Stud 9:1

Rome Statute of the International Criminal Court, 2000. https://www.icc-cpi.int/nr/rdonlyres/ea9aeff7-5752-4f84-be94-0a655eb30e16/0/rome_statute_english.pdf. Accessed 04 Dec 2016

South Sudan situation – Information sharing portal (2016) WFP (1 November 2016). http://data.unhcr.org/SouthSudan/regional.php

South Sudan: UN peacekeeping chief sets up task force after probe into mission's performance (2016) UN News Centre (3 November 2016). http://www.un.org/apps/news/story.asp?NewsID=55471. Accessed 3 Nov 2016

Sudan: Independence through Civil Wars, 1956–2005 (2011) The Enough Project (3 December 2011). http://www.enoughproject.org/blogs/sudan-brief-history-1956. Accessed 22 Oct 2016

Thakur R (1994) From peacekeeping to peace enforcement: the UN operation in Somalia. J Mod Afr Stud 32(3):387–410

The Comprehensive Peace Agreement Between The Government of The Republic of The Sudan and The Sudan People's Liberation Movement/Sudan People's Liberation Army, signed on January 9, 2005. http://unmis.unmissions.org/Portals/UNMIS/Documents/General/cpa-en.pdf. Accessed 04 Dec 2016

The IGAD region (2016) IGAD (14 October 2016). https://igad.int/index.php/about-us/the-igad-region. Accessed 20 Oct 2016

Top South Sudan officials directed or knew about acts of violence in war-torn nation, sanctions committee chair tells Security Council (2016) UN News Centre (19 February 2016). https://www.un.org/press/en/2016/sc12251.doc.htm. Accessed 29 Oct 2016

Totten C (2009) The International Criminal Court and truth commissions: a framework for cross-interaction in the Sudan and beyond. Northwest J Int Hum Rights 7(1):1–33. http://scholarlycommons.law.northwestern.edu/njihr/vol7/iss1/1. Accessed 05 Dec 2016

U.N. council in South Sudan to press government to cooperate or face arms embargo (2016) Reuters (3 September 2016). http://www.reuters.com/article/us-southsudan-security-un-idUSKCN1190NW. Accessed 15 Oct 2016

UN (2016) Report of the Secretary-General on South Sudan (20 June 2016). UN Doc. S/2016/552

UN boss denies links with South Sudanese rebels (2014) Sudan Tribune (3 April 2014). http://www.sudantribune.com/spip.php?article50528. Accessed 3 Nov 2016

UN mission 'extremely concerned' over increased incidents of violence across South Sudan (2016) UN News Centre (12 October 2016). http://www.un.org/apps/news/story.asp?NewsID=55273#.WBRwaPkrLIU. Accessed 15 Oct 2016

UN peacekeeping chief says S Sudan deliberately delaying protection force (2016) Radio Tamazuj (19 October 2016). https://radiotamazuj.org/en/article/un-peacekeeping-chief-says-s-sudan-deliberately-delaying-protection-force. Accessed 1 Nov 2016

UNMISS (2014) Report, Conflict in South Sudan – a human rights report (8 May 2014). https://unmiss.unmissions.org/sites/default/files/unmiss_conflict_in_south_sudan_-_a_human_rights_report.pdf

Unprecedented level of food insecurity in South Sudan, UN agencies war (2016) WFP (29 June 2016). http://www.wfp.org/news/news-release/unprecedented-level-food-insecurity-south-sudan-un-agencies-warn

UNSC Resolution 2327 (2016) on South Sudan, 16 December 2016. https://www.un.org/press/en/2016/sc12634.doc.htm. Accessed 17 Dec 2016

Vidmar J (2012) South Sudan and the international legal framework governing the emergence and delimitation of new states. Texas Int Law J 47(3):541–559

Williams PD (2016) Key questions for South Sudan's new protection force. IPI Global Observatory (12 September 2016). https://theglobalobservatory.org/2016/09/south-sudan-regional-protection-force-kiir-unmiss/. Accessed 3 Nov 2016

Yihdego Z (2009) Darfur and humanitarian law: the protection of civilians and civilian objects. J Conflict Secur Law 14(1):37–69

Jasmin Hansohm is currently an intern at the ICTY and Assistant Editor of the EtYIL; she holds an LL.B. (Hons) from the University of Aberdeen and an LL.M. from Queen Mary, University of London.

Zeray Yihdego is a Reader in International law at the University of Aberdeen. The authors recognise the extensive and constructive comments provided for by Prof Melaku Desta and the comments offered by Dr Ian Taggart, all errors and omissions are of the authors.

CPSIA information can be obtained
at www.ICGtesting.com
Printed in the USA
LVOW05*0725211117
557155LV00011B/74/P

9 783319 558974